Praise for
Youth and Post-conflict Reconstruction
Agents of Change

"This book serves as an important addition to the body of literature which looks at the relationship between youth and conflict. While the wealth of literature around this subject focuses on the potential for destabilization as a result of a youth bulge, this publication contributes an important step in beginning to identify what the proper steps of addressing youth needs in the post-conflict setting should look like, as well as some of the expected results when theses needs are addressed. The volume is unique in its approach to carefully consider independent variables such as international involvement related to youth, domestic youth policy, and cultural and environmental factors."

—**L. Randolph Carter,** Center for Peacebuilding International

"An ambitious and detailed study of a vitally important issue, this book offers significant insights about youth and conflict. Timely and very well-written, Schwartz has successfully synthesized a number of different variables, theories, cases, and policy areas, into a compelling and useful analysis. This book will be of interest to students, scholars, NGO personnel and policymakers worldwide."

—**Siobhan McEvoy-Levy,** Butler University and author of *Troublemakers or Peacemakers? Youth and Post-Accord Peacebuilding*

"Stephanie Schwartz' book on youth in post-conflict reconstruction is a very welcome addition to the literature on youth and violence. Schwartz forcefully argues that we need to pay attention to the positive roles that youth may play in post-conflict reconstruction. Most importantly, she identifies and discusses strategies that may contribute to breaking the cycle of violence. This book will help change the perception of youth as primarily being a threat to one of youth representing an opportunity."

—**Henrik Urdal,** The International Peace Research Institute, Oslo (PRIO)

D1125091

YOUTH AND POST-CONFLICT RECONSTRUCTION

YOUTH
AND POST-CONFLICT RECONSTRUCTION
A G E N T S O F C H A N G E

STEPHANIE SCHWARTZ

UNITED STATES INSTITUTE OF PEACE PRESS
Washington, D.C.

UNITED STATES INSTITUTE OF PEACE
1200 17th Street, NW, Suite 200
Washington, DC 20036-3011
www.usip.org

Library of Congress Cataloging-in-Publication Data

Schwartz, Stephanie.
Youth and post-conflict reconstruction: agents of change / Stephanie Schwartz.
    p. cm.
Includes bibliographical references and index.
ISBN 978-1-60127-049-8 (pbk. : alk. paper)
1. Youth and war. 2. Youth and peace. 3. Youth in development. 4. Postwar reconstruction—Social aspects. I. Title.
HQ799.2.W37S33 2010
303.6'60835—dc22

2009040607

Contents

Acknowledgments

This book would not be possible without the support of teachers, colleagues, friends, and family. I am indebted to many of my colleagues at the United States Institute of Peace for their contributions and guidance, in particular to David Smock, vice president, Center for Mediation and Conflict Resolution. The insightful comments of the three anonymous reviewers, and the persistence and patience of editor Michael J. Carr were invaluable to the project. Finally, with great appreciation, warmest thanks to Douglas Foyle of Wesleyan University, whose guidance was pivotal in bringing this book to life, and to my parents, Bob and Shelley Schwartz, for their unflagging support.

Tables and Figures

Foreword

During my career working in post-conflict zones, I have seen and experienced all types of reconstruction efforts. Some have failed and others have been successes. Each had its own set of goals, parameters, and subjects, but few have focused on engagement with youth in peacebuilding after war. Youth are pivotal to the success or failure of any post-conflict peacebuilding or development exercise, especially in those countries in which they participated in the conflict. Stephanie Schwartz's book, *Youth and Post-conflict Reconstruction: Agents of Change,* is a remarkable and welcome volume that focuses on this neglected group.

This book not only asks what role youth can play in post-conflict reconstruction but also features the author's finding that youths in war-torn societies are neither necessarily forces of instability nor passive victims, as they are often popularly portrayed. They themselves can be agents of peace given the right constellation of reconstruction programs. As Schwartz argues, this constellation must not only address the protection and reintegration needs of youths but also empower them.

My own experience in working with youth in Africa confirms this thesis. I have witnessed a great number of cases where efforts fall apart due to the lack of attention to youth empowerment. At the same time, I have also seen the difference young people can make toward establishing a lasting peace, particularly in circumstances where individual attention has been giving to the young person or persons.

A few years ago, I met "Andy," a youngster from Uganda who at the tender age of nine was abducted and enlisted into the Lord's Resistance Army (LRA). During his conscription Andy was forced by a commander to kill his own brother in a most brutal fashion. Six years later, Andy escaped from the LRA. With his parents having long since fallen victim to the LRA, he located an aunt with whom he was able to settle. However, unable to cope with his profound sense of guilt over what he had done to his brother, he had trouble adapting to his new-found freedom and constantly contemplated suicide.

It was at this point that I was introduced to Andy through the nongovernmental organization Invisible Children. I immediately understood how psychologically destructive his experiences had been and asked him what, if anything, he needed to move forward. He replied that he wanted to see and speak to the commander who had made that fateful order for him to kill his older brother. I agreed to help him and quickly tracked down the commander, who by this time had been granted amnesty. At first the commander was unwilling to meet Andy. He told me that he had started a new life and did not wish to face old demons. However, over time, I made him see that without this meeting, Andy would never be able to move on.

When the commander and the boy first met, the boy was trembling, overcome with raw emotion. The commander did not even recall who he was, which suggested to me just how unremarkable—and common—that day must have been for him. Even so, Andy proceeded to recount the story of his brother's death, so upset he could barely get the words out. After listening to Andy, the commander said that he wished he could change what happened, but that he could not and was sorry for what he had done. To my surprise, as the conversation drew to a close, Andy shook the commander's hand, and then gave him a hug. With the help of his aunt and Invisible Children, Andy now attends university in Uganda and regularly speaks to young children about the need to stay in school and work hard. Although Andy knows his wounds will never completely heal, he no longer sees himself as a killer, but as a role model and future leader.

Another young person that came to mind while I read this volume was "Renaldo," who fought in Mozambique's civil war as a young boy and who benefited from the government's disarmament, demobilization, and reintegration (DDR) program in the late 1990s. The DDR program helped the country transition from war to peace by ensuring a safe environment, encouraging ex-combatants to reintegrate with society. While Renaldo received food, a stipend, and education and was reunited with family, allowing him a fresh start, he too suffered from guilt because of his participation in war. Even with all the support from the DDR program, Renaldo never felt like he belonged. Although his material needs were met, the reintegration side of the program did not include a psychosocial element. Fortunately, soon after Renaldo began his new life, he took an interest in soccer and began playing with a local team. The experience helped him understand rules and fair play and gave him the opportunity to socialize with other children—as children—again.

As time passed, teachers and other students came to recognize his talent on the field. He gradually rose up the ranks, as coaches continually recommended him to more accomplished leagues and teams, and he eventually became a member of Mozambique's national soccer team. I met him after he was already famous, a leader to his community. Knowing the horrors he had experienced as a youth, I could not help but be struck by his remarkable transformation—how someone's sense of self and worth could be so radically altered in a short number of years.

While individual cases are important, I have also seen the change that occurs in larger groups within society with the right type of support. Just as war has witnessed the forced conscription of boys, it has also witnessed the forced conscription of girls, who are at times overlooked in reconstruction programming. While boys are abducted solely to become fighters and killers, young girls are abducted not only to fight in the bush but also to serve as sex slaves, cooks, porters, and child bearers. Indeed, senior soldiers take several wives at a time, including very young girls, to service their needs and provide them with children. Those girls who bear children are known as child mothers.

Child mothers lucky enough to avoid death and to escape with their children often face rejection by the very societies from which they were stolen. Some return to families that are simply too impoverished to feed additional mouths, while others are turned away for having given birth to children of killers. Although most of these girls are eager to enroll in a formal education program and become productive members of society, with no one to take care of their children and little chance of finding potential mates, they must abandon such hopes.

With the help of local and international programs, many of these child mothers have bonded together in the face of this rejection and formed local education groups of their own in Sierra Leone, Liberia, and Uganda. Through these groups, they receive education in a trade. For example, they might learn how to make jewelry, how to weave baskets, or how to run a catering business. Members of these groups then help one another sell their products locally, nationally, and even internationally. Through these businesses, the child mothers earn money to support themselves and their children. This success has also enabled some girls to help support their extended families or to find new husbands. Having met many of these girls through my own work in Uganda and elsewhere, I have witnessed firsthand how they define themselves not by the crushing poverty, abuse, and social rejection that they once experienced, but by what they have since accomplished and by the space that they have created for themselves in society.

I relate these stories not only in support of this volume's central argument, but also to help put a face to the subject matter that Schwartz so assuredly examines on the following pages. I know from both personal and professional experience that the stories that I have presented here are the rare exception, and not the common rule. But I specifically chose to relate such inspirational examples of success to highlight a common thread that runs through them and that should run through all post-conflict protection, reintegration, and empowerment programs. That thread is identity—or, more specifically, the reconstruction of identity. We should not forget that when we speak of reconstruction, we are not just speaking about the reconstruction of countries or societies, but of individual lives—in short, of a person's sense of self and worth. Although not all youth will be able to draw on the emotional maturity of Andy, the physical gifts of Renaldo, or the supportive network of the child mothers to transform themselves, it is my hope that scholars will draw on this volume and continue to develop this vital line of inquiry. I also hope that policymakers and practitioners will draw on the singular findings in this book when designing their own courses of action so that one day all youths in post-conflict societies may truly be agents of change.

—Betty Bigombe

1

Youth and Post-conflict Reconstruction: An Analytical Framework

"Now, I have been demobilized and I am with my family. It is good to be home, but I have nothing to do. I would like to study or work, but I have no money, there is no training and there is no work. I feel sad, because I feel unhelpful to my family. I am at home but I am worthless. During the day I try not to think of my life as a fighter, because it makes me cry, but sometimes I think maybe I should go back to the armed groups." (John, 15, Democratic Republic of Congo)[1]

"I'm trying to join the Children's Club so we can work together as children to help our community. We don't have water or toilets here, and we don't even have proper shelter to live in. So we'll come together and help each other to help organizations promote our community." (Hawa, 16, Sierra Leone)[2]

John's and Hawa's stories, above, represent the increasing number of youth in conflict zones who face severe obstacles as they move from war to civilian life. These young people, many of whom grew up knowing only a life of war, must not only navigate their country's peacebuilding and reconstruction processes, but also enter the adult world, gain access to education, and earn money to support their families. And yet, while the role of youth during conflict has been studied at length, the impact of a large youth population during post-conflict reconstruction has been largely overlooked.[3] Significant gaps remain in our understanding of how the post-conflict reconstruction process affects young people and of the role youth play in determining its success.

---

1. Amnesty International, "Democratic Republic of Congo: Children at War, Creating Hope for the Future," report, Oct. 10, 2006, www.amnesty.org/document.php?lang=e&id=engafr620172006 (accessed Sept. 1, 2009).

2. Matt Hobson, "Forgotten Casualties of War: Girls in Armed Conflict," Save the Children report, 2005, www.reliefweb.int/rw/lib.nsf/db900SID/EVIU6BSFEG?OpenDocument (accessed Sept. 1, 2009).

3. Jo Boyden and Joanna de Berry, *Children and Youth on the Front Line: Ethnography, Armed Conflict and Displacement*, vol. 14, Studies in Forced Migration (New York: Berghahn, 2004); Paul Collier and Anke Hoeffler, "Greed and Grievance in Civil War," *Oxford Economic Papers* 56, no. 4 (2004): 563–94; P. W. Singer, *Children at War* (New York: Pantheon, 2005); Henrik Urdal, "A Clash of Generations? Youth Bulges and Political Violence," *International Studies Quarterly* 50, no. 3 (2006); Fareed Zakaria, "The Politics of Rage: Why Do They Hate Us?" *Newsweek*, Oct. 15, 2001.

Most of the research on youth focuses on young men, suggesting that a large proportion of male youth will increase the likelihood of conflict, or on children's rights, painting young people as passive victims in a world broken by adults.[4] But pigeonholing youth either as destabilizers or as passive victims oversimplifies the evidence: although young people do participate in conflict and help incite it, there are also many examples of young men and women becoming leaders in peacebuilding and contributing to the reconstruction process. In part, young people's choice between resorting to violence and contributing to peace can be influenced by intervening efforts during a post-conflict reconstruction process.[5] Because of this dual potential, management of the youth transition from war to peace is integral to breaking the cycle of violence that leads to civil war and instability.[6] As young adults become the next generation to lead their countries, their experiences during the reconstruction period will affect their understandings of peace and conflict and, therefore, have the potential to guide the national trajectory toward either reconciliation or renewed conflict.

The process of post-conflict reconstruction, and the youth demographic's role in it, is drawing increasing attention from scholars and policymakers.[7] Intrastate conflict is the dominant form of war today, and young people are increasingly involved as active participants.[8] As the international community seeks to promote stability and maintain peace after civil wars, it must seek to understand how to make post-conflict reconstruction efforts as successful as possible while also addressing the needs of the young people affected by conflict.

Post-conflict reconstruction and nation building involves a wide range of actors, with youth representing just one sector. Youth have been major stakeholders in many recent civil conflicts, including those in Northern Ireland, Israel-Palestine, Iraq, Colombia, Sierra Leone, and Nigeria. And yet, they continue to be underrepresented in peace processes despite the clear evidence of their potential to affect the prospects for durable peace. Youth gangs in South Africa continue to destabilize the country, and youth militancy plagues the

---

4. See Urdal, "A Clash of Generations?"; Collier and Hoeffler, "Greed and Grievance in Civil War"; Zakaria, "The Politics of Rage."

5. See Yvonne Kemper, "Youth in War-to-Peace Transitions: Approaches by International Organizations," *Berghof Report* no. 10 (2005): 8, www.berghof-center.org/uploads/download/br10e.pdf (accessed Sept. 1, 2009); Siobhán McEvoy-Levy, ed., *Troublemakers or Peacemakers? Youth and Post-Accord Peace Building* (South Bend, Ind.: University of Notre Dame Press, 2006); Jeannie Annan, Christopher Blattman, and Roger Horton, "The State of Youth and Youth Protection in Northern Uganda: Findings from the Survey of War Affected Youth (SWAY)," report for UNICEF Uganda, 2006, www.sway-uganda.org (accessed Sept. 1, 2009).

6. For a discussion of the structural and psychological factors in building durable peace, see Malvern Lumsden, "Breaking the Cycle of Violence," *Journal of Peace Research* 34, no. 4 (1997).

7. Annan, Blattman, and Horton, "The State of Youth and Youth Protection in Northern Uganda," iii.

8. Compared to the 25 interstate wars fought from 1945 to 1999, with 3.33 million battle deaths, there were approximately 127 civil wars in the same period, in 73 different countries, with a death toll of 16.2 million. J. D. Fearon and D. D. Laitin, "Ethnicity, Insurgency, and Civil War," *American Political Science Review* 97, no. 1 (2003). See also Singer, *Children at War.*

Niger Delta. Meanwhile, former youth combatants have contributed to community reconciliation and development projects in Mozambique and Kosovo and started taxi associations in Sierra Leone, and youth groups in Belfast have worked with local peacebuilding organizations to promote social development in their communities.

John and Hawa, too, demonstrate that young people's agency in post-conflict situations is not necessarily predetermined by their age or experience in war. Both served in armed groups during their countries' civil wars, and as each conflict moved toward resolution and began the transition to peace, John and Hawa embarked on distinctly different paths. Whereas John is contemplating rejoining an armed group, Hawa has a clear idea of how to make her voice heard while she makes a positive difference in her community. Both these stories reflect the experiences of millions of other young people affected by armed conflict, who must make choices about how they will survive and succeed in the future. This study seeks to understand better the factors that influence these choices, by answering these questions:

What causes young people like John to consider returning to the life of a fighter while others, like Hawa, choose to work and hope for a better future?

- Can actions be taken in the reconstruction process to break the cycle of violence so that young people like John choose to remain in civilian society rather than take up arms?
- If so, what structures can be put in place so that the Hawas of the world can better contribute to their societies?

To answer these questions, this study uses three cases of post-conflict reconstruction—Mozambique, the Democratic Republic of the Congo (DRC), and Kosovo—to explore how structural factors such as domestic policy, non-governmental organizations (NGO) programming, international interventions, and cultural context affect and are affected by young people's role in post-conflict situations.[9] The hypotheses drawn from these comparisons can help guide future research, both on the role of youth in post-conflict reconstruction and on reconstruction actors' ability to facilitate the youth population's war-to-peace transition.

The rest of this chapter will consider the existing knowledge about youth roles in conflict and outline the methodological framework of the study. A review of the literature outlines the dominant structures for studying youth in conflict, highlights key gaps in the current scholarship, and provides background information on several factors critical to analyzing the case studies. Such factors include the importance of the process of disarmament, demobilization, and reintegration (DDR) in the reconstruction framework, and the impact of the

---

9. Whereas this study examines the interconnected structural factors that affect youth behavior, for a thorough examination of why young people choose specifically to become soldiers, see Rachel Brett and Irma Specht, *Young Soldiers: Why They Choose to Fight* (Boulder, Colo.: Lynne Rienner), 2004.

rising trend of NGOs' involvement in reconstruction processes. The final theory presented is the overarching hypothesis explored in the case studies: that youth are dynamic actors and that their influence on the post-conflict environment depends on how well the post-conflict reconstruction process meets specific needs of protection, reintegration, and sociopolitical empowerment. The chapter then concludes with a discussion of the study's methodology.

Youth in Post-conflict Reconstruction: A Theoretical Framework

Defining "Youth"

Defining "youth," as distinct from "child" and "adult," is a complicated task, yet an essential one if we are to get an accurate picture of issues specific to youth, and of the role youth play in post-conflict reconstruction. Moreover, the definition is not just a question of semantics. These issues have concrete effects on the ways that reconstruction actors design and implement programs intended to serve this population.

The difficulties in defining "youth" fall into three broad categories, each providing important insights on the structures for dealing with youth in the post-conflict environment. We must grapple with legal definitions of "child" and "adult," conceptions of childhood and adulthood altered by experiences in conflict, and manipulation of the labels "children" and "youth."

Locating Youth between the Legal Definitions of "Child" and "Adult"

With the Convention on the Rights of the Child, the international community has created a legal distinction between "child" and "adult," defining a child as "every human being below the age of 18 years unless under the law applicable to the child, majority is attained earlier."[10] Recently, the United Nations and other international institutions have acknowledged (though not legally) the existence of a youth demographic that does not fit either definition precisely. These distinctions often conflict or overlap, making pinpointing "youth" within legal and working definitions quite problematic.[11] For example, the World Health Organization (WHO) designates three different categories

---

10. United Nations, "Convention on the Rights of the Child," A/RES/44/25 of 20 November 1989, www.un.org/documents/ga/res/44/a44r025.htm (accessed Oct. 22, 2009).

11. Under the legal status of the Convention on the Rights of the Child (CRC), a "child" is every human below age 18, unless legal majority is attained earlier. But whereas the Optional Protocol to the CRC on the Involvement of Children in Armed Conflict (2002) affirms the special rights of children under the age of 18 during conflict, the CRC itself and the Rome Statute of 2002 allow for voluntary recruitment of children over age 15 into armed forces. See Kemper, "Youth in War-to-Peace Transitions," 8; United Nations, "Convention on the Rights of the Child"; United Nations, "Optional Protocol to the Convention on the Rights of the Child on the Sale of Children, Child Prostitution and Child Pornography," A/RES/54/263 of 25 May 2000; United Nations, Rome Statute of the International Criminal Court, adopted July 17, 1998, http://untreaty.un.org/cod/icc/statute/romefra.htm (accessed Sept. 1, 2009).

of youth—adolescents (10–19 years old), youth (15–24 years old), and young people (10–24 years old)—whereas the UN program on youth defines youth as those age 15–24.[12]

Moreover, these age-defined boundaries do not capture conceptions of "youth" across cultures. Chronological definitions of youth common in the West promote an individualistic understanding of development outside social contexts: youth is determined simply by age, not in reference to one's interaction with other people or events. This view is in direct contrast to other cultural interpretations, where the idea of youth may be understood as community dependent or developing through a social dynamic. Some cultures, for example, see youth as the time before certain life events, such as marriage, land ownership, or rights of passage.[13] In these cases, age may be a common characteristic of youth, but not the defining criterion, and a person maybe considered a youth well past the Western age-defined cutoff.[14]

While chronological definitions may not provide the best understanding of who youth are, what is important is that there is a gradation between child, youth, and adult—that the characteristics that define a child differ from those of a youth, and that the youth identity is strongly characterized by the state of transition from child to adult. Especially important in a conflict situation, childhood and youth are also identified by a lack of access to political power. The age-bound definitions simply serve as an indicator of this stage between childhood and adulthood.

The differences between the legal and operational definitions of youth are particularly important for this study. International policymakers and non-governmental actors often focus their attention on children in conflict, since the international legal definitions create a practical framework for addressing child-specific needs. Yet, while the definition of "young adult" may vary in cultural contexts, youth have different needs from children, and more potential to influence the reconstruction process. The combined transition that youth face in post-conflict societies, from war to peace on a political level and from child to adult on a social level, requires the international community to tailor programming for a specific set of needs going well beyond rights protection. Therefore, operations under a children's framework are often inadequate.

Conceptions of Childhood and Adulthood Altered by Experiences in Conflict

To further complicate the issue, when children and youth live through times of war or crisis, the normal designations of childhood and adulthood may be subject to change. Experiencing extreme crisis is generally associated with a

---

12. Kemper, "Youth in War-to-Peace Transitions," 8.
13. Ibid.
14. McEvoy-Levy, *Troublemakers or Peacemakers?* 4.

loss of "innocence," forcing children to "grow up" faster and often causing psychological damage in its wake.[15] For instance, children's or youth's experiences in war, as soldiers, rebels, refugees, or sexual slaves, can drastically change their psychological state and their own personal identity as child, youth, or adult. Many children and youth may become orphans, mothers, or heads of household, responsible for taking care of themselves and other family members. While these individuals may not have satisfied other cultural criteria of adulthood, such as age, "financial independence, marriage, initiation rites, or the right to vote or full judicial liability," their responsibilities as head of household force them into an adult's world.[16] This creates a tension between the reality of children and youth assuming adult responsibilities, and the economic and sociocultural restraints that deny them the power that adults wield in the greater political and social community.

Manipulation of the Labels "Child" and "Youth"

Finally, different actors manipulate labels of "child," "youth," and "adult" to gain advantages in public opinion. For instance, because the term "child" carries both social and legal obligations of protection, it is often used by NGOs and other outside actors to cite human rights violations or by individuals trying to benefit from programs that are legally obligated to protect children.[17] Conversely, officials may rely on stereotypical connotations of the term "youth" to invoke images of menacing gangs or rioting students to enforce legal culpability, whereas youth activists may call themselves "children" to avoid punishment.[18] Both the media and conflict participants use these connotations to manipulate public opinion and policy agendas.

To facilitate comparisons across the three case countries, this study focuses on individuals age 10–24, corresponding to the WHO definition of "young people." This definition is the most useful because it covers the typically defined adolescent age group (15–24) along with members of the younger population who, having lived through times of crisis, may in fact be filling youth or adult roles. While a chronological definition is not ideal, it is necessary for a consistent cross-case comparison. Where appropriate, discussion of each case will take cultural context into account.

Evaluating Post-conflict Reconstruction

Just as we must define "youth" to examine that demographic's impact on post-

---

15. Kemper, "Youth in War-to-Peace Transitions," 8.

16. Ibid.

17. Jo Boyden and Gillian Mann, "Children's Risk, Resilience and Coping in Extreme Situations," in *Handbook for Working with Children and Youth: Pathways to Resilience across Cultures and Contexts*, ed. Michael Ungar (Thousand Oaks, Calif.: SAGE, 2005).

18. Ibid.

conflict reconstruction, we must also define "post-conflict reconstruction" and understand how other scholars have attempted to evaluate the success or failure of reconstruction efforts.

Functions of Post-conflict Reconstruction

First, the phrase "post-conflict reconstruction" is loosely used to describe a number of situations: nation building, postaccord peacekeeping, and reconciliation can all fall under the umbrella of post-conflict reconstruction. Paraphrasing former UN Secretary-General Boutros Boutros-Ghali's 1992 report "An Agenda for Peace," reconstruction can be defined as "foster[ing] economic and social cooperation with the purpose of building confidence among previously warring parties; developing the social, political and economic infrastructure to prevent future violence; and laying the foundations for a durable peace."[19] For instance, this definition would include operations as wide-ranging as the Marshall Plan in Germany, where the United States helped restore the infrastructures of enemies defeated in war, and the reconciliation efforts in Rwanda after the 1994 genocide. It is also important to note that this definition includes achieving both a "negative peace," by preventing reincitation of violence and establishing law and order, and a "positive peace," by supporting political, social, and economic systems that can help the country develop and maintain stability.[20]

While post-conflict reconstruction takes many different forms, a few key elements are generally acknowledged as critical to the process. According to the Center for Strategic and International Studies' Post-conflict Reconstruction Project, the four essential pillars of reconstruction are security and public safety, justice and reconciliation, governance and participation, and economic and social progress.[21] Within each of these groupings are certain reforms that leaders in the field identify as necessary for successful reconstruction. For instance, to establish safety and security and reform the security sector (police force, military, and so on), one of the first requirements of a successful reconstruction program is the DDR of former combatants.

"DDR" refers to any program that encompasses three broad functions: First, disarmament is the collection and disposal of weapons used by former combatants. Demobilization involves disbanding military structures to transform from a wartime to a peacetime environment. Both disarmament and demobilization are therefore more in line with the "negative" goals of reconstruction, seeking to dismantle the structures of war to prevent further outbreaks of violence.

---

19. Michael W. Doyle and Nicholas Sambanis, *Making War and Building Peace: United Nations Peace Operations* (Princeton, N.J.: Princeton University Press, 2006), 11.

20. For definitions of positive and negative peace, see Johan Galtung, *Peace by Peaceful Means: Peace and Conflict, Development and Civilization.* (Oslo: International Peace Research Institute, 1996).

21. Center for Strategic and International Studies (CSIS), "Post-conflict Reconstruction Project," www.csis.org/isp/pcr/ (accessed Sept. 1, 2009).

Reintegration, on the other hand, goes further, to facilitate long-term peace and the return of former combatants to civilian life. This process often involves training and support programs that enable ex-combatants and their dependents to adapt and succeed in peacetime social, political, and economic life.

Successful DDR programs can significantly contribute to the stability of the post-conflict community and reduce the potential for future violence. But ineffective DDR programs that only partially disarm, demobilize, and reintegrate combatants or do not include all three tasks over time can perpetuate instability. For example, if a DDR program does not find and dispose of weapons caches hidden by competing factions or does not provide adequate support so that ex-combatants can find jobs and return to their families, many former combatants will have the means or incentive (or both) to return to violence rather than struggle with civilian life.[22]

In recent conflicts, militias' ranks have increasingly filled with children and youth, calling attention to the specific issue of disarming, demobilizing, and reintegrating child soldiers. But because of the legal distinction between child and adult, these child-specific DDR programs operate under a children's rights framework and, therefore, tend to focus solely on protection and family reunification. As a result, they are not always as adept at serving the young adult population's full array of needs. Moreover, while in many respects the distinctions between child and adult are useful and necessary to protect children during the DDR process, the differences in the programming can also cause tension over who gets what resources. For instance, under international law, an 18-year-old is left out of the "child" category and, therefore, does not have access to the psychosocial and reintegration resources provided to children, whereas a 16-year-old who led her peers in battle may require support beyond just helping locate her family. These situations have led young soldiers in DDR processes to protest, and sometimes even riot, if they did not receive the same reintegration stipend and resources as the adults they fought alongside.

The United Nations has identified some guiding principles that, if followed, enable DRR programs to address youth needs successfully. According to these principles, successful youth DDR will (1) involve effective coordination between programs for children and those for adults, to "make sure that people who started out as child soldiers but are now 18 receive proper support"; (2) provide for long-term sustainability by fully reintegrating youth rather than separating them from their peers; and (3) "do no harm," by planning a smooth transition and recognizing youth as an asset in the reconstruction process. This third task can be achieved by "dealing with root causes of youth's participation in armed conflicts; understanding the youth labour market and increasing the employability of youth so they are not trapped in poverty; addressing the health needs

---

22. Ibid.

of youth . . . , assisting youth who have child-care responsibilities; and opening up opportunities for further education and training."[23]

Measuring Success in Post-conflict Reconstruction

While the overarching reconstruction goals of creating stability and durable peace are quite logical, the method for achieving them isn't. To develop better methods for reconstruction, scholars have sought to understand key variables affecting stability after civil wars and to measure the relative success of different cases of post-conflict reconstruction.[24]

Most studies that try to evaluate the success or failure of reconstruction efforts focus on broad factors, such as the settlement agreement, regime type, international environment, or third-party enforcement, that are commonly believed to affect the peace process. One example of this approach is Hartzell, Hoddie, and Rothchild's method, which explores the impact of these and other variables on the post–civil-war environment by testing them against the number of months, up to five years, that the ensuing peace endured.[25] This method helps researchers isolate the degree to which certain variables affected the peacebuilding process, and gives practitioners who facilitate these efforts a better idea of what factors may help or hinder them along the way.

But the same logic has not been used to examine the impact of the youth demographic as one of the broad issues affecting the reconstruction process. While there is a growing body of literature on the correlations between youth, stability, and conflict causation, this book provides a systematic analysis of the youth cohort's effects, positive and negative, on the *post-conflict* environment. This is not to say that the youth demographic is the lynchpin in the success or failure of reconstruction, but exploring the interaction between youth and the post-conflict reconstruction process can help further our understanding of youth roles in conflict and of the ways that the international community can tailor youth programming to improve reconstruction programs.

---

23. United Nations, "Integrated Disarmament, Demobilization and Reintegration Standards: Module 5.20 Youth and DDR," www.unddr.org/iddrs/framework.php (accessed Sept. 1, 2009).

24. Caroline Hartzell, Matthew Hoddie, and Donald Rothchild, "Stabilizing the Peace after Civil War: An Investigation of Some Key Variables," *International Organization* 55, no. 1 (2001); Matthew Hoddie and Caroline Hartzell, "Signals of Reconciliation: Institution-Building and the Resolution of Civil Wars," *International Studies Review* 7, no. 1 (2005).

25. Hartzell, Hoddie, and Rothchild divide these variables into these categories: "settlement environment," or the structural characteristics of the country where the civil war occurred, such as the former regime type, the prevailing international system, and characteristics of the country and of the war itself; and the "settlement arrangement," which includes the specifics of the peace agreement, such as whether it partitions territorial autonomy or provides for power sharing and whether there was third-party enforcement or involvement. These factors are then coded and analyzed against the number of months, up to five years after the conflict, that peace endured. The five-year period of analysis allowed the test to demonstrate the short-term durability of the arrangement, allow for changes over time, and predict the likelihood of long-term stability, since civil wars have only rarely resumed after five years of peace. Ibid., 187.

General Trends in Youth-in-Conflict Literature

While there is a wide variety of scholarship on youth in conflict, less is known about the role of youth in a post-conflict scenario. There are, however, a number of recent studies that attempt to understand youth roles after conflict, and how the tensions between child and youth paradigms manifest in reconstruction policy. These studies tend to focus on three main issues: (1) child soldiers, (2) the structural roles of the youth demographic, and (3) the potential for youth agency in post-conflict reconstruction.

Child Soldiers

One of the main trends of research on youth in conflict deals with the humanitarian and legal issues of child soldiers. Young men have historically been targeted as the most capable trained soldiers, and armies have always recruited them. But in the past fifty years, the role of younger adolescents and children in armed conflict has risen dramatically. Technological innovations that allow for lighter and more easily manipulated weapons, combined with growing motivations such as extreme poverty and insecurity, increase children's and youth's capacity to participate in conflict, and their likelihood of being recruited. Girls and boys are wielding firearms and serving as spies, messengers, cooks, and sexual slaves for older troops.[26] Some are forced into service, while others volunteer for a variety of reasons, including poverty, lack of education and employment opportunities, self-defense, culture, and political ideology.[27]

> "I was abducted by Renamo in April 1980 when I had been given the chance to go to my home village to say goodbye to my parents [after transferring to a new school]. I was to go and study administration in a church-related centre. But I never got to go there." (Armando, Mozambique, 37 years old in 2006)[28]

> "I joined [President Laurent] Kabila's army when I was 13 because my home had been looted and my parents were gone. As I was then on my own, I decided to become a soldier." (Young boy, DRC)[29]

> "We were very happy to travel in their Pajero [four-wheel-drive jeep]. At that time of my life I did not know about war. . . . I used to see the LTTE soldiers come into the area I lived. They were very smartly dressed in uniforms. I used to admire them with the buttons and nicely polished guns. They go about in big cars and carry big guns. . . . I was drawn to them and wanted to join them." (Ajith, Sri Lanka)[30]

---

26. For more information on child soldiers, see Singer, *Children at War.*

27. See Brett and Specht, *Young Soldiers: Why They Choose to Fight.*

28. Bram Posthumus, *Struggles in Peacetime: Working with Ex-combatants in Mozambique: Their Work, Their Frustrations and Successes* (Amsterdam: NiZA, 2006).

29. Quote from Singer, *Children at War.*

30. Brett and Specht, *Young Soldiers: Why They Choose to Fight.*

In part as a reaction to the plight of child soldiers, a strong international movement has brought attention to the issue of children affected by armed conflict. The international community ratified a number of different documents, including the Convention on the Rights of the Child (CRC), which defined the special political, social, and economic rights of children[31] and, to reduce the incidence of child soldiering, put restrictions on the minimum legal age for recruiting soldiers.[32] But even though the international community paid special attention to children's issues and established a legal framework for their protection, the topic of *youth* in conflict has attracted much less attention. The disparity is understandable. Children are vulnerable and depend on adults. Because they cannot care for themselves, they easily become the innocent victims of conflict. Youth, on the other hand, have greater capacity than children to think for themselves and carry out actions on their own behalf. Thus, instead of being seen as innocent victims of conflict, youth are stereotyped as mischievous instigators, and much of the literature on youth in conflict focuses on their destabilizing potential.[33] Yet, although the CRC deems any person under age 18 a child, there is no clear-cut and universally applicable demarcation in development such that a 17-year-old soldier is an innocent victim and a 19-year-old is a troublemaker.[34] This blurred distinction between child and youth creates ambiguity and tension around how to deal politically and socially with young adults and adolescents involved in conflict.

Along with their efforts centered on the issue of child soldiering, many international organizations active in post-conflict areas work under a "rights-based" approach, trying to ensure the security of children and provide for their basic needs based on the legal provisions of the CRC.[35] These efforts are generally more advocacy related and often manifest in policies and programs designed to reunite orphans with their families; provide food, shelter, and health care; and establish social outreach and primary education programs. While these organizations provide many needed services, the overall approach is incomplete, especially in reaching out to older youth. The rights-based approach is limited first by an age 18 cutoff, which excludes a significant proportion of youth from the benefits of advocacy and protection programs. More significantly, the rights-based approach is limited by its underlying assumption that children need special protection because they are innocent and dependent actors in an adult world.

---

31. United Nations, "Convention on the Rights of the Child."

32. The CRC forbids recruitment of children under 18 into the armed forces, although the Optional Protocol allows for the voluntary (as opposed to forced) recruitment of children as young as 15. Ibid.

33. Jack Goldstone, "Youth and Conflict: A Toolkit for Intervention," USAID, Office of Conflict Management and Mitigation, Conflict Toolkit, 2004, www.usaid.gov/our_work/cross-cutting_programs/conflict/publications/docs/CMM_Youth_and_Conflict_Toolkit_April_2005.pdf (accessed Sept. 1, 2009); Urdal, "A Clash of Generations?"

34. McEvoy-Levy, *Troublemakers or Peacemakers?*

35. Kemper, "Youth in War-to-Peace Transitions."

Applying this logic to young people who held considerable power during wartime leaves no room for their agency in the programming itself or in the broader context of the conflict and the peacemaking process.

Structural Role of the Youth Demographic

The three main theories relevant to the relationship between youth and post-conflict reconstruction are the *youth bulge theory*, which emphasizes population structures, the *greed-grievance model*, which emphasizes decision-making structures, and the *spoiler theory*, which emphasizes power structures.

Youth bulge theory. Youth bulge theory[36] examines the likelihood of conflict based on the logic that a large proportion of young men in the population will make a country more vulnerable to instability. This argument proposes that the sheer number of young men in a country or region affects the decision-making framework, increasing both the motives and the opportunity for political violence.[37] For example, when a disproportionately large population of young people is seeking jobs or to enroll in university, a country's infrastructure will not have enough space to accommodate the demand. As a result, grievances such as poverty and unemployment will be amplified, increasing the motivation toward violence and rebellion.[38] This pattern is astutely summarized by a youth interviewer in Pakistan: "So, in an area where economic opportunities are scarce, education is not free, where no law can be extended, [and] the border area has been at war for the last 24 years: could one expect some positive changes other than fighting Jihad."[39] Indeed, without economic opportunity or access to a political platform to have their voices heard, the logic of violence emerges as a rational—and, seemingly, the most effective—means for youth to make demands and engage the system.[40]

Greed-grievance model. Paul Collier and Anke Hoeffler examine the motive and opportunity for violence with an econometric model to predict conflict.[41] Their greed-grievance model uses a kind of cost-benefit analysis to understand what conditions make it easier for violent groups to recruit members. This thinking identifies several factors that can affect the opportunity-cost structure in ways that make joining rebel organizations a rational choice. "Opportunity

---

36. Urdal, "A Clash of Generations?"; Zakaria, "The Politics of Rage."

37. It is important to note that Urdal's study examines young men's decisions to join an existing organization and does not look at the likelihood of young men forming a new organization or working together through collective action. Therefore, Urdal is saying that a large proportion of young men, combined with institutional crowding, increases the likelihood that young men will turn to violence to express their grievances if the structures to do so, such as rebel organizations, are already in place. Urdal, "A Clash of Generations?" 607–9.

38. Ibid., 609.

39. Brett and Specht, *Young Soldiers: Why They Choose to Fight.*

40. Urdal, "A Clash of Generations?" 612–13; Collier and Hoeffler, "Greed and Grievance in Civil War," 569; Zakaria, "The Politics of Rage."

41. Collier and Hoeffler, "Greed and Grievance in Civil War."

cost" refers to the foregone benefits in choosing one action (e.g., joining a rebel organization or using violence to fight for a cause) over another action (e.g., staging a peaceful protest or lobbying for a change in policy). Joining a violent group means making certain sacrifices, such as leaving one's family or job, that are enough to prevent some people from joining. But young men, who have fewer family obligations than their elders, fewer employment opportunities, and fewer political options, have a correspondingly lower cost to joining a rebel group. Membership in these groups is also quite enticing, since those who join will be guaranteed benefits including food, education, camaraderie, and power, as these young soldiers demonstrate:

> "I heard that the rebels at least were eating. So I joined them." (Ikombi, young soldier in DRC)[42]

> "You got like a buzz when you done it, like I don't know, all the adrenaline and all. Like when you pick the gun up." (Billy, Northern Ireland)[43]

Therefore, a large youth cohort with low opportunity costs is ripe for recruiting by rebel groups.[44]

Both the youth bulge and greed-grievance models address the youth demographic's potential to cause conflict, but they say nothing about the youth role either during the conflict or in a post-conflict reconstruction process. Indeed, a large proportion of youth in the population can also threaten stability during the reconstruction process. And the opportunity-cost structures described by Urdal and Collier and Hoeffler may continue to drive the decision-making process in the post-conflict environment, although (for some, anyway) the shoe may now be on the other foot. That is, as young people are forced to cope with the terror of war and as many become heads of households, they face new responsibilities and may see violence as less productive than peaceful pursuits. The intervening effects of reconstruction actors can also change the cost-benefit structure: if reconstruction policy provides opportunities for a transition to civilian life (such as transitional stipends, vocational training, access to education, and other sociopolitical empowerment programming), the potential benefits of returning to civilian life may outweigh those of staying with a rebel group. Thus, we see that although these two models help explain the relationship between youth and conflict causation, neither provides a complete analytic structure for understanding the role and impact of the youth population once the conflict has begun and after it is over.

Spoiler theory: The third approach relevant to youth roles in conflict comes from spoiler theory, which examines the behavior of elite individuals or groups

---

42. Paul Salopek, "The Guns of Africa: Violence-Wracked Nations Are Dumping Grounds for World's Arsenals," *Chicago Tribune* via *Seattle Times*, Feb. 27, 2002.

43. Brett and Specht, *Young Soldiers: Why They Choose to Fight.*

44. Collier and Hoeffler, "Greed and Grievance in Civil War."

seeking to thwart a peace process.[45] Recently, Kelly M. Greenhill and Solomon Major reframed the spoiler problem in terms of how an individual's or group's structural and situational capacity determines its behavior.[46] This *"capabilities model"* argues that spoilers act based on a cost-benefit structure of cooperation versus continuation of conflict. This model also adds to the paradigm the category of "latent spoilers," defined as groups of "determined but weak actors who would oppose the implementation of a peace accord, if only they had the material wherewithal to do so."[47]

While spoiler theory focuses on elites, the capabilities model can apply to youth behavior if a large youth cohort is understood as a latent spoiler. Youth who once held relatively powerful positions during wartime, as soldiers or troop captains wielding the threat of violence, will face a different power structure in peacetime. Despite their high expectations for what a resolution of the conflict might bring, in a peacetime environment youth are likely to lose much of the power they once held, face inadequate economic opportunity, and lack access to a political forum to make their voices heard. This forces a cost-benefit analysis similar to that described in the greed-grievance model, as youth choose whether to cooperate with a peace agreement or continue using violence. For instance, if they keep fighting, they maintain their sense of belonging in a community and the power implicit in being armed. This sense of camaraderie and power is reflected in the comments of young people from various conflict zones:

> "When you feel the heat in a neighborhood, when you begin to fire shots around, you start to smoke marijuana, you're almost the tough guy of the neighborhood. Then people see, this guy's like that, not a—you see?" (Carlos, Colombia)[48]

> "Because you have been separated from your families for such a long time, it was natural to forge new bonds, most likely with your immediate colleagues. We did not really have complete families anymore. So the people you were with all the time in the military became your new family." (Paulo Andrasson Vinte, reflecting on his reintegration after being in the armed forces in Mozambique)[49]

> "I had many friends in the bush. Whenever I fell behind during the fighting, they'd help me get back to my unit. One time, we were in the north, and we were attacked by the Kamajors [government-allied militia in Sierra Leone]. I was in a house, and I didn't know what was going on. When I came out, one of my friends killed the Kamajor who wanted to kill me." ("I.," Sierra Leone)[50]

---

45. This sense of the term "spoiler" was coined by Stephen J. Stedman in 1997 as a term to describe elites who are party to a conflict and who strive to hamper the peace process. Stephen Stedman, "Spoiler Problems in Peace Processes," *International Security* 22, no. 2 (1997).

46. Kelly M. Greenhill and Solomon Major, "The Perils of Profiling: Civil War Spoilers and the Collapse of Intrastate Peace Accords," *International Security* 31, no. 3 (2006).

47. Ibid., 9–10.

48. Brett and Specht, *Young Soldiers: Why They Choose to Fight.*

49. Posthumus, *Struggles in Peacetime.*

50. Singer, *Children at War,* 89–90.

By contrast, in civilian society these young people could be shunned from their homes and face unemployment, no access to education, and, because of their young age, no significant political power. As result, youth's "expected utility of continuing to fight" (what Greenhill and Major characterize as the most important factor in determining spoiler behavior) may be greater than the perceived benefits of integrating into the peace regime.[51] This is similar to the cost-benefit analysis that drives elite spoiler behavior. But because youth are not as able as elites to manipulate the peace process, they may choose other ways to continue to fight, ranging on a spectrum from demonstrating to riots, joining street gangs, or even rejoining militias.

The youth bulge, greed-grievance, and capabilities models all demonstrate the strength of a structurally based analysis in determining actors' behavior in conflict environments. While these models tend to see youth as a destabilizing factor, this type of analysis suggests that the nature of youth behavior in conflict is not predetermined—that youth roles have the potential to change given the proper conditions. If this is indeed the case, examining the conditions that youth face in a post-conflict society can help intervening actors find ways to change incentive structures that lead youth toward destabilizing behavior, and instead invest young people in the peace process. If reconstruction policies could make it more rewarding for youth to work with the peace process than to use violence, not only would it be more difficult for armed groups to recruit young people, but these same young people might instead choose to contribute positively to the peace process and the security of their communities. For instance, if youth were given access to education, training, and tools to earn an income; had the opportunity to participate in community crime patrols; or could join youth groups with a true voice in local politics, they would have both the opportunity and the incentive to contribute to the rebuilding process.

Understanding the dynamic of incentive structures during post-conflict reconstruction requires an analysis of the various types and relative success of intervening policies and programs. Since a post-conflict state may also be faced with humanitarian crises such as mass displacement, disease, and destruction of infrastructure, the factors shaping the incentive structure for youth may be related to a variety of needs that were not present in the preconflict scenario. The three case studies will serve as a springboard to further examine the role of youth as potential latent spoilers and the impact of changing structural dynamics on determining youth behavior during the post-conflict reconstruction period.

Youth Agency in Post-conflict Reconstruction
Even combined, the youth bulge literature's focus on the youth population's potentially destabilizing characteristics, and the protection issues addressed by

---

51. Ibid., 12.

the scholarship on child soldiers do not provide an adequate model for under-standing youth behavior in the post-conflict environment. However, there is an emerging field that acknowledges young people's more dynamic role in post-accord peacebuilding. Two recent models, for instance, point out the limited conception of youth roles reflected in current approaches and argue for a more holistic understanding of youth behavior in post-conflict reconstruction.

Approaches to youth programming. Yvonne Kemper, in her report "Youth in War-to-Peace Transitions: Approaches of International Organizations," provides a useful model for understanding the limits of various approaches used to address youth issues during post-conflict reconstruction. Kemper divides the approaches into three distinct categories: rights-based, economic, and sociopolitical. Each approach has significant value for the reconstruction process, reflects a differ-ent understanding of children and youth needs, and addresses a different time frame in youth development in conflict situations. For instance, as previously discussed, the rights-based approach focuses mainly on preventive policy, view-ing children as victims of a hostile situation that undermines their legal human rights. Programs using this framework tend to concentrate on reuniting children with their families, educating communities about protecting children's rights, and providing temporary food and shelter.

An economic approach moves a bit further away from the emphasis on the child's passive role. Instead, similar to the greed-grievance model, an economic approach views youth as decision makers in the marketplace, who make rational decisions in pursuit of their best interests.[52] This approach is driven by young people's potential role either as an easily exploitable resource for conflict produc-tion (e.g., as a soldier, sex slave, or spy) or as a resource for a productive peacetime economy (e.g., as a student, microentrepreneur, or worker). The corresponding programming is therefore aimed at the short-term reintegration of youth into pro-ductive economic activity, often through vocational training, job placement, or access to microbusiness lending. But just as the rights-based approach is limited by its underlying principles, the economic approach is limited because it reduc-es youth to being merely a resource available for manipulation and, therefore, "inadvertently accepts th[e] narrow view of those who exploit them and carries on myths of youth's inherent violence."[53]

Under the rights-based and economic models, the goal is to help children and youth fulfill their potential along a spectrum of potential roles as passive social and economic actors. While this conception of possible roles for children and youth may be descriptively accurate, it is not complete. Young people do fill these roles; however, they are not limited to them. Youth also have the poten-tial to act as social and political agents who can contribute to the post-conflict

---

52. Kemper, "Youth in War-to-Peace Transitions," 25.

53. Ibid., 27.

reconstruction process. In this respect, a sociopolitical approach to youth programming regards youth as vital members of civil society and understands the precarious long-term dynamic whereby youth can be active agents in the community, both as potential spoilers and as peacebuilders. Recognizing this potential, these sociopolitical empowerment programs may support youth civil society groups to do community service projects or engage with their local government; establish and train an independent youth parliament; or use the arts, media, or journalism as a platform for youth to engage in community dialogue. While sociopolitical youth programming is the least common of the three approaches, successful sociopolitical programs have the potential to help "rebuild war-torn societies through and by youth."[54]

Although each of the three types of programming provides a distinct value to the reconstruction process, one approach is typically favored over another, and evidence from conflict zones suggests that "there appears to be a mismatch between the needs of youth and the programs on offer. Current programming focuses primarily on humanitarian needs and psychological support (broadly defined) with less emphasis on education and economic interventions. Moreover, programs and spending also appear to be more oriented towards children rather than adults."[55] As Kemper and Annan, Blattman, and Horton suggest, programming should be more inclusive of young adults, and a holistic perspective on youth programming should include all three approaches and recognize youth's agency as social, economic, and political actors.

Youth's dual role in post-conflict reconstruction. Siobhán McEvoy-Levy, in her recent works "Youth as Social and Political Agents: Issues in Post-Settlement Peace Building" and *Troublemakers or Peacemakers? Youth and Post-Accord Peace Building*, portrays youth as dynamic agents who embody the dual task of the postaccord peace process.[56] Youth can be both positive and negative agents during reconstruction. Young people in post-conflict zones have organized student community service projects, taught their peers about conflict resolution and health issues, and started a union of taxi and motorbike drivers to serve their community. By contrast, youth can also start street gangs, join terrorist organizations, or riot in the streets. As the two quotes below show, many young people in areas of conflict believe that they have a stake in the conflict and that they can affect their communities, through either violence or peacebuilding.

---

54. Ibid., 36.

55. Annan, Blattman, and Horton, "The State of Youth and Youth Protection in Northern Uganda," vii.

56. Siobhán McEvoy-Levy, "Youth as Social and Political Agents: Issues in Post-Settlement Peace Building," Kroc Institute Occasional Paper no. 21, 2001, www.ciaonet.org/wps/mcs01/index.html (accessed Sept. 1, 2009); McEvoy-Levy, *Troublemakers or Peacemakers?*

"I'm willing to give my young life for the land that belongs to my grandparents. I didn't fight for glory, I fought for freedom." (Bashkim H., 16, Gjakova/Djakovica, Kosovo, on joining the KLA)[57]

"When young people have more self-confidence and opportunities to express our views, we will be able to protect ourselves and transform our communities." (Emmanuel, co-founder of GYFA, a youth-run education and advocacy group in Northern Uganda)[58]

The roles that youth choose to take on may change over time and, either actively or passively, contribute to peace or instability. However, an understanding of youth roles in conflict is incomplete without both sides of the equation: as perpetrators and victims of violence, and as leaders of grassroots peace efforts. Although ignoring young people's potential multiplicity of roles may not be fatal to the reconstruction process, it may cause prolonged instability. Dealing with youth issues is central to fostering a sustainable peace.[59]

Moreover, McEvoy-Levy proposes that the endurance of peace will depend "on whether the next generations accept or reject it, how they are socialized during the peace process and their perceptions of what that peace has achieved."[60] If, during the peacebuilding process, youth are given venues in which they can succeed, have their voices heard, and participate in decision making in their communities, they may be more inclined to trust in the peace process and strive to further it when they become their countries' leaders. But if youth needs are ignored, disenchantment with the peace process will affect how these young people interact with state institutions and deal with community issues in the future.

Although the literature on youth in conflict and youth agency includes a number of different causal theories and several in-depth single-case studies, there is no cohesive study of the youth demographic's role in post-conflict and peacemaking processes that derives conclusions from cross-case comparisons. As Kemper's work shows, to develop programs that better cater to youth needs, it is important to understand the effects that the policies of local, international, and third-party institutions have on the emergence and impact of youth participation. This study attempts to fill that gap.

Youth Policies in Post-conflict Reconstruction: The Role of NGOs

NGOs have become one of the leading types of institutional actors responsible for implementing post-conflict reconstruction programs, particularly for youth.

---

57. Jane Lowicki and Allison A. Pillsbury, "Making the Choice for a Better Life: Promoting the Protection and Capacity of Kosovo's Youth," Women's Commission report, 2001, www.womenscommission.org/pdf/yu_adol.pdf (accessed Sept. 1, 2009).

58. Women's Commission for Refugee Women and Children, "Youth Speak Out: New Voices on the Protection and Participation of Young People Affected by Armed Conflict," report, 2005, www.womenscommission.org/pdf/cap_ysofinal_rev.pdf (accessed Sept. 1, 2009).

59. McEvoy-Levy, "Youth as Social and Political Agents," 5–6.

60. Ibid., 5.

While international organizations, such as the United Nations, and aid organizations of foreign countries, such as the United States Agency for International Development (USAID), are active players in post-conflict reconstruction, they often depend on local and international NGO (iNGO) partners to help implement their programs. The abundant and increasing activity of non-governmental actors has created a situation where NGOs with specific grants and objectives are better suited than international organizations to tailor programs to youth issues, and NGOs have thus taken a more dominant role in dealing with the 15 to 24-year-old demographic. Therefore, any analysis of the impact of youth programming during post-conflict reconstruction must include an examination of NGO involvement.

The trend of rising NGO involvement in conflict and post-conflict situations has been discussed at length in recent literature as part of a global phenomenon that is shifting power away from states and into the hands of multinational corporations and organizations. The power and influence that NGOs wield is impressive. According to J. T. Mathews, in the late 1990s, NGOs were providing "more official development assistance than the entire U.N. system (excluding the World Bank and the International Monetary Fund)."[61] NGOs' activity within conflict zones is also growing rapidly.

With the help of various NGO programs, youth in post-conflict situations actively contribute to community safety, crime prevention, economic development, and peacebuilding efforts.[62] However, this vast expansion of non-governmental action in conflict zones may also bring severe costs. Specifically in conflict situations involving humanitarian and refugee crises, the presence of numerous organizations and an abundant supply of aid can worsen the situation by prolonging the war and even serving as a catalyst for the spread of conflict.[63] For instance, in refugee camps it is extremely difficult to separate noncombatants from rebels seeking to use the humanitarian assistance to recuperate their armies and continue to launch attacks from a safe haven, as happened in the DRC in the aftermath of the Rwandan genocide.[64]

While NGO efforts may be humanitarian and altruistic in nature, the competitive environment in which they exist can change the way these organizations behave, to the detriment of the populations they originally sought to serve. Cooley and Ron (2002) use a political-economic model to explain NGO behavior that is out of sync with originally stated humanitarian goals.[65] Their model

61. J. T. Mathews, "Power Shift," *Foreign Affairs* 76, no. 1 (1997).

62. Steve Seigel, Frederick Barton, and Karin von Hippel, *Engaging Youth to Build Safer Communities: A Report of the CSIS Post-conflict Reconstruction Project*, Aug. 2006 (Washington, D.C.: CSIS Press, 2006).

63. Sarah Kenyon Lischer, *Dangerous Sanctuaries: Refugee Camps, Civil War, and the Dilemmas of Humanitarian Aid* (Ithaca, NY: Cornell University Press, 2005), 73.

64. Ibid.

65. Alexander Cooley and James Ron, "The NGO Scramble: Organizational Insecurity and the Political Economy of Transnational Action," *International Security* 27, no. 1 (2002): 9.

shows that as the number of NGOs operating within a sector increases, competition among NGOs also increases as they vie for limited funding resources. This marketization of the NGO community through competitive bidding and renewable contracts provides incentives for "dysfunctional" behavior, whereby NGO operations may resemble profit-seeking companies and lose sight of humanitarian and nonprofit objectives.[66]

Since NGOs play such a dominant role in facilitating youth programming during reconstruction, to understand youth behavior in post-conflict environments we must first understand how NGO involvement affects the youth demographic. On one hand, as Kemper demonstrates, NGOs' potential for helping youth can vary depending on the type of programming (rights-based, economic, or sociopolitical). But how the program design translates into impact on the ground is equally important, and this may depend on how well NGOs are able to avoid the traps of competition and successfully coordinate their efforts. While the original intentions and policies may be positive, youth-oriented NGO programs can and do suffer from the same malfunctions described by Cooley and Ron and by Lischer, and the resulting inter-NGO competition can end up having a net negative impact on youth development and the post-conflict reconstruction process. Therefore, to assess the relative and net impacts of NGO programming, this study includes an analysis of the types of NGO programming provided during the reconstruction process, along with an examination of the inter-NGO atmosphere, including competition and coordination among NGOs and with international organizations.

Summary of Existing Literature

The theories discussed in this chapter suggest a broad range of hypotheses regarding the impact of youth populations on post-conflict stability. Negative causal hypotheses, such as the youth bulge and spoiler logic, predict that large youth cohorts increase the likelihood of instability. These arguments focus on overarching structural conditions, such as the lack of economic resources, unemployment, land scarcity, and urban crowding, which lower the opportunity cost of joining armed groups. These conditions, combined with technological developments and changes in modern warfare, make young people an easily exploitable resource, likely to express their frustration through violence.[67]

On the other side of the spectrum, scholars posit a dynamic theory of the role of youth in conflict. In contrast to the youth bulge and spoiler models, this theory demonstrates that youth are on the front lines, both in war and in grass-roots efforts for mobilizing peace. The agency that youth have in wartime can be

---

66. Ibid., 6.
67. Singer, *Children at War*, 55.

Table 1.1 Theories Relating Youth and Conflict in Existing Literature

Theory	Logic	Driving Forces Affecting Youth Behavior
Youth Bulge	A large population of young men is a potentially destabilizing force because this demographic has particular motive and incentive to resort to violence.	Lack of opportunity, few obligations
Greed-Grievance	The opportunity-cost structure in the decision-making process for involvement in conflict highlights young men as an especially dangerous and destabilizing population because their low opportunity cost in joining rebel forces makes them easy targets for recruitment.	Unemployment, institutional crowding
Spoiler	Certain actors may have incentives to disrupt the negotiation or peacemaking process, depending on personality and structural conditions. Youth may be a potential demographic of "latent spoilers" who, given the means, would obstruct the conflict resolution process.	Lack of access to political and economic structures
Dynamic role	Youth have the potential to act as both destructive and constructive sociopolitical agents. The types of policies implemented during the reconstruction process, from child protection to economic and sociopolitical empowerment, reflect conceptions of the youth role in conflict. These conceptual frameworks of various programs may either limit or empower youth in exerting a positive influence on the peacebuilding process.	Type and effectiveness of youth policy and programming

redirected to efforts to build safer communities. For instance, young people who have served as soldiers and, in many cases, been in charge of other soldiers, have developed certain leadership and social skills that may be used in peacebuilding and security programs, as seen, for instance, in Liberia and South Africa, where youth volunteer in crime patrols and community peace worker programs.[68] In the short run, these programs provide youth with an outlet for their energy, and a constructive way to have the camaraderie and agency they had during wartime. In return for young people's time and service to the community, NGOs may provide them with career counseling or training in leadership or life skills. In the long run, the programs establish youth ownership and buy-in to peacebuilding processes and shape the political attitudes and skills of the younger generation in a positive direction, to support a durable peace. (Table 1.1 summarizes these existing perspectives.)

---

68. Seigel, Barton, and Von Hippel, *Engaging Youth to Build Safer Communities.*

While these theories cover a broad range of potential youth roles, many questions remain unanswered. Each of the arguments discussed so far presents an idea of youth's potential impact or role in conflict, yet none provides an adequate model to explain why some children, like John, may choose destabilizing behavior while others, like Hawa, choose to contribute to their community. The different structural characteristics that create incentives for young people to turn to violent behaviors have been explored at length in the context of conflict causation. But the possibility that structural characteristics or intervening programming could create a generation of peacebuilders rather than terrorists and rebels has largely been ignored. Further, while the success of post-conflict reconstruction has been evaluated via several different variables, there has not been a cohesive study examining the youth demographic's impact on stability during post-conflict reconstruction.

Causal Expectations: Key Lessons from Mozambique, the DRC, and Kosovo

The evidence developed in the following three case studies supports the expectation that a high proportion of youth in the population does not automatically presage instability. Moreover, the study reveals a number of key lessons for understanding youth roles in post-conflict situations:

- *Youth are not simply a force for instability; they are also agents of peace. Their role, whether positive or negative, is shaped by the structures of the reconstruction process.* The youth population's influence on the level of stability during post-conflict reconstruction is highly conditional. The institutional context and impact of intervening reconstruction policy can have a great effect on whether youth become a part of the ongoing conflict or a part of the solution. The types of policies implemented and the efficiency with which they are carried out are integral in shaping this youth role. If reconstruction actors recognize the special needs of the youth demographic and carry out comprehensive reintegration and empowerment policies, not only can youth's negative potential be quelled, but their energies can be redirected toward peacebuilding and nation-building activities, contributing to the safety, security, and progress of their community.

- *Successful reconstruction involving the youth demographic does not require specific youth policy or an onslaught of youth-oriented NGOs. Rather, it depends on how effectively reconstruction actors fulfill certain critical functions.* The reconstruction programs that best channel youth's positive potential are those that efficiently meet the critical functions of protection, reintegration, and empowerment, thereby facilitating young people's positive transition from war to peace. For instance, whereas family reunification policies were necessary for child protection, they are not always effective in preventing young people from rejoining armed groups. Rather, it is the programs that go further, providing quality social and economic reintegration programming, education opportunities, and platforms for youth voices to be heard in the reconstruction debate, that are the most successful in preventing youth from resorting to violence. When these programs were successful, they not only prevented violence, they also helped young people become agents of peace and development through community service programs in refugee camps, conflict resolution and interethnic dialogue programs in their communities, and even youth parliaments.

Protection, reintegration, and empowerment are the three critical youth needs that must be met in post-conflict environments. Protection programs address the need for safety, security, and health care. Reintegration programs help young people adjust to peacetime life and reestablish a sense of belonging in a community. Empowerment, or capacity building, through basic or vocational education, gives young people the skills they need to succeed economically. Sociopolitical empowerment programs, though not necessarily critical to the immediate reconstruction process, give youth platforms to make their voices heard in decision-making processes and ongoing community dialogue.

Again, this does not mean that there must be a specific youth policy or a large number of organizations working on youth programs, but only that these youth needs must be effectively met. *Who* performs these functions appears not to matter as long as *someone* is doing them. In fact, community-based programming that addresses these critical youth needs can be just as effective and influential as youth-specific programming. A broad range of actors, including the international community, NGOs, and local religious leaders, can help fulfill these needs and facilitate youth's transition from war to peace.

- *To harness young people's potential as peacebuilders, post-conflict actors must bridge the gap from advocacy to empowerment.* Most of the programs for young people during post-conflict reconstruction are child-oriented, emphasizing psychosocial and protection issues over educational and economic activities. Protection, psychosocial care, and community advocacy are critical to helping young children affected by war, but these types of programs are insufficient for older youth, who are important social and political actors in the reconstruction process. Whereas an advocacy framework is well suited to providing protection and lessening the youth demographic's negative potential, sociopolitical and empowerment approaches have proved more effective in guiding young people to become forces of positive change in their communities.

- *The sequence of youth programming is also key.* The case studies also suggest that youth programming that successfully addresses the critical youth needs is not enough—the *sequence* in which it meets those needs is equally important. For instance, for youth capacity-building efforts to succeed, the immediate survival needs of food, shelter, and safety must first be met, followed by reintegration. Different post-conflict environments may require that more attention be paid to resolving immediate security issues, while others may allow for immediate implementation of youth capacity-building programming.

Because successful youth policy is contingent both on structural conditions (such as the degree of humanitarian crisis and the state of existing educational and economic institutions) and on the sequencing of programming, the level of effort need not be extreme as long as it meets the critical demands of the youth demographic at each stage. If intervening actors cannot establish protection for youth, help them reintegrate into their communities, and provide effective empowerment and capacity-building programs, there is a greater likelihood that youth will emerge as a negative or destabilizing factor during the reconstruction process. But if those needs are met, more youth choose to participate as agents of peace, reconciliation, and community development. Chapter 5 gives an in-depth discussion of sequencing in youth programming and post-conflict reconstruction, integrating lessons demonstrated in the case studies.

Methodology

Since youth's role in post-conflict reconstruction has been studied far less than its role in conflict causation, hypotheses are needed associating youth population levels with reconstruction outcomes. Therefore, this study is structured with a hypothesis-generating focus and a heuristic case study design. This type of research design uses detailed case examinations to generate hypotheses and research questions that will lead to more refined hypotheses, addressing more specific ends.[69]

Stephen van Evera, in his *Guide to Methods for Students of Political Science*, notes that hypotheses can be generated both through the "controlled comparison" of case studies, whereby "the investigator infers hypotheses from contrasts or similarities in aspects of several cases," and through "congruence procedures," which explore "within-case correlation between the study variables and other phenomena."[70] This study uses both methods to compare the similarities and

---

69. See Stephen van Evera, *Guide to Methods for Students of Political Science* (Ithaca, N.Y.: Cornell University Press, 1997); Harry Eckstein, "Case Study and Theory in Political Science," in *Handbook of Political Science*, ed. Fred I. Greenstein and Nelson W. Polsby (Reading, Mass.: Addison-Wesley, 1975).

70. Van Evera, *Guide to Methods for Students of Political Science*, 68–69.

differences in the reconstruction process in Mozambique, the DRC, and Kosovo and to uncover possible causal relationships between the variables and the role of youth during and after periods of conflict.

While this type of research design can yield new insights, the purpose of the inquiry is not to generate firm conclusions about youth in the post-conflict reconstruction process. Rather, the goal is to gather, explore, and compare the available data to better locate and define possible causal relationships. By allowing for both in-case and cross-case evaluation of the different variables on the overall level of post-conflict stability, the case study design makes possible a cohesive and comparative analysis of the relationships among youth, intervening reconstruction actors, and stability, in a field where no similar studies exist. The study's value, then, is not in drawing finite conclusions but in identifying future avenues for exploration and development in the field.

Case Selection

The cases were selected to permit the best possible comparative research design. The standards for choosing the cases were drawn from Van Evera's designations of eleven criteria for case selection. Specifically, cases were chosen based on how they fulfilled the requirements of data richness; extreme values on the independent variable, dependent variable, or condition variables; and divergence of competing theories' predictions of the case.[71] Several different cases of post-conflict reconstruction were vetted across potential variables to construct a group of cases that were similar enough to allow comparison yet different enough to provide variability. These variables included the proportion of youth in the population, level of international involvement, and relative outcomes of stability. Finally, whereas two cases would have been too few to make significant comparisons, space constraints precluded using more than three.

The three cases that were chosen—Mozambique, the DRC, and Kosovo— exhibit a number of similarities. Each case involves a postaccord environment where reconstruction activity has occurred involving differing degrees of domestic and international influence. All three cases had a relatively large youth cohort in the population and also significant youth involvement in the conflict itself. Also, each conflict meets the defining criteria of a civil war rather than simply an insurgency.[72]

Variability is built into the design for the dependent variable *level of instability*, since the case studies fall along a spectrum of success (and failure) in achieving

---

71. Ibid., 88.

72. Whereas a civil war is defined as a war between opposing groups from the same country, a rebellion is a "condition of revolt against a government that is less than an organized revolution and that is not recognized as belligerency." *Merriam-Webster's Collegiate Dictionary*, 11th ed. (Springfield, Mass.: Merriam-Webster, 2003).

post-conflict stability, ranging from Mozambique—often considered the "poster child" of reconstruction—to the DRC, which has experienced a return to conflict in some areas and exemplifies the regionalization and spread of conflict. Kosovo represents the middle case, with evidence of successful peacebuilding and increased security but also ongoing tension and violence. Geographic variation permits a broader scope of inquiry and of potential inferences. While using two cases from sub-Saharan Africa provides for similarities in initial conditions, using Kosovo allows for cross-regional comparison, with the expectation that reconstruction policy and international involvement in the European context may differ from that in African conflicts. The differences in the cases, as well as the potential problems with comparison, are discussed in chapter 5's evaluation of the inferences drawn from the three case studies.

Several cases that could have been included were left out of the research design, for various reasons. First, for some cases, data on the reconstruction process was not readily available. Also, some cases were left out because they did not present a sufficiently conclusive or extreme value of stability or instability. For instance, Sierra Leone, Liberia, and Guinea were all considered as potential cases for comparison against Mozambique, but data on the conflicts in Liberia and Guinea were initially less available than that for the DRC, and this posed a potentially significant obstacle to the study's success.[73] The DRC was chosen over Sierra Leone because it represented a more extreme variation on the level of stability and could be considered as a potential case of reconstruction failure compared to the success in Mozambique.[74] While a research design including Mozambique, Sierra Leone, and the DRC might have been just as appropriate, with Sierra Leone representing the medium in comparison to the "stable" and "unstable" environments in Mozambique and the DRC, the types of issues raised regarding the youth demographic may have been more limited than with the inclusion of a case from a different region. For instance, all three African cases involve widespread use of child soldiers. But youth involvement in conflict is not limited to child soldiering; thus, examining cases where this was not the main issue adds a useful degree of variability.

The cross-regional comparison also enlarges the scope of inquiry by allowing for a comparison between the international community's role in a generally more developed region and in a less developed region.

---

73. The availability of data was based on initial searches in a number of social science databases, including the Social Science Citation Index, H. W. Wilson Databases Social Sciences Full Text, and PAISInternational.

74. The reconstruction process in Sierra Leone has seen elements of both success and failure, particularly concerning the youth demographic. Although it is an important case for understanding the roles of youth in post-conflict reconstruction, it was not selected for this study, because it has not experienced a level of instability as decisive as in the DRC. For more information on the conflict in Sierra Leone and on the roles of youth there, see Michael Chege, "Sierra Leone: The State that Came Back from the Dead," *Washington Quarterly* 25, no. 3 (2002); Angela McIntyre, "Children and Youth in Sierra Leone's Peace-Building Process," *African Security Review* 12, no. 2 (2003); Krjin Peters, "From Weapons to Wheels: Young Sierra Leonean Ex-Combatants Become Motorbike Taxi-Riders," *Journal of Peace Conflict and Development* 10, no. 10 (2007).

Variable Structure and Coding Methods

For each case, the study considers the influence of several independent variables on the level of stability during the first five years of the reconstruction process.[75] To begin, the dependent variable *instability* is defined in terms of political violence, riots and demonstrations, terrorism, tension between opposing parties and within the general population, and participation in rebel or violent groups that both hinders the progress of peace and reconstruction and is connected or related to youth activity. To evaluate and support findings on the level of instability, data on levels of violence and tension were gathered from various sources, including the "Political Scene" sections of the Economist Intelligence Unit's Country Profiles and its Country Reports,[76] which provide quarterly updates with an archive that spans the time frame of each study. Ratings from the Global Peace Index,[77] the 2008 Ibrahim Index of African Governance,[78] Failed States Index,[79] and RiskMap 2008[80] were also used to guide the analysis on a number of key stability factors and to support the stability ratings developed in the case studies. From these data, instability is coded along a scale with graduations of extreme, high, medium, and low. An extreme coding reflects a reincitation of violence at or near the levels experienced during the conflict. A high level of instability indicates the existence of numerous instances of prolonged violence, rioting, or terrorism that is politically motivated. A medium level of instability describes a situation in which tensions may be high but instances of violence or rioting are not prolonged or directly politically motivated. Finally, a low level of

75. If the conflict took place far enough in the past such that data is available for more than five years after the peace accord, it is also included in the individual analysis, but not in the cross-case comparisons.

76. The Economist Intelligence Unit (EIU) is an electronic database providing expert analysis on over two hundred countries. Economist Intelligence Unit, "Country Report," 1996–2009, www.eiu.com (subscription only, accessed Sept. 1, 2009).

77. The Global Peace Index 2008 ranks 121 nations according to their relative peacefulness, using 24 indicators, ranging from a nation's level of military expenditure to its relations with neighboring countries and the level of respect for human rights. Vision of Humanity, "Global Peace Index," www.visionofhumanity.com/rankings/ (accessed Sept. 1, 2009).

78. The Ibrahim Index of African Governance ranks sub-Saharan African nations according to the quality of governance in five key areas: safety and security; rule of law, transparency, and corruption; participation and human rights; sustainable economic development; and human development.
Mo Ibrahim Foundation, "2008 Ibrahim Index of African Governance," www.moibrahimfoundation.org/the-index.asp (accessed Sept. 1, 2009).

79. The Failed States Index ranks countries based on social, economic, and political pressures that may predict state failure. To evaluate each country, the index uses the Conflict Assessment System Tool (CAST). Failed States Index, www.fundforpeace.org/web/index.php?option=com_content&task=view&id=99&Itemid=140 (accessed Sept. 1, 2009).

80. The RiskMap 2008 assesses the level of political and security risk for businesses looking to operate in foreign countries. The political risk rating gauges "the likelihood of state or non-state political actors negatively affecting business operations in a country," whereas the security risk rating gauges the likelihood of "state or non-state actors engaging in actions that harm the financial, physical and human assets of a company." Control Risks Group, *RiskMap 2008* (London: Control Risks, 2007), www.controlrisks.com/default.aspx?page=1096 (accessed Sept. 4, 2009).

instability reflects an environment with very few incidences of violence. In this case, if some violence exists, it is not necessarily politically motivated.

The analysis of independent variables begins with an evaluation of macroeconomic and demographic factors that describe the post-conflict situation. This includes an examination of the proportion of youth age 10–24 in the population, the level of youth involvement in the conflict, and the degree to which youth were affected by the conflict. These indicators are evaluated as high, medium, or low. *High* represents a large proportion of youth in the population compared to the global baselines, and a large proportion of youth affected by the conflict, measured through youth participation in armed groups, number of displaced youth (internally or as refugees), level of youth unemployment, and destruction of schools. *Medium* represents a youth population proportion on par with the baselines, and moderate youth levels of participation in conflict, internal and external displacement, and unemployment. A rating of *low* indicates a proportion of youth in the population below the baselines, relatively little youth participation in armed groups, low youth displacement and unemployment, and little destruction of schools. In addition, the macroeconomic and demographic variables include data on the level of unemployment and the gross national income (GNI) per capita. Each of these indicators is then coded as *high, medium,* or *low* compared to a regional baseline.

The analysis then divides the reconstruction policy into four broad categories of independent variables, each coded to reflect its level of influence on the youth demographic in the reconstruction process. The coding scheme for these variables uses two analytical determinants. First, each variable is coded as having either a positive or a negative *directional* impact. Then the level of the directional impact is graded as *low, medium,* or *high.*

The first independent variable, *international involvement,* includes policies ranging from the specific stipulations of the peace treaty to the involvement of foreign governments and the impact of the United Nations or other international organizations. This involvement includes, for instance, how the peace treaty establishes the DDR process, what type of peacekeeping mission the United Nations or other regional organization arranged, and an evaluation of the type and impact of the youth-specific programs that these organizations implemented.

The *domestic policy* variable reflects the national government's reconstruction policies as they affect the youth demographic. For instance, this includes how local officials handle education and employment programming during the reconstruction process. The variable may also include nationally run demobilization and reintegration programs, such as family reunification or other youth-specific policies.

Both the international involvement and domestic policy variables are coded as having a *positive* impact if the overall effect of the programs and policies moved the country toward peace and stability, and a *negative* impact if the programs, taken together, hindered the reconstruction process or moved the country toward reincitation of the conflict. The variables are coded as having *high*, *medium*, or *low* impact, depending on the extent to which the actors' positive or negative impact was felt across the conflict: a *high* level indicating widespread influence on the process, a *medium* level indicating a substantial degree of influence, and a *low* level indicating influence felt in individual situations rather than on a large scale.

The *NGO involvement* variable examines the level of efforts, coordination, type, and quality of programming implemented by non-governmental organizations during the reconstruction process. This includes an examination of certain key NGO programs, along with an evaluation of how well coordination efforts were facilitated and whether competition influenced the efficacy of NGO operations. The coding for *NGO involvement* uses the same measurement of *positive* or *negative* impact used to assess the domestic policy and international involvement variables. The level of the positive or negative impact is then graded as *high*, *medium*, or *low*, depending on how the level of NGO efforts (number of NGOs active relative to the situation), the efficacy of their coordination, and the quality of programming affected the general trajectory of positive or negative impact. A *high* impact indicates that NGOs had a widespread influence on reconstruction outcomes, *medium* indicates a significant though not extensive impact, and *low* indicates that NGOs had nominal or anecdotal impact but, due to mitigating factors (which may include poor coordination or high competition), did not exert great influence on the overall process and the youth demographic.

The final variable, *cultural/environmental factors*, isolates certain circumstantial characteristics and their impact on the youth demographic and the overarching reconstruction process. These factors include cultural characteristics, religious practices relevant to the reconstruction process, and environmental issues, such as the type of terrain or accessibility of transportation infrastructure, that affected the outcome of reconstruction efforts. The cultural/environmental factors are then coded as having a *positive* impact if they helped enable successful reconstruction policy, or a *negative* impact if they hindered the reconstruction process. The level of impact ranges from *low*, affecting only certain programs or communities, to *medium*, substantially affecting reconstruction efforts, to *high*, exerting effects that are felt structurally across the reconstruction process.

Missing Data

Due to a lack of availability, data is missing from portions of the analysis. Most notably, statistical data for Kosovo is hard to come by, as most databases include Kosovo as a part of Serbia. Therefore, Kosovo-specific data is used where available, but if it is unavailable, the corresponding information for Serbia is used as a proxy, and the discrepancy is indicated in the analysis. Also, some information, particularly for the African cases, is simply unavailable due to the lack of up-to-date surveys. For instance, while statistics on youth unemployment are available for Kosovo, unemployment information is less accurate for Mozambique and represents the overall unemployment rate, and unemployment data is not available at all for the DRC. Whereas population data is on hand for Mozambique and the DRC, data for Kosovo, which was not considered an independent nation until February 2008, is not as available. The missing data creates an unavoidable discrepancy in the analysis, but wherever possible, substitute measures are provided, or it is otherwise indicated that the specific data is missing and not included in the study.

Also, not every case country is included in each of the stability indices. The Global Peace Index does not include information on the DRC, and the Ibrahim Index of African Governance covers only sub-Saharan countries. However, the broad range of resources used in evaluating stability compensates for gaps in the availability of established peace-and-stability rankings, and for each case at least three different indices are used to derive an accurate description of the level of stability.

For an evaluation of the programs and policies implemented during the reconstruction process, the study uses reports from the implementing agencies, along with analytical accounts by various scholars and international agencies. Each case study attempts to provide as inclusive an account of the reconstruction process as possible, but space constraints and data availability limit the focus to the main actors and the most significant programs.

The Cases and Conclusions

Each of the next three chapters examines one of the three cases, and a concluding discussion follows, drawing together the observations and trends set forth in this chapter. Chapter 2, the Mozambique case study, evaluates the reconstruction processes that led to one of the most successful peacebuilding efforts to date in sub-Saharan Africa. Mozambique is a particularly interesting case because the reconstruction program was able to meet youth needs without a specifically youth-focused policy. Chapter 3 examines the extreme opposite case: the Democratic Republic of the Congo. The DRC is the case with the most instability, and it is also characterized by an extremely high involvement of child and youth soldiers in both the initial conflict and the perpetuation of violence. Chapter 4 moves inward from the two extremes to the case of Kosovo, a territory with one of the world's highest proportions of youth in the population, which saw an extremely high level of involvement from the international community directed toward the youth demographic—with unclear results. The final chapter explores the similarities and differences among the cases, and the potential implications for youth policy and post-conflict reconstruction. It concludes with a discussion of the questions generated from the case study analyses and the potential directions for future research on the role of youth in post-conflict reconstruction.

The case studies and comparisons not only provide insight for scholars in the field but may also help policymakers and practitioners see the dynamic role that youth play in conflict. With a more complete understanding of youth as active players in both destabilization and peacebuilding, reconstruction actors can better facilitate young people's transition from war to peace and guide their untapped potential toward rebuilding communities and supporting durable peace in areas torn apart by conflict.

2

Mozambique: The "Poster Child" for Reconstruction

The fifteen-year civil war (1977–92) in Mozambique left behind a legacy of human rights abuses and systematic violence against civilians, with armed young men and boys responsible for most of the atrocities. The war devastated the country, costing the lives of nearly one million Mozambicans and displacing over five million. Over the course of the war, 250,000 children were separated from their families.[1] The extremely high level of child and youth involvement in the conflict set the tone of the international community's reaction, bringing the issue of child soldiering to the forefront of international dialogue. Moreover, it presented a significant complication to the post-conflict reconstruction environment: a generation of young men socialized in war. And yet, despite the years of violence and upheaval and without a specific international policy directed at reintegrating the large youth population that had participated in the conflict, Mozambique emerged from its civil war as the most stable of the three cases studied. Moreover, it has become a model for successful post-conflict reconstruction in sub-Saharan Africa.

That Mozambique overcame the potentially destabilizing problem of the youth bulge is all the more surprising considering that, unlike in many other reconstruction processes, Mozambique was not flooded with international organizations or NGOs dedicated to peacebuilding or reconstruction. In fact, the UN mission to Mozambique, though significant in size and capacity, did not create or implement a comprehensive policy to deal with youth and child soldiers as a distinct population. Therefore, the relative success in Mozambique is especially intriguing because it directly contradicts the assumption that successfully countering the youth demographic's potentially negative impact and meeting young people's needs during post-conflict reconstruction requires a high level of involvement and programming tailored exclusively to youth and children.

---

1. USAID, "Children and War: The Mozambique Experience," undated project report, http://pdf.usaid.gov/pdf_docs/PNABY287.pdf (accessed Sept. 1, 2009).

The key to this puzzle lies in how effectively Mozambique and the international actors involved implemented the reconstruction program. For instance, the United Nations ran an especially efficient mission to disarm, demobilize, and reintegrate ex-combatants. Except for one program that demobilized about 850 child soldiers, this process did not include a policy specifically on demobilizing and reintegrating children or youth. Instead, all ex-combatants age 16 and older, many of whom were former child soldiers, were included in the overarching demobilization and reintegration process. Whereas the UN policies were designed to meet community needs as a whole (with young people benefiting from many community programs, such as the building of schools and hospitals), NGOs filled in gaps with targeted youth programs. These combined efforts effectively met young people's short- and medium-term needs, from the initial need for protection to community reintegration and, in some cases, social empowerment as community peacebuilders.

One of the most important aspects of the reconstruction program was the emphasis placed on reintegration as part of the DDR process. The United Nations was moderately successful in reintegrating demobilized soldiers back into their home communities in a timely manner, armed with some form of support that would help them build a civilian life. Where the United Nations could not satisfy specific youth needs, a few NGOs and domestic actors efficiently and successfully provided advocacy, reintegration, and youth empowerment programming. Through the combination of the UN DDR programs and NGO efforts that prevented former child soldiers from being drafted into the army and that also provided youth with the skills to become peacebuilders in their home communities, the dangerous potential of the large youth population was largely avoided. In fact, when given the opportunity, many young people contributed to the community-building and reconciliation process.

Background

The conflict in Mozambique emerged directly from its colonial heritage. Therefore, to have a complete understanding of the situation facing reconstruction actors in 1992, the case study must begin with an examination of the country's colonial history. Unlike Great Britain and France, which were highly efficient in creating an infrastructure for extracting raw materials from their protectorates, the Portuguese struggled to profit from their colonial endeavor. The more industrialized metropolises sought to expand their capitalist structure both by extracting raw materials and by investing in markets and infrastructure within their colonies to expand their home economies. Portugal, by contrast, did not have the capacity to create such a colonial structure and instead sought only to extract resources and foreign exchange from Mozambique and Angola while investing little in the colonies' infrastructure and internal markets.[2] Despite Mozambique's prime shipping location, the railroad system, which would have promoted trade between the African colonies and with other European nations (particularly the British), was never completed. Any infrastructure that was developed was contained in the main cities of Lourenço Marques (later Maputo) and the port city of Beira. As a result, the various provinces "developed largely in isolation from each other," creating a modern colonial state characterized by "a high degree of dis-integration."[3] With the flight of the Portuguese population (and their capital) after 1975, newly independent Mozambique was faced with the task of building a modern infrastructure virtually from scratch.

While the colonizers' lack of investment in basic physical and institutional infrastructure would prove a great detriment to human development, their lack of investment in the indoctrination of native Mozambicans into the colonial system had a beneficial effect, allowing the many indigenous cultures and religions to survive. Mozambican culture, largely dominated by traditional animistic religions, included a wealth of knowledge in traditional medicine and healing, along with philosophical understandings of relationships among individuals, society, and the universe.[4] Traditional understandings of justice and peace would play a crucial role in the transition from civil war to peace in Mozambique as traditional spiritual leaders and healers, or curandeiros, guided communities through grassroots reconciliation, reintegration, and justice efforts.

The civil war that ended in 1992 grew directly from anticolonial and nationalist sentiments and the Mozambican movement for independence. After World War II, when the British and the French began to dismantle their empires, the Portuguese tried hard to retain their colonies.[5] In response, indigenous anticolonial organizations in Mozambique came together in 1962 to form the Frente de Libertação de Moçambique (Liberation Front of Mozambique), more commonly known by its acronym, Frelimo. In September 1964, Frelimo launched an armed campaign to overthrow the colonial government.[6] Portugal could not contain the insurgency, and following a military coup in Lisbon in 1974, Mozambique gained its independence on June 25, 1975. Frelimo, with uncontested control of the newly independent government, aligned itself with the Soviet Union as a Marxist-Leninist party.[7]

---

2. Malyn Newitt, *A History of Mozambique* (Bloomington, Ind.: Indiana University Press, 1995), 392.

3. Ibid., 397.

4. Ibid., 157.

5. For example, in the 1950s, Portugal changed its constitution to use the word "overseas province" instead of "colony" to emphasize the claim that "the African territories and Portugal formed a single indivisible country." Ibid., 473.

6. Chris Alden, *Mozambique and the Construction of the New African State: From Negotiations to Nation Building* (New York: Palgrave, 2001), 5.

7. In 1989, Frelimo officially dropped its Marxist-Leninist affiliation. Ibid.

With the help of the Soviet Union and its client states, Frelimo began its rule in Mozambique by forming a single-party socialist state. Although Frelimo tried to organize a number of progressive initiatives in health and education, it soon succumbed to a more radical authoritarian doctrine, banning strikes, limiting religious activity, and nationalizing certain sectors of the economy. In seeking to mobilize Mozambique's workers and peasants, it tended to "ride roughshod" over the complex cultural composition, including the various regional, ethnic, and religious divides that existed within Mozambican society.[8]

Opposition to Frelimo emerged largely from an external context. Along with Frelimo's domestic endeavors, it began a foreign policy campaign that placed sanctions on Rhodesia (now Zimbabwe), cutting off the landlocked country from the port city of Beira. In addition to this grievance, the white-minority governments of Rhodesia and apartheid South Africa had a vested interest in fueling an insurgency in Mozambique because they felt threatened by the collapse of white colonial rule in Mozambique and Angola and by Frelimo's support for "black" nationalist movements inside Rhodesia. As a result, Rhodesia began launching direct attacks into Mozambique, and the Rhodesian secret service, eventually with the help of the South African military, fostered the development of an internal insurgent group, the Resistência Nacional Moçambicana (Mozambican National Resistance), or Renamo.

The conflict in Mozambique is often simplistically portrayed as an externally driven Cold War-era proxy conflict.[9] But several internal factors were easily as divisive as the superpowers' Cold War rivalry. While the conflict, though fueled by regional tensions, was largely a political struggle between the pro-Soviet, socialist Frelimo and the pro-Western, free-market Renamo, Renamo did attempt to ground the insurgency within the domestic population. Made up largely of mercenaries and forced recruits (often kidnapped children), Renamo "prey[ed] upon the 'regional sensibilities' and 'traditional' loyalties that Frelimo disregarded."[10] The Rhodesians were not manufacturing an insurgency amid a population completely satisfied with its government. Domestic anti-Frelimo sentiment was rife, along with other ethnic, religious, and territorial tensions. For instance, while the conflict did not pit one religion against another, Renamo sought to mobilize the more ardent religious community members who were opposed to the absolute secularism espoused by the Frelimo government.[11] Also, while Frelimo initially had support throughout the country, its power base was

---

8. Taisier Mohamed Ahmed Ali and Robert O. Matthews, *Civil Wars in Africa: Roots and Resolution* (Montreal: McGill-Queen's University Press, 1999), 127–28.

9. For an example, see Mary H. Moran and M. Anne Pitcher, "The 'Basket Case' and the 'Poster Child': Explaining the End of Civil Conflicts in Liberia and Mozambique," *Third World Quarterly* 25, no. 3 (2004). In the article, the background to the Mozambique conflict is a standard characterization emphasizing the Cold War alignments over the internal aspects of the conflict.

10. Ali and Matthews, *Civil Wars in Africa*, 128.

11. Cobban, *Amnesty after Atrocity?* 145.

concentrated in the north—the first area to be liberated from Portuguese rule. Many of Renamo's commanders were members of the Ndau ethnic group, residing in the center of Mozambique (not coincidentally, the area most accessible to Rhodesians). However, these divisions did not become the mobilizing cause for resistance. Because Renamo did not have the internal capacity to develop as a powerful insurgency on its own, it depended on support from Rhodesia and South Africa, which drove the antisocialist cause.[12]

Although internal tensions played a part, the struggle is best characterized as an ideological war brought in from the outside, which then became an internal struggle between domestic actors for the spoils of office.[13] The predominance of ideological rather than ethnic, religious, or territorial dimensions is evident in the many cases of family members who fought for opposing sides during the war.[14]

In 1980–81, Renamo, with the help of the South African military, began a bloody campaign of destabilization against the Frelimo regime, which would escalate to full-scale civil war.[15] To complicate matters, the Frelimo government allowed the African National Congress (ANC), an organization ardently opposed to the apartheid regime in South Africa, to take up residence in Mozambique and launch sabotage campaigns into South Africa.

In 1983, Mozambique and South Africa attempted to reach a compromise over the situation. The efforts culminated in the 1984 Nkomati Accord, in which Mozambique agreed to curb ANC activities in exchange for South Africa's withdrawal of support from Renamo. But despite the agreement, South African officials continued to support the Renamo insurgency. With the mysterious death of Mozambican President Samora Machel in a plane crash over South Africa in 1986, the Nkomati Accord collapsed.

The civil war in Mozambique continued because neither side could win a definitive victory. By the late 1980s, both Renamo and Frelimo depended on external resources for their campaigns, and a changing regional and international climate threatened to cut off this support: Nelson Mandela's release from prison in 1990 signaled the end of South Africa's involvement in Mozambique's internal affairs, and Mikhail Gorbachev's political and economic reforms in the Soviet Union foreshadowed the dwindling Soviet role. Also, domestic conditions in Mozambique had deteriorated until, by 1989, thousands were on the verge of starvation.[16]

---

12. William Minter, *Apartheid's Contras: An Inquiry into the Roots of War in Angola and Mozambique* (Johannesburg: Witwatersrand University Press, 1994).

13. Ali and Matthews, *Civil Wars in Africa*, 129.

14. For a discussion of how the nature of ethnic and religious tensions, as well as other factors specific to the Mozambican civil war, differ from those in the DRC and Kosovo, see chapter 5.

15. By 1980, the transfer of power as Rhodesia became Zimbabwe lessened that country's influence on the conflict, and South Africa became Renamo's dominant supporter.

16. Alden, *Mozambique and the Construction of the New African State*, 21–24.

Eventually, unable to bear the costs of continued conflict, the war-weary country moved toward a negotiated settlement. The shift toward negotiations began in 1989, facilitated by representatives of Catholic and Protestant churches through the Mozambican Christian Council and the Italian government. In 1992, the General Peace Agreement (GPA) was signed in Rome, establishing an official nationwide cease-fire. The GPA also outlined the process of initiating democratic elections and committed both parties to participate in a DDR program for ex-combatants.

The United Nations took over control of the reconstruction effort, which was lauded at the time as one of its most comprehensive and successful campaigns. Since 1994, however, the UN Mission to Mozambique (ONUMOZ) has been criticized for various aspects of its program, including delays in mobilization, failure to adequately address the issues of child soldiers and land mines, and an incomplete DDR program. Nonetheless, despite growing tensions during the campaign period, in 1994 Mozambique held its first democratic elections, and the government has survived without any significant renewal of violence.

Today Mozambique continues to struggle with long-term development. Since the civil war, the country has experienced significant economic growth rates, though it remains one of the poorest in the world, with a GDP per capita of US$350 ($1,500 PPP), and with 64.8 percent of the population living on less than $1 per day.[17] In 2000 and 2001, Mozambique suffered crisis-level flooding that severely injured the developing infrastructure. Despite debt relief programs, the country still depends on foreign assistance for most of its budget.

Perhaps one of the most tragic legacies of the civil war in Mozambique is the widespread practice of child soldiering. While Renamo was particularly active in forcibly recruiting and kidnapping children to serve in its guerrilla forces, both parties used child soldiers, and firsthand accounts of the violence in Mozambique note that young boys were responsible for carrying out much of the violence and terrorism against civilians. Because of the high degree of youth involvement during the conflict, upon resolution of the war, Mozambique and the international actors involved during the transition process had to develop methods to reintegrate this population of children and youth back into normal civilian life.

Children and youth in Mozambique continue to suffer from a number of threats, particularly the prevalence of HIV/AIDS: in Mozambique, 14,300 15-to-24-year-olds, along with 140,000 children under 14 years old, are living with HIV. Approximately 1.5 million of Mozambique's children are orphans, and 470,000 children have lost one or both parents to AIDS.[18]

---

17. Mo Ibrahim Foundation, "Ibrahim Index of African Governance," www.moibrahimfoundation.org/the-index.asp (accessed Sept. 1, 2009). According to the Human Development Index (calculated for 2005), Mozambique ranks 101st of 108 developing countries on progress in poverty and human development.

18. UNICEF, "Mozambique: Background and Statistics," www.unicef.org/infobycountry/mozambique_statistics.html#25 (accessed Sept. 2, 2009).

While Mozambique's youth continue to face a number of significant obstacles, the country as a whole has moved away from the history of conflict and emerged as "one of the international community's few success stories on the African continent."[19] As demonstrated in the following analysis, the relatively effective fulfillment of youth needs proved to be an essential factor in the successful reconstruction process. What is most striking, however, is that the reconstruction community was able to fulfill those requirements without a specific policy targeting the youth demographic.

The following sections will show that whereas the international community provided vital programming in DDR and the return of refugees, a few markedly successful NGOs played a large part in fulfilling youth-specific needs. Also, the policy of amnesty after the war created an environment more amenable to reconciliation and acceptance of former combatants back into civilian life. Finally, the cultural environment in Mozambique and the traditional and religious leaders played a critical part in facilitating the difficult task of uniting communities and reintegrating young ex-combatants—many of whom had committed numerous atrocities during the war—back into their communities in a culturally legitimate manner. Through these combined policies and characteristics, the reconstruction program in Mozambique effectively prevented youth from emerging as a destabilizing force during the peacebuilding process.

Variable Analysis: Impact on Youth and Stability

Youth Demographic Variables

To understand the implications of youth policy in each case study and make comparisons across the cases, it is important to outline the general situation facing youth in each country at the outset of the reconstruction period. Of particular interest are the proportion of youth in the population and how they were affected by the war, the state of the education system, and the level of unemployment, since these indicators illuminate both the degree of youth involvement in each conflict and the obstacles that youth must overcome to make a successful war-to-peace transition.

Population

From 1993 to 1997 (in the years immediately following the GPA in 1992), Mozambique had a relatively high proportion of youth in the population, with 10- to 24-year-olds making up roughly one-third of the population and with a nearly equal ratio of males to females. The median age nationwide was 18.[20] Children

---

19. Alden, *Mozambique and the Construction of the New African State*, xiii.

20. U.S. Census Bureau, *International Data Base* (www.census.gov/ipc/www/idb/index.php (accessed Sept. 1, 2009). Although this proportion is just above average for sub-Saharan Africa (where 10- to 24-year-olds

and youth were greatly affected by the war—about 60 percent of the one million people killed during the conflict were children.[21]

Youth Refugees and Soldiers

Mozambique's civil war resulted in 1.5 million to 1.7 million refugees and 3 million to 4.3 million internally displaced people (IDPs) out of a total population of 13.2 million.[22] The United Nations High Commissioner for Refugees (UNHCR) reported that half the refugees returning after the war were under age 15.[23] According to an evaluation conducted for the International Labour Organization (ILO), one of the consequences of the displacement and destabilization was the increase in the number of so-called street children.[24] As of 1997, Mozambique's Ministry of Culture, Youth, and Sport reported that there were 11,000 to 12,000 children in the streets in the capital city, Maputo, and 30,000 in total throughout Mozambique. Many of the street children in the neighboring Zimbabwean capital, Harare, also claimed they were Mozambican refugees. When questioned, these children said they had come to Zimbabwe because they found "nothing to do in Mozambique" and little chance of work. Despite the evidence that after repatriation some of the younger refugees returned to their former countries of asylum to seek work (often at the prompting of their families), UNHCR reported that there were no large-scale backflows of refugees and that the potential issue of unaccompanied minors abandoned in the refugee population was largely avoided.[25]

The conflict in Mozambique has also become infamous for both parties' exploitation of child soldiers. Although both Frelimo and Renamo abducted children to use as soldiers, Renamo's tactics were decried across the international community as especially cruel for socializing children into war by subjecting them to a period of terror and abuse.[26] It is estimated that Renamo used at least

---

made up 32 percent of the 1996 regional population), it is considerably higher than the global figure (27.9 percent in 1996) and a full 12 percentage points higher than in more developed countries, where 10– to 24-year-olds averaged only 20 percent of the 1996 population.

21. Sarah Aird, Boia Efraime, Jr., and Antoinette Errante, "Mozambique: The Battle Continues for Former Child Soldiers," Youth Advocate Program International resource paper, 2001, www.nabuur.com/files/attach/2008/07/task/doc_44537b29343bb.pdf (accessed Sept. 1, 2009).

22. Ibid., 3; Stuart Maslen, "The Reintegration of War-Affected Youth: The Experience of Mozambique," report, International Labour Organization, Geneva, 1997, www.ilo.org/public/english/employment/crisis/download/maslen.pdf (accessed Sept. 1, 2009). U.S. Census Bureau, *International Data Base*.

23. Peter Walker, "Mozambique: Reintegration Strategy," unpublished report, Office of the United Nations High Commissioner for Refugees, 1994.

24. This term encompasses both children *of* the street (those who are orphaned or abandoned and are living in the streets) and children *on* the street (those who live with families by night but work in the streets during the day to support their families). Maslen, *The Reintegration of War-Affected Youth.*

25. Jeff Crisp et al., "Rebuilding a War-Torn Society: A Review of the UNHCR Reintegration Programme for Mozambican Returnees," *Refugee Studies Quarterly* 16, no. 2 (1997).

26. Neil G. Boothby and Christine M. Knudsen, "Children of the Gun," *Scientific American* 282, no. 6 (2000): 62; UNICEF, "The State of the World's Children 1996," report, 1996, www.unicef.org/sowc96/

10,000 child soldiers, and estimates suggest that over one-quarter of former soldiers in Mozambique were recruited when they were younger than 18.[27] Of the 92,881 officially demobilized soldiers, 4,678 were under age 13 when recruited, 6,289 were age 14 to 15, and 13,982 were age 16 to 17—accounting for almost 28 percent (25,498) of demobilized soldiers.[28] Half the demobilized soldiers were under 31 at the time of demobilization.[29] These statistics indicate that while children as young as 6 years old were recruited, most demobilized child soldiers fell into the "youth" demographic of 10 to 24 years old at the age of recruitment, and most served in the militias for over five years.[30]

While much less is known about the gender disaggregation of youth and child soldiers, UNHCR estimated that a significant proportion of the returning refugee population were female heads of households.[31] In the initial surveys of the former military bases, over 40 percent of the 2,000 documented children were female. However, no females were included in the one official child-soldier demobilization program, and only 1.5 percent of the officially demobilized soldiers were female.[32]

Education

The conflict in Mozambique inevitably disrupted and damaged the education system. An estimated 600,000 children were deprived of regular education, either by their recruitment into the armed forces or by the destruction of roughly half (2,500) of Mozambique's primary schools along with 22 secondary schools and 36 boarding schools.[33] Many children, like Lídia Mangueze Huó, were kidnapped walking to school. Lidia, who was 16 when she was kidnapped, states, "It was certainly not voluntary. I wanted to be a doctor."[34]

In 1995, the adult literacy rate was 38.7 percent.[35] While civil war invariably destroys infrastructure, the extreme to which Mozambique's already struggling education system suffered from the conflict is astounding. Consequently, education became a priority in domestic policy during post-conflict reconstruction.

(accessed Sept. 1, 2009).

27. Boothby and Knudsen, "Children of the Gun," 60.

28. Action for the Rights of Children (ARC), "Critical Issues: Child Soldiers," UNHCR and International Save the Children Alliance, report, 2001, www.unhcr.org/3f83de714.html (accessed Sept. 1, 2009), 134.

29. Ibid.

30. Ibid.

31. UNHCR, "Mozambique: Reintegration Strategy."

32. ARC, "Critical Issues: Child Soldiers." This program, facilitated by Save the Children, USA, demobilized and reunited 850 male child-soldiers with their families and conducted follow-up research on their reintegration into society.

33. Aird, Efraime, and Errante, "Mozambique: The Battle Continues for Former Child Soldiers," 3.

34. Posthumus, *Struggles in Peacetime*.

35. World Bank, "World Development Indicators," World Bank annual report, www.worldbank.org/data/wdi/home.html (accessed Sept. 1, 2009).

Unemployment

Most work in Mozambique is agricultural, usually subsistence farming, although many workers in the south have traditionally migrated to work on mines and farms in South Africa.[36] The vast majority of those joining the labor market are self-employed or work in family businesses or small-scale agriculture.[37] In 1997, it was estimated that only 1 in 6 members of the workforce was waged, and only 1 in 123 was an employer.[38]

Although unemployment statistics in Mozambique are not readily available, there is evidence of high levels of unemployment after the conflict. In 1996, Minister of Labour Guilherme Mavila announced that the official rate of unemployment was 7.2 percent, but admitted that this figure was a gross underestimate. Mr. Mavila stated that the real rate was likely more than half the economically active population.[39] According to the U.S. Central Intelligence Agency's and other estimates, the unemployment rate in Mozambique in 1997 was estimated at 21 percent.[40]

Coding

Mozambique is rated as having a high percentage both of youth in the population and of youth involvement in conflict. As stated earlier, the proportion of youth in the population is on par for sub-Saharan Africa at the time (32 percent) but higher than the world average (29 percent) and significantly higher than the average for more developed countries (21 percent).[41] The numbers of children and youth involved as soldiers or displaced by the conflict are also markedly high compared to the total number of soldiers involved in the conflict, with 28 percent of the combatants being under age 17 when recruited, and over half under age 30.

International Policy's Impact on Youth and Stabilization

Because the internal conflict in Mozambique had involved a number of regional and international actors, the peacebuilding process received significant international attention. Although individual nations were involved in the peace talks, the most active international player was ONUMOZ. After the United Nations' problematic experiences in peacebuilding in Angola and Cambodia, the UN

---

36. Maslen, *The Reintegration of War-Affected Youth.*

37. U.S. Department of State, "Background Note: Mozambique," www.state.gov/r/pa/ei/bgn/7035.htm (accessed Sept. 1, 2009); Maslen, *The Reintegration of War-Affected Youth.*

38. Maslen, *The Reintegration of War-Affected Youth.*

39. Ibid.

40. Central Intelligence Agency (CIA), "The World Factbook: Mozambique," www.cia.gov/library/publications/the-world-factbook/geos/mz.html (accessed Sept. 1, 2009).

41. U.S. Census Bureau, *International Data Base.*

mission was determined to work with local and international actors to establish a successful, effective, and complete peacekeeping operation in Mozambique. The most relevant UN programs for youth in the post-conflict environment were the demobilization and reintegration programs. However, it is important to note that the UN policies and programs were highly coordinated between the United Nations and NGOs, particularly in implementing DDR. Therefore, the influence of the United Nations must be understood in some respects as interrelated with that of NGOs.

The Peace Accord

The GPA contained a number of different prescriptions that indirectly affected youth in Mozambique. First, the GPA established UN involvement in Mozambique, calling for the United Nations to monitor the cease-fire, assist in election planning, and provide humanitarian assistance. The agreement also established a timetable for implementing the treaty, including a commitment by both parties to fully demobilize soldiers by April 1993.[42] At the time, the United Nations did not recognize soldiers younger than 16 for inclusion in official demobilization programs, nor did the operations delineate specific programs for soldiers of different ages. Therefore, there was no established mechanism to deal with the large population of child soldiers.

The GPA also outlined the structure for a new Mozambican army, to be composed of former government and Renamo forces.[43] This meant that some former child soldiers who had been forcibly and illegally recruited could be subject to continued service in the armed forces. (However, a strong movement headed by an NGO, discussed later in this chapter, successfully prevented the conscription of former child soldiers.)

In this case, while the text of the peace treaty did not directly address the youth demographic or the issue of child soldiers and reintegration, its specifications created both positive and negative consequences for Mozambican youth. For instance, while child soldiers were not legally eligible to receive benefits from the DDR program, the treaty did create a binding agreement for both sides to commit to demilitarization programs, and youth soldiers over 16 received the same treatment and resources in this process as older soldiers.

Foreign Government Involvement

Aside from representation within the United Nations and through international NGOs, foreign governments were not deeply involved in post-conflict reconstruction in Mozambique. They were, however, quite involved in negotiating the GPA. The governments of Zimbabwe, Botswana, Kenya, South Africa, and

---

42. Alden, *Mozambique and the Construction of the New African State*, 36.

43. Conciliation Resources, *General Peace Agreement for Mozambique*, 1992, Protocol IV, www.c-r.org/our-work/accord/mozambique/rome-protocol4.php (accessed Sept. 2, 2009).

Malawi all took active part in the negotiations in Rome, and members of the Italian government, along with international Catholic Church organizations, were the official mediators for the negotiations. Representatives from the United States, the UK, France, and Portugal were also present as observers. These Western nations served as representatives to the Supervisory and Monitoring Commission, which oversaw the implementation of the GPA.[44]

USAID, which has been active in Mozambique since 1984, assisted in the postaccord transition process by providing support for a number of different demobilization and humanitarian assistance programs. These programs dealt with demobilization, demining, elections, rehabilitation of roads and bridges, and provision of seeds, tools, and health services to millions of Mozambicans displaced by war and drought.

Aside from the USAID presence and foreign governments' involvement in negotiating the GPA, foreign governments did not have a significant effect on the post-conflict reconstruction policy, nor did they cater directly to the youth demographic.

United Nations Involvement (ONUMOZ)

Background. Although the United Nations was only an observer at the GPA negotiations in Rome, it took on a significant and largely unprecedented[45] role in both implementing the treaty and orchestrating the reconstruction process, from organizing and coordinating demobilization to working with aid agencies to provide humanitarian services and facilitate refugee reintegration programs. Considering the large proportion of young people in the militias and in the population of refugees and IDPs, the UN-coordinated demilitarization and humanitarian assistance programs were essential in facilitating the youth transition from war to peace.

After its official establishment in December 1992, ONUMOZ would operate for two years, ending its mandate with the successful national elections in 1994.[46] Over those two years, ONUMOZ deployed 6,576 military personnel and 1,087 civilian police observers and was supported by gross financing of US$492.6 million.[47] The operation emphasized four main goals: maintaining the cease-fire, demilitarizing the country, providing humanitarian assistance, and monitoring elections.

Although the primary goals of carrying out a swift and thorough demobilization and reintegration program seems straightforward enough, the DDR

---

44. Alden, *Mozambique and the Construction of the New African State*, 37.

45. According to Christopher Alden, the "UN would have to play a role in the peace process which extended well beyond that of previous missions, with the exception of UNTAC in Cambodia." Alden, *Mozambique and the Construction of the New African State*, 36.

46. ONUMOZ was established by UN Security Council Resolution 797 (Dec. 3, 1992).

47. United Nations, "Mozambique—ONUMOZ: Facts and Figures," www.un.org/Depts/dpko/dpko/co_mission/onumozF.html (accessed Sept. 5, 2009).

program in Mozambique cannot be understood independently of the UN experience in Angola. The disarmament and demobilization process in Angola was, by all accounts, a disaster. The failure to adequately disarm ex-combatants before elections were held opened the door to a resurgence of the war when election results were contested. In light of these events, UN officials in Mozambique were ardently committed to disarming and demobilizing all former government and Renamo forces before elections were held.[48] Essentially, the goal of the demilitarization program in Mozambique was to create a "negative peace." That is, officials hoped to prevent violence in the short term and also foster medium-term stability by giving demobilized soldiers skills training, information, and basic provisions including food, shelter, and medical aid while in the cantonment areas, and monetary stipends and agricultural kits for their return home.[49] For young people, ONUMOZ sought to achieve its goal of negative peace through a DDR program that gave them basic psychosocial support and skills training but did not empower them in the long term as active participants in the reconstruction and peacebuilding process.

ONUMOZ's DDR program: ONUMOZ was tasked with the disarmament, demobilization, and reintegration of approximately 63,000 government troops and 30,000 opposition forces.[50] Children under 16 were excluded from this process; those 16 and older were allowed to participate. The ONUMOZ program designated forty-nine assembly areas where former combatants would be held for no more than ten weeks. The DDR process included a variety of programs to begin the psychological, economic, and political reintegration into civilian life. Programs included education and recreational activities, job placement, and information about the peace process. Provisions were also given to the soldiers' wives and children who were living in military camps. The Technical Unit was designated to implement these programs in coordination with the International Organization for Migration (IOM), which worked to arrange transport of demobilized soldiers and their families to their preferred destinations.[51]

Along with the demobilization program, the United Nations instituted a reintegration strategy with a four-pronged approach to meet ONUMOZ's short- and medium-term stability goals. The Reintegration Support Scheme (RSS) provided a monthly financial subsidy (for eighteen months) to all ex-combatants, with the amount of the subsidy pegged to the former soldier's rank.[52] This was

---

48. Secretary-General Boutros Boutros-Ghali said, "In the light of the recent experience in Angola, I believe it to be of critical importance that the elections should not take place until the military aspects of the agreement have been fully implemented." Alden, *Mozambique and the Construction of the New African State*, 39.

49. Galtung, *Peace by Peaceful Means*.

50. Chris Alden, "Making Old Soldiers Fade Away: Lessons from the Reintegration of Demobilized Soldiers in Mozambique," *Security Dialogue* 33, no. 3 (2002): 343.

51. Alden, *Mozambique and the Construction of the New African State*, 40–41.

52. The lowest-ranking officers received MT75,000 (US$15), and the highest-ranking officers received MT1,270,080 (US$130). Alden, "Making Old Soldiers Fade Away," 344.

intended to provide a "safety net" of guaranteed income so that ex-combatants returning to civilian life could have enough time to secure work. The program also operated with the underlying assumption that most of the ex-soldiers came from poor backgrounds and would prefer to return to working the land rather than seek paid work in the cities.[53] Each ex-combatant received an agricultural kit, including tools and seeds, in the hope that this would encourage demobilized soldiers to return to rural or agricultural communities, where unskilled labor was available.

The second aspect of the reintegration strategy was the Information and Referral Service, implemented by the IOM (and later integrated into the Provincial Fund). This provided ex-combatants with information and counseling on such things as how to work with the demobilization process (for example, where to pick up their monthly payments) and where to find employment opportunities.

The third component of the reintegration strategy was the Occupational Skills Development (OSD) program, implemented by the ILO. This program provided ex-combatants with various types of formal vocational training that would give them the skills and tools they needed to start their own businesses.[54] The final element of the RSS, the Provincial Fund, launched in 1994, provided resources for extending the Information and Referral Service, and funding for demobilized soldiers to pursue entrepreneurial projects.

DDR implementation. Overall, the demobilization and reintegration programs were relatively successful. However, there were instances of lengthy delays in the cantonment process, and infighting both within the UN system and between the United Nations and NGOs.[55] Early on in the mission, there were a number of allegations of UN soldiers' involvement in child prostitution and abuse, and when an investigatory commission confirmed the accusations, the United Nations dismissed the offenders.[56] Among the worst problems in the demobilization program itself were the many delays and the United Nations' slow reaction to the situation on the ground: although the GPA was signed in October 1992, ONUMOZ was not fully operational until June 1993 and did not deploy troops until August, well after the GPA's April deadline for full demobilization. By November 1993, only twenty of the forty-nine assembly areas were open to receive troops, with the remaining twenty-nine opening in February 1994. Because of these delays, soldiers were detained for much longer than originally planned. As a result, soldiers in the assembly areas rioted or caused disturbances, including "attacks on UN officials, taking hostages in the camps, blocking major roads in

---

53. Ibid.

54. Ibid., 345.

55. Alden, *Mozambique and the Construction of the New African State*, 50–51.

56. Ibid., 52; Richard Synge, *Mozambique: UN Peacekeeping in Action, 1992–1994*, (Washington, DC: United States Institute of Peace Press, 1997); Graça Machel, "The Impact of Armed Conflict on Children," report for UNICEF, 1996, www.unicef.org/graca/ (accessed Sept. 1, 2009).

the area or looting in neighboring towns."[57] Despite the setbacks, the demobilization process was complete by August 1994, before the general elections were held. In total, 64,130 government forces and 22,637 Renamo forces were officially demobilized. Over half these ex-combatants (56 percent) were younger than 31, and 28 percent were under 18 when recruited.[58]

One of the major causes behind the delay in the demobilization program was the issue of child soldiers. While it was widely known that both sides forcibly recruited children during the war, at first neither side admitted to such practices. These attempts to cover up the use of child soldiers, particularly by Renamo, delayed the official demobilization program because the Renamo territory could not be opened for general access until UNICEF, in coordination with the International Committee of the Red Cross (ICRC) and Save the Children, had instituted a reunification and repatriation program for child soldiers living on the Renamo bases. Although there were an estimated 10,000 Renamo child soldiers, only 2,000 were officially documented. Of these 2,000, only 850 boys participated in the children's DDR program. UNICEF also organized a follow-up home visitation program with the participants so that social workers could monitor the children's progress in reintegrating into their communities. These 850 children also received basic education services, trauma counseling, and occupational apprenticeships as part of the UNICEF program.[59]

Many children not included in the official UNICEF demobilization process tried to return home on their own. Noticing this gap in services, a number of NGOs instituted their own reunification programs.[60] However, because there was no structured method for dealing with child soldiers, reintegration was largely left up to the communities themselves.

There is some evidence that former child soldiers, both those included and those excluded from official programs, were dissatisfied with the process. Some children who were kept out of the official UN program voiced complaints that they were soldiers, too, and deserved access to the demobilization programs, and instead resorted to crime, such as banditry and theft. Others complained about the pension system, since pensions were given only to soldiers on the government side who were 18 or older when they were drafted or who had served for more than ten years. This essentially excluded any child soldier from receiving a pension, even if they were old enough to participate in the adult demobilization

57. Alden, *Mozambique and the Construction of the New African State*, 54. For further discussion of the riots and violence in the assembly areas, see the section "Dependent Variable: Level of Stability as Affected by Youth," later in this chapter.

58. ARC, "Critical Issues: Child Soldiers," 134.

59. Aird, Efraime, and Errante, "Mozambique: The Battle Continues for Former Child Soldiers," 7.

60. For example, the Youth Social Reintegration Programme was established specifically to find child soldiers' families and reunite them in their homes. Eventually, the Youth Social Reintegration Program developed longer-term reintegration programs aimed at helping these children cope with their experiences and empowering them for future success.

process.[61] One child soldier is quoted as saying, "We make money by selling guns from arsenals. Some of our people also engage in banditry to get extras. It's a way to survive."[62]

Although this rule fueled resentment, providing stipends to demobilized child soldiers is a sensitive issue because it can spark problems that hinder the reintegration process. For example, in cases where child soldiers did receive stipends, this caused frustration among peers who did not go through any official demobilization program. It also contributed to stigmatization of child soldiers and can drive some children to join armed groups in order to receive the cash for demobilization. Therefore, today the United Nations recommends that cash stipends not be given to demobilized child solders.[63] For Mozambique, the issue was complicated by the fact that many soldiers who were recruited as children were over 18 at the time of demobilization but were still unable to receive the pension.

Despite the setbacks in the DDR process, each of the reintegration programs conducted by the United Nations reported that all ex-combatants were successfully reintegrated into society.[64] However, the international community's idea of success may be simply the lack of outright violence during and after the disarmament and reintegration period. Aside from delays and protests in the assembly camps, and incidences of low-level criminal or gang activity, the violent reaction that the United Nations had anticipated (and deeply feared in light of experiences in Angola) did not occur. The instances of low-level violence that did take place, including the rioting in the assembly areas, were isolated incidents or were related to crime, rather than being politically motivated to reincite the war. A study prepared for the IOM reported, "In no cases did [demobilized soldiers] show disposition towards violence or social disruption. The importance of military structures has clearly waned and community structures (family, traditional authority, community organizations) seem to have replaced military structures in assisting with conflict resolution, problem solving and social support."[65] In this case, it seems that the United Nations was successful in achieving its initial goal of "negative peace."[66]

The reintegration program was one of the most comprehensive undertaken through a UN peacekeeping mission, with $95 million spent implementing four

---

61. Maslen, *The Reintegration of War-Affected Youth.*

62. Aird, Efraime, and Errante, "Mozambique: The Battle Continues for Former Child Soldiers," 5.

63. United Nations, "United Nations Integrated DDR Standards," www.unddr.org/iddrs/framework.php (accessed Sept. 1, 2009).

64. Alden, "Making Old Soldiers Fade Away," 345. However, as Alden points out, some of the reintegration programs were more successful than others. Specifically, the Occupational Skills Development program, conducted by the ILO, was particularly inefficient in providing demobilized soldiers with skills they could use upon returning to civilian life.

65. Maslen, *The Reintegration of War-Affected Youth.*

66. Alden, "Making Old Soldiers Fade Away," 351.

different reintegration approaches.[67] However, despite the massive and highly coordinated reintegration effort, there were a number of difficulties. Interviews with community leaders indicate that many Mozambicans did not share the view of the United Nations and international agencies that reintegration was fully achieved. Instead, these leaders comment on the remaining need for a comprehensive "social peace," with particular attention to issues of vocational training, disabled war veterans, and victims of land mines.[68]

Specifically, the OSD vocational training program was largely ineffective. Only one in six demobilized soldiers received vocational training.[69] Also, the program did not conduct initial surveys that would have provided a general picture of the economic landscape and the sectors with potential employment opportunities. As a result, many of those demobilized soldiers who received vocational training were then "thrown into a labour market where there were no vacancies" or else had new skills inapplicable to the area to which they were returning.[70] For instance, some of the demobilized soldiers were trained to be electricians but were returning to areas without electricity.[71] This was a serious handicap for youth and child soldiers who needed to earn an income upon returning to their community, as attested by the child soldiers quoted below, who were demobilized at the Lhanguene Rehabilitation Center in Maputo:

> "I think the war was evil. It delayed my life and I needed to make money once I got home."

> "Those who did not go to the war had the time to earn some money, but I had nothing after the war."

> "I had no resources; I had to begin everything from the beginning."[72]

Also, competition between the implementing agents in different regions meant that ex-soldiers in one region did not have access to the same resources or programs as those in other regions.[73] The OSD and the Provincial Fund operated in separate districts. Therefore, where some demobilized soldiers had access to vocational training but no subsidized income-generating opportunities, others received support from the Provincial Fund but did not have access to the vocational training courses.

---

67. Ibid., 341.

68. Ibid., 351.

69. Ibid.

70. Maslen, *The Reintegration of War-Affected Youth*.

71. Ibid.

72. Neil Boothby, Jennifer Crawford, and Jason Halperin, "Mozambique Child Soldier Life Outcome Study: Lessons Learned in Rehabilitation and Reintegration Efforts," *Global Public Health* 1, no. 1 (2006): 87–107.

73. Alden, "Making Old Soldiers Fade Away," 348.

Despite the deficiencies in the DDR program (particularly in the vocational training activities), the reintegration assistance was a positive contribution to the reconstruction process.[74] Although child soldiers under age 16 were explicitly excluded from these programs,[75] a large percentage of the beneficiaries were youth (51 percent were between ages 16 and 31), and youth were largely given the same opportunities as adults in the program.[76]

UN humanitarian assistance: In addition to the demobilization and reintegration programs for ex-combatants, the United Nations also implemented a number of humanitarian programs aimed at reintegrating the refugee population. With a massive influx of over 1 million returning refugees, ONUMOZ was faced with managing a huge humanitarian effort. Instead of coordinating all the programs internally, it devised a way to pool the resources of NGOs and foreign development assistance programs, to address all the various needs without creating redundant programs or stirring resentment between the United Nations and NGO communities. The UNHCR also used this NGO coordination policy in implementing its various repatriation and reintegration activities.[77] While the program was designed to smooth relationships between the United Nations and NGOs, relations were not always amicable, and some NGOs, faced with delays in the UN operation, began acting outside the UN-orchestrated effort. (For more detail on this relationship, see the NGO section of this chapter.)

The original UNHCR strategy document emphasized the need for programs catering to both women and young people. But the organization decided that the best strategy for addressing the acute and distinct needs of the women and youth living in the refugee camps would be to target specific districts rather than population categories, facilitating a "transition from emergency relief and initial reconstruction to longer-term development."[78] This way, instead of providing direct services to benefit individual groups, ONUMOZ could, for example, rebuild schools or health centers, thus meeting immediate youth needs while providing long-term benefits to the entire community.

The UNHCR's main method for carrying out humanitarian assistance was through "quick impact projects," or QIPs. These are "small-scale interventions made up of simple inputs and activities, intended to be an immediate injection of support to meet community-based needs in different sectors of assistance."[79] One of the QIPs' main successes was rehabilitating or building, and staffing a number of schools and health centers and providing all returnees with access

---

74. Maslen, *The Reintegration of War-Affected Youth.*

75. Ibid.

76. ARC, "Critical Issues: Child Soldiers," 134.

77. Crisp et al., "Rebuilding a War-Torn Society."

78. UNHCR, "Mozambique: Reintegration Strategy," sections 10 and 14.

79. Crisp et al., "Rebuilding a War-Torn Society."

to basic services. The rehabilitation of the education system infrastructure was particularly important in light of the widespread destruction of schools during the conflict. Without the opportunity to go to school, return to a sense of normality, and potentially earn an income, many young people might have resorted to violent behavior in the immediate aftermath of the conflict.

The QIPs were helpful during the emergency period immediately following the war, yet the long-term goals remain unmet, as evidenced by the current languishing state of human development in Mozambique. With the ONUMOZ mandate officially terminated in 1994, by 1997 the cycle of reintegration efforts had largely ended: the money had dried up and most of the UN and UN-funded programs left the country.[80] Long-term efforts from the United Nations were left to programs developed through the United Nations Development Program (UNDP).

Coding

The international efforts in Mozambique are rated as having a medium-level positive impact.[81] The efforts are coded as positive because the United Nations and regional involvement, particularly in facilitating the DDR program and refugee reunification, played a significant role in moving the national trajectory toward peace and stability. The medium level of impact reflects the fact that while ONUMOZ and its partnering UN agencies had a widespread influence on the reconstruction process, their impact on the youth demographic was significant, but not necessarily sufficient, leaving a number of holes for other agencies to fill in order for successful reconstruction to occur.

NGO Involvement: Impact on Youth and Stability

The role of NGOs in Mozambique's reconstruction process is particularly relevant for understanding the youth demographic's transition from war to peace. While youth benefited from both the UN demobilization program and the UN-HCR reintegration efforts, neither program specifically targeted youth as an at-risk demographic. But NGOs were free to focus on the youth population and were relatively successful in filling the gaps left open by the UN programs.

The UN-NGO Relationship

Coordination between the United Nations and NGOs implementing reconstruction programs is essential to success—without coordination, reconstruction efforts can be delayed, programs may operate without the proper resources, and redundancies and competition occur at the expense of those in need. In the case

---

80. Alden, *Mozambique and the Construction of the New African State.*

81. For coding definitions, see pages 27–29 in chapter 1.

of Mozambique, coordination worked in the favor of several youth-related programs, allowing the United Nations and NGOs to pool resources and allowing NGOs to easily fill gaps left by the UN program.

Mozambique's reconstruction program was structured to include coordination between the United Nations and NGOs already on the ground. As a result of experiences in Cambodia, where there was marked tension between the United Nations and humanitarian agencies already working in the field, the plan for Mozambique was to use UN agencies, such as the United Nations Office for the Coordination of Humanitarian Assistance (UNOHAC), as coordination units to facilitate all reconstruction programs.[82] The coordination structure was intended not only to prevent duplicating efforts and competition but also to allow the United Nations access to the NGOs' broad and deep knowledge of local conditions and to their assistance programs already in place.

While the initial plans made clear the strong desire for a smooth and beneficial relationship between NGOs and the United Nations, cooperation did not always happen. There were a number of instances of successful coordinated efforts between the United Nations and NGOs, such as the combined work of UNICEF, Save the Children, and the International Red Cross to demobilize the 850 Renamo child soldiers. UNICEF also created a network of NGOs to provide assistance to the burgeoning number of street children. The various NGOs in the network provided shelter, health care, basic education, recreation, family reunification, and skills training to children living in the streets (or working the streets) as a result of the war.[83]

But there was also considerable friction among the donor community, NGOs, and the United Nations. Specifically, several NGOs and donors were frustrated by the United Nations' slow progress and viewed the coordination effort as too authoritarian.[84] While this friction undoubtedly hampered the program's efficiency, it is unlikely that any operation of this scale could come off without some interagency squabbling. Despite the controversy and the slow progress by the UNOHAC and the UNHCR, the benefits of coordination were acknowledged throughout the community. For instance, the UNHCR created a comprehensive national database that pooled information from numerous organizations to facilitate their humanitarian assistance programs.[85] And there was no evidence of NGOs exacerbating existing problems through disputes with the United Nations or through inter-NGO competition.

---

82. Alden, *Mozambique and the Construction of the New African State*, 43.

83. This network was focused on family and community reunification and, therefore, did not work with NGOs that did not follow the established government policy on reunification with communities of origin. Maslen, *The Reintegration of War-Affected Youth*.

84. Ibid., 57.

85. Ibid., 58.

Associação Reconstruindo a Esperança (Rebuilding Hope Association)

Apart from the coordinated UN-NGO efforts, several successful NGOs dealt specifically with youth needs that fell through the cracks of the UN structure. One problem arose from overreported troop numbers and a lack of volunteers in the Mozambique military. To correct the situation, former combatants were subject to compulsory military conscription into what had been intended to be a voluntary Mozambican defense force.[86] The draft would involve all former soldiers over age 18, thus including many who had been abducted as children into the Renamo or government forces. The mandatory conscription of former child soldiers not only presented a human rights issue but also would likely have fueled great unrest among Mozambican youth who were unwilling to serve in the army.

In response, several child advocacy groups, led by the local NGO Associação Reconstruindo a Esperança (Rebuilding Hope Association), launched a successful public campaign to exempt former child soldiers from military conscription and institute a screening process for those who volunteered. In addition to its work to prevent the conscription of former child soldiers, Rebuilding Hope was quite successful in developing psychosocial reintegration programs, aligned with local cultural and religious practices, for former child soldiers and their families. The program successfully reintegrated 600 male and female child soldiers and has received international recognition for its efforts.

ProPaz

While Rebuilding Hope focused on protecting young people, another successful NGO, ProPaz, was able to harness young people's potential to contribute positively to the peacebuilding process. ProPaz began operating in Mozambique in 1995 as a partnership of two organizations already working with former combatants: the Demobilized Soldiers Organization (AMODEG) and the Disabled Veterans Association. ProPaz sought to provide conflict resolution training to young ex-combatants struggling to reintegrate into their home communities. To accomplish this goal, it created working groups so that youth from both parties could discuss their experiences and needs and participate in leadership training and conflict resolution workshops. As a result of the workshops and other ProPaz-facilitated community outreach programs, many youth were accepted into their communities and no longer seen as violent. Some participants went on to become community leaders or were later employed by ProPaz. Others became official ProPaz "peace promoters," traveling to other communities to continue conflict resolution activities. For example, in one community, dialogue participants discussed what peace would look like in their community and concluded that peace would be a safe space, where children could play without fear

---

86. Ibid.

of stepping on a land mine. As a result of these discussions, a number of former soldiers voluntarily came forward and gave police information on where they had planted land mines and revealed where a cache of small arms was hidden. These ex-combatants went on to work with local officials in efforts to make the area safe. Armando Messitera Muharu, abducted at age 11 and demobilized in 1993 at age 24, tells of his involvement with AMODEG and ProPaz:

> I decided to go to Quelimane and there I became vice co-ordinator of AMODEG. It was practical work, not political. After all, all those who had been demobilized had the same rights. And through my work in AMODEG I was able to convince my colleagues in Renamo that the war was truly over. You could do that by getting together with the Frelimo soldiers and exchange our experiences. That worked, it helped overcome fear. People were very afraid; they were fearful of coming out of the bush. Talk, that is what you need to do. Never stop talking.
>
> It is the same with ProPaz. We do palestras (a combination of lecture and discussion), we talk, we debate, we educate people about peace and talk about ways to solve conflicts, about the dangers of having arms hidden in communities. We do this in the entire province. We have trained others to do the same work in the districts, and we have also worked with Handicap International, an international NGO that helps landmine victims.[87]

Since 1995, ProPaz has trained 150 ex-combatants as peace promoters and has involved over 1,000 people in peacebuilding activities. These peace promoters work in 100 communities in six of Mozambique's ten provinces and are organizing more conflict resolution teams.[88]

Another organization that developed out of the reconstruction process is the youth led, youth-run volunteer network Associação Juvenil para o Desenvolvimento do Voluntariado em Moçambique (AJUDE, or the Youth Development and Volunteer Association of Mozambique). The organization was founded in 1993 by a group of students at the Higher Institute for International Relations to provide a venue for young people to participate actively in reconstruction. AJUDE focused on hosting work camps to mobilize youth in urban and rural communities through volunteerism and community results-based projects. In 2009, ADJUDE continues to sponsor work camps, provide skills training, and host cultural exchange programs with other youth organizations in southern Africa and worldwide.[89]

Today a number of issues still remain for NGOs to tackle in Mozambique, particularly regarding land mines, disabled youth, and gender issues. Nevertheless, the proactive and coordinated efforts by NGOs to tackle youth issues and fill gaps

87. Armando Messitera Muharu was 37 years old in 2006, when this report was published. Posthumus, "Struggles in Peacetime."

88. InterAct, "Action Plan for Children in Armed Conflict," Newsletter no. 4, Nov. 1999, www.iss.co.za/Pubs/Newsletters/InterAct/InterAct4.html (accessed Sept. 6, 2009); Lynette Parker, "Organizing Ex-Combatants for Peace in Mozambique," Restorative Justice Online, 2007, www.restorativejustice.org/editions/2007/april2007/mozambique (accessed Sept. 6, 2009).

89. See AJUDE, "Associação Juvenil para o Desenvolvimento do Voluntariado em Moçambique," www.ajude.org.mz/ (accessed Sept. 1, 2009); Canada World Youth, "Partner Organizations," www.canadaworldyouth.org/en/Content.aspx?PageId=66 (accessed Sept. 5, 2009).

left from the UN program had direct positive results for reintegration in the immediate aftermath of the war.

Coding

Mozambique receives a medium-level positive impact coding for NGO involvement. The NGO variable is rated medium level because, although several NGOs were involved in Mozambique, the level of involvement was not extremely high and did not overwhelm the reconstruction scene to the exclusion of local peacebuilding efforts. Also, coordination was relatively successful and did not impair the overall process. The evidence also indicates that the NGOs operating in Mozambique had a positive impact on the youth demographic, meeting a number of critical needs, including protecting former child soldiers from conscription, as well as reintegration and reconciliation support.

Domestic Policy

Reunification

Most of the domestic policies regarding children and youth were government-sponsored reunification and education programs. During the conflict, the government's official policy toward children involved in the conflict was to reunite children with their families in the shortest time possible.[90] Most of these reunification programs involved some kind of family tracing, contacting the families, and transporting children back to their home villages, where they might have follow-up reintegration support. This program, initially implemented by the Ministry of Health, was later integrated into a larger effort with the creation of the Programme for Family Localization and Reunification, which coordinated efforts from numerous organizations including the Mozambican Women Organization, the Mozambican Youth Organization, and local church groups.[91]

Education

In addition to the official reunification programs, after the civil war the Ministry of Education began to rebuild (literally) the education system. The ministry instituted mandatory seven-year primary education and began an effort, in coordination with the United Nations and NGOs, to repair a physical infrastructure devastated by war and to design a comprehensive education strategy. By 1997, of the 60 percent of primary schools destroyed by the war, 96 percent had been rebuilt. School enrollment rose from 1.2 million in 1992 to 1.7 million by 1997.[92]

---

90. Miguel A Máusse, "The Social Reintegration of the Child Involved in Armed Conflict in Mozambique," in Monograph no. 37, "Child Soldiers in Africa," 1999, www.iss.co.za/Pubs/Monographs/No37/TheSocialReintegration.html (accessed Sept. 7, 2009).

91. Ibid.

92. Economist Intelligence Unit, "Country Report: Mozambique Malawi," Oct. 1997, www.eiu.com

Despite the increase in numbers, as of 1998, the proportion of students repeating grades was still very high, with almost one-quarter of lower primary students repeating. While this statistic indicates a low quality of primary education, it is not unusual for underdeveloped countries in the region to have a high proportion of repeating students.[93]

Amnesty

Finally, another significant domestic policy was the Frelimo government's granting of retrospective blanket amnesty to all individuals. Often, communities rejected children and youth who were involved in the war, because of their history of violence. But this blanket amnesty, although not specifically directed toward youth, not only freed these ex-combatants from legal culpability but also helped assuage resentments by contributing to a general ethos of accepting ex-combatants back into their home communities.[94]

Coding

Domestic policy in Mozambique is coded as having a medium-level positive impact. The emergency reunification programs, education reforms, and amnesty policy were all helpful in reintegrating the youth demographic. The coding is medium level because, although the domestic policy orientation covered both the short and long term, its impact on the overall process was significant but not extensive.

Impact of Cultural and Environmental Factors

While the efforts of international interventions, NGOs, and domestic agents were generally beneficial to the reintegration of youth into Mozambican civil society, the vast majority of programs did not directly target the youth demographic. However, an examination of Mozambique's cultural and religious environment helps explain how the reconstruction effort was able to fulfill critical youth needs during the reconstruction process.

As explained earlier, Mozambique's atypical colonial experience left intact strong and active traditional cultures and religious communities. These traditional belief systems served as a vehicle for accepting former soldiers back into community life. In Mozambique, the traditional view of violence and war is very different from Western conceptualizations. Fernando Manuel Dos Santos Zimba, a traditional healer, or curandeiro, explained his view of the violence:

(subscription only, accessed Sept. 1, 2009). The proportion of school-age children attending school rose from 45 percent in 1990 to 55 percent in 2002.

93. Tuomas Takala, "Making Educational Policy under Influence of External Assistance and National Politics—a Comparative Analysis of the Education Sector Policy Documents of Ethiopia, Mozambique, Namibia, and Zambia," *International Journal of Educational Development* 18, no. 4 (1998): 326.

94. Cobban, *Amnesty after Atrocity?*

If someone is violent, then that is not a normal state of affairs. It must be a spiritual problem he's suffering from, and this must be dealt with through traditional medicine. Someone who kills another person ... must have some kind of wrong spirit with him.[95]

Another curandeiro explained,

Many of these boys never wanted to fight, they did not know what it meant to fight ... you see, if you kill someone, their soul stays with you. The souls of the murdered follow these soldiers back to their homes and their families, back to their communities to cause problems. . . . These soldiers ... have learned to use violence. Their own souls have been corrupted by what they have seen and done. . . . We have to take this violence out of these people, we have to teach them how to live nonviolent lives like they did before.[96]

In keeping with this spiritual conception of violence, many Mozambican communities were deeply committed to leaving the conflict in the past and helping former combatants—or even those who experienced or witnessed the violence of war—to move beyond their violent past.

To make this spiritual transition, many Mozambican communities relied on traditional healers, who would guide returnees through rituals and ceremonies to begin their reintegration into the community. While the specific rituals and religions varied, the communities' acceptance and belief in the rituals was widespread.[97] Professor Alcinda Honwana describes one such reintegration ritual:

[The traditional healer] took the boy to the bush, where a small hut covered in dry grass had been built. The boy, dressed in the dirty clothes he brought from the rebel camp, entered the hut and undressed himself. Then the hut was set on fire, and an adult relative helped the boy out. The hut, the clothes, and everything else that the boy brought from the camp had to be burnt. This symbolized the rupture with the past.[98]

The boy then went on to perform other rituals that would help cleanse his body and give him strength. The entire ritual was public, with relatives and neighbors assisting the healer, performing specific roles, or simply observing. In other cases, the reintegration rituals were more private, focusing on the personal significance of absolving the returnee of sins committed during the war. For instance, one former soldier said that he participated in a purification ritual because "during the war I might have stepped over a place where people were killed, or I might have shot someone."[99] Another former child soldier explained that the importance of a traditional ceremony is one's acceptance back into his community:

I came back from war and used language of the other side, the language from the war. After the ceremony, I was familiar with the language here. After the ceremony people in general treated me well—before the ceremony people treated me badly. When I returned some people didn't talk to me as they thought I would teach them bad things

---

95. Ibid., 157.
96. Ibid., 158.
97. Ibid., 159–65.
98. Ibid., 159.
99. Ibid., 161.

that were learned there [in the war]. In a progressive way people started to like me more and stopped excluding me.[100]

It is clear that these symbolic rituals of purification were important both to individual returnees and to their communities. In fact, traditional healing played such a crucial role during the reconstruction process that many NGOs acknowledged its significance, either (like ProPaz) by working directly with the religious leaders or by keeping their distance to avoid delegitimizing the process.[101]

While there is ongoing debate on how much the practices of traditional healing and justice affected the reintegration process, the basic tenets, as explained by the curandeiros, are strikingly similar to the principles behind many official truth and reconciliation commissions. These reconciliation efforts aimed to acknowledge a lasting memory of what happened but also created a space for forgiveness and acceptance back into the community.[102] Also, while this process was used for children and youth returning from war, as well as for other older members of the community, the different rituals used were recognized as appropriate for the individuals undergoing them. While the extent to which traditional healing helped the Mozambican population cope with the atrocities of war may be uncertain, the role of indigenous culture and religion has clearly been a significant factor in the successful transition of youth from war to peace.

Coding

Cultural factors in Mozambique had a medium-level positive impact on the youth demographic and the overall reconstruction process. While traditional religious practices helped facilitate the successful reintegration of former soldiers on the community level, they did not have a major effect on the greater reconstruction process.

Dependent Variable: Level of Stability as Affected by Youth

Any country emerging from civil war may see fluctuating levels of stability after a cease-fire and peace accord are signed. A complete and immediate cessation of violence is highly unlikely. In the case of Mozambique, while there continue to be many instances of low-level violence, the country seems to have emerged from the twelve-year civil war without any significant reincitation of politically motivated or destabilizing violence.

---

100.   Boothby, Neil, Jennifer Crawford, and Jason Halperin, "Mozambique Child Soldier Life Outcome Study: Lessons Learned in Rehabilitation and Reintegration Efforts."

101.   Alden, "Making Old Soldiers Fade Away," 352; Cobban, *Amnesty after Atrocity?* 160.

102.   Cardinal Alexandre Dos Santos, in his interview, pointed to a scar from an accident and said, "I look at that scar and remember the accident that caused it. The wound no longer hurts at all. But it is important to remember what happened so I don't make the same mistake again." Cobban, *Amnesty after Atrocity?* 161.

Over the course of the UN mission, most reported violence involved soldiers waiting in the assembly areas for the demobilization process to take place. Many of the demobilized soldiers, disarmed and confined to the monotony of life in the assembly areas, were frustrated with the delayed progress.[103] Also, it appears that Renamo officials, in convincing soldiers to submit to the demobilization process, had made "elaborate promises," including assurances about the condition of the camps, substantial payments, and a speedy return to their homes.[104] The frustrations from unmet expectations and long-term confinement led to several disturbances in the assembly areas and to attacks on UN or government officials. Soldiers cited a number of different reasons for the violence. In Renamo camps, the complaints usually stemmed from inadequate facilities and shortages in food and clothing.[105] In the government/Frelimo camps, the complaints were more about the demobilization process itself, as soldiers were frustrated from being detained without knowing when they were going to be released.[106] As of September 1, 1994, a total of thirty-seven incidents were reported in the Renamo assembly areas, and forty in government assembly areas.[107] However, while these riots and incidents were serious, they did not indicate the demobilizing soldiers' desire to continue the war, but rather their frustrations over not receiving the treatment and benefits they believed they were entitled to. Aside from the incidents of violence in the assembly areas, there were no significant breaks in the cease-fire during 1992–94.

By 1994, the level of instability in Mozambique had improved dramatically. A number of security risks continued to arise, however, especially in the months preceding the election in 1996. Data from the Economist Intelligence Unit (EIU) country profiles from 1996 notes the emergence of a new violent gang called Chimwenje, operating in the west-central region of Mozambique and allegedly harboring Zimbabwean dissidents. It is unclear, however, what the group's specific goals were. EIU reports from 1996 also indicate an increasing fear of violence from both parties, as Frelimo in particular may have had an electoral interest in cultivating the fear that Renamo was prepared to reincite the violence. But by 1997, a strong Frelimo campaign against Renamo's illegal control of territory and attacks on Frelimo property had quelled the violence.[108]

---

103. Chris Alden, "The UN and the Resolution of Conflict in Mozambique," *Journal of Modern African Studies* 33, no. 1 (1995): 117.

104. Alden, *Mozambique and the Construction of the New African State*, 54.

105. João Paulo Borges Coelho and Alex Vines, "Pilot Study on Demobilization and Reintegration of Ex-combatants in Mozambique," report, Oxford Refugee Studies Programme, 1994, University of Oxford.

106. For example, on May 27, 1994, soldiers in the Frelimo assembly area forwarded a letter of demands to the UN military observers: "With respect we like to know why the demob process stopped? We are here for a long time without any definite answers. For this reason, we are demanding to know the exact dates for the next demob here in Rio Save. . . . If Rio Save receives more soldiers . . . and still we don't receive any answer, we are not sure who we are going to kill—the Camp Commander or ONUMOZ group. We are tired and bored of staying here . . . we have the right to know our rights . . . ." Ibid.

107. Alden, *Mozambique and the Construction of the New African State*, 55.

108. Economist Intelligence Unit, "Country Report: Mozambique Malawi," Oct. 1997, www.eiu.com

The emergence of low-level violence, road banditry, and gang-related activity became a significant security risk. The 1996 and 1997 EIU reports note the increasing level of violent crime, particularly in Sofala, Zambezia, and Tete provinces and on the main road connecting Maputo to the South African border. Although the level of road banditry and violence reached a "crisis point" in 1996, much of the violence was controlled within the year with the deployment of paramilitary police units and regular provincial police patrols.

Chris Alden reported that the organization behind the gang violence was thought to have its roots in the upper echelons of former militaries. Alden's interviews show that some middle- and high-ranking officers were frustrated with the demobilization program, which they viewed as oriented toward the "common" soldier and "irrelevant to [professional soldiers'] needs and backgrounds," and turned instead to lucrative and powerful positions within the developing ranks of organized crime:

> The connection between criminal gangs operating in Mozambique in the areas of illegal arms sales, stolen vehicles, and the burgeoning drugs trade and former military officers also had its origin in the failings of the demilitarization programme. Tailored to meet the needs of the top brass—with its pension support provisions—and the foot soldier—with its disbursement of "kits" containing hoes, seeds, and a bucket—the reintegration programme neglected to address the concerns of the government's middle ranking officer class. An elite product of the Soviet and Eastern European (and Cuban in some cases) training programmes in political and military schools, with the onset of peace, these officers found themselves with neither the prestige of position nor the income and privileges accorded to military service during the civil war.[109]

According to Alden, these officers used their organizational skills to become leaders in the "criminal underworld," often generating incomes rivaling those from the army or police.

Other reports, however, link the criminal activity to increasingly marginalized youth, particularly in overcrowded cities with few employment opportunities.[110] Specifically, one of Mozambique's two national trade unions, the Organizacionão dos Tralhadores de Moçambique, expressed concern that because of shortcomings in the demobilization and reintegration program and a lack of income-generating opportunities, young people might resort to drug use, stealing, or road banditry.[111]

The frequency of violence and road banditry may also be linked to the proliferation of cross-border arms trafficking, particularly between Mozambique and South Africa.[112] The control of weapons caches from the disarmament process

---

(subscription only, accessed Sept. 1, 2009).

109. Alden, "Making Old Soldiers Fade Away," 350; Alden, *Mozambique and the Construction of the New African State*, 113–14.

110. Maslen, *The Reintegration of War-Affected Youth*; Aird, Efraime, and Errante, "Mozambique: The Battle Continues for Former Child Soldiers."

111. Maslen, *The Reintegration of War-Affected Youth*.

112. Economist Intelligence Unit, "Country Report: Mozambique Malawi," Oct. 1996, www.eiu.com (subscription only, accessed Sept. 1, 2009).

was particularly problematic, with weapons stockpiles going unreported and parties failing to turn over their weapons.[113] Still, although the ease of access to small arms supported emerging gang activity and banditry, there is little evidence that this activity was politically motivated or aimed at destabilizing the situation to return the country to a state of civil war. Rather, the criminal activities appear to have been economically motivated, since weapons trade may have been one of the most profitable forms of informal commerce, particularly for youth.

Mozambique has emerged from the conflict's end in 1992 to become a relatively stable society with no significant violent political movements:

- Mozambique earned an 86.1 out of 100 on the 2008 Ibrahim Index of African Governance's rating for Safety and Security in 2000, 2002, and 2005.[114] Only six countries rank higher for all three years. The subcategories for which Mozambique received less than 100 were ease of access to small arms, and level of violent crime.
- According to the Global Peace Index, Mozambique received an overall score for 2007 of 1.909 on a scale of 1 to 5, with 1 signifying most peaceful and 5 signifying least peaceful.[115] On subindexes related to stability, ranging from 1 (very low) to 5 (very high), it received a 3 for level of organized internal conflict, and 2's for level of political instability, likelihood of violent demonstrations, and level of violent crime.
- On the Failed States Index, Mozambique is rated at "warning" level for risk in 2005–07, although it dropped from the rank of forty-second most at risk for conflict in 2005 to eighty-first in 2007 (among all states worldwide).[116]
- RiskMap 2008 places Mozambique at the medium level for political and security risks to foreign business.

These indexes show that while Mozambique is still struggling with the same issues that many developing states must confront, it is no longer at a crisis level of conflict and, in fact, is relatively peaceful as of 2007. While issues such as arms availability and violent crime continue to present a problem, the political structure has been able to survive without any large-scale waves of violence. Moreover, while there was some youth involvement in low-level violent crimes such as banditry, the youth demographic did not appear to have a large destabilizing impact.

---

113. Alden, *Mozambique and the Construction of the New African State*, 113.

114. The scale ranges from 0 (least safe and secure) to 100 (most safe and secure).

115. This score ranked Mozambique fiftieth most peaceful of 121 countries.

116. The Failed States Index ranks countries' vulnerability to state collapse, on a four-category scale from "sustainable" (least vulnerable to collapse) through "moderate" and "warning," to "alert" (most vulnerable to collapse).

Although the success of Mozambique's economic and democratic development after 1992 is sometimes exaggerated, the lack of sustained or large-scale civil unrest and violence is noteworthy.[117] The country faced some overwhelming development issues, including massive flooding in 2000 and 2001, which could have put great political strain on a country recently emerging from civil war.[118] But Mozambique dealt with these disasters and other economic and political issues with no resurgence of widespread violence. The successful elections of 1994, 1999, and 2004, along with the country's high marks in safety and security and overall peace from the Ibrahim Index and the Global Peace Index, are clear evidence.

Coding

For the first five years after the conflict, Mozambique is coded as maintaining a low level of instability as affected by youth. The coding reflects the evidence that there was relatively no sustained politically motivated violence, breaking of the cease-fire, or emergence of politically motivated violent crime during 1992–97. While some reports link youth to the emergence of gang and criminal activity, this did not have a significant destabilizing effect on the reconstruction process. Instances of medium levels of violence during the delays in the disarmament process and surrounding the election were not directly related to youth, nor did they significantly impede the overall transition from war to peace or prevent the creation of a generally stable environment.

Summary Impacts of Variables

Tables 2.1 through 2.7 summarize the information conveyed in this chapter, synthesizing the details in each variable and showing the variable's impact on the youth demographic and on the general level of stability in Mozambique. Tables 2.1 through 2.5 deal with independent variables and tables 2.6 and 2.7 with dependent variables.

---

117. Alden, *Mozambique and the Construction of the New African State* 66, 97.

118. Cobban, *Amnesty after Atrocity?*, 162–63.

Table 2.1. Mozambique: International Involvement

Variables	Program Specifics	Impact
Treaty	• Establishes DDR program under UN; no other specific impact on youth	Low positive impact
Foreign Governments	• Involvement in negotiation process • Humanitarian aid	Low positive impact
United Nations	• DDR • Humanitarian aid, refugee reintegration • "Quick impact projects"	High positive impact
Time Frame	• Short to medium term	Effective in alloted time frame, but lacking long-term vision
Overall Effectiveness		**Medium positive impact**

Table 2.2. Mozambique: NGO Involvement

Variables	Program Specifics	Impact
Coordination	• Clear coordination mechanism • Despite instances of poor cooperation, relatively successful coordination helps facilitate the process	Medium positive impact
Types of Programming	• Psychosocial support • Reintegration • Advocacy (e.g., exempting former child soldiers from military conscription) • Humanitarian • Conflict resolution—youth empowerment	Medium positive impact; effective at filling in and complementing the international program; successfully met critical youth needs in the short term
Level of Efforts (number of NGOs or international personnel)	• Medium level • NGOs operating were relatively successful and effective	Medium positive impact
Time Frame	• Short to medium term • Successful in time frame, but most programs did not go long term	Low positive impact
Overall Effectiveness		**Medium positive impact**

Table 2.3. Mozambique: Domestic Policy

Variables	Program Specifics	Impact
Focus on Youth	• Some focus on youth in emergency efforts and long-term education policy, though most policies affect youth only indirectly	Medium positive impact
Types of Programming	• Education reform • Reunification (emergency relief) • Amnesty	Medium positive impact
Overall Effectiveness		**Medium positive impact**

Table 2.4. Mozambique: Cultural and Environmental Factors

Variables	Role	Impact
Religion and Religious Practices	• Helped facilitate reintegration of former child soldiers back into their home communities	Medium positive impact
Overall Effectiveness		**Medium positive impact**

Table 2.5. Mozambique: Demographic and Objective Statistics

Population Age 10–24	• 33% of population age 10–24 • Total population (1993): 13,691,368
	Baseline • Average for sub-Saharan Africa: 32% in 1997 • Average for more developed states: 21% in 1997
Level of Youth Participation	• Over 10,000 of 93,000 soldiers were under 18 at time of demobilization • 28% under age 17 at recruitment • 50% under age 31 at recruitment • 30,000 "street children" as of 1997 • No accurage statistics available for level of youth participation in reintegration programs, youth-driven clubs, volunteer associations, etc.
Unemployment	• Estimated at 21% in 2007
GNI per Capita	• US$210 (2000)
	Baseline • Average for sub-Saharan Africa (2000): US$485.10
Overall Coding	• **High proportion of youth in the population** • **High level of youth involvement in the conflict**

Baseline population statistics taken from U.S. Census Bureau, "International Data Base," Sept. 2009, www.census.gov/ipc/www/idb/ (accessed Sept. 1, 2009). Baseline for GNI per capita taken from World Bank, "Key Development Data and Statistics," http://web.worldbankd.org/WBSITE/EXTERNAL/DATASTATISTICS/0,content/MDK:20535285~menuPK:1390200~pagePK:64133150~piPK:64133175~theSitePK:239419,00.html (accessed Sept. 1, 2009).

Table 2.6. Mozambique: Level of Instability

Overall Description of Instability	• Significant drop in level of violence after conflict; no reincitation of conflict • Some rioting in DDR assembly areas • Low-level violence, road banditry, crime
Youth Involvement	• Marginalized youth a contributing factor in increasing criminal activity, although no evidence for a significant link to youth as the driving force • Rioting at DDR assembly areas includes many former child soldiers and youth old enough to submit to the DDR process
Youth's Effects on Overall Level of Instability	Low level of instability, with low levels of youth participation in politically motivated violence and crime. Despite high levels of youth involvement in the conflict, youth do not structurally affect stability or contribute to ongoing conflict. Some instances of youth having positive impact by contributing to increased stability

Table 2.7. Mozambique: Supporting Indicators of Level of Instability

Ibrahim Index of African Governance	• Safety and Security: 86.1/100 (100 = most secure)
Global Peace Index	• 1.909 on a scale of 1–5 (1 = most peaceful)
Failed States Index	• "Warning" level for risk of collapse or conflict • From 2005 to 2007, improved from 45th to 81st most likely to fail
RiskMap 2008	• Medium political risk • Medium security risk

Conclusion

On the surface, the success of the post-conflict reconstruction process in Mozambique is surprising, since the international community's programs did not include cohesive child- and youth-specific policies. But Mozambique's relative success in meeting the youth demographic's needs is not a fluke. Rather, the combined impact of a few key factors explains how the country overcame the potentially dangerous youth bulge situation and experienced one of the more successful periods of modern post-conflict reconstruction in sub-Saharan Africa. These are perhaps the most important of these factors:

- an effective international effort to disarm and reintegrate older youth
- the successful efforts by NGOs to fill gaps in UN programming, particularly for child soldiers

- the positive impact of the cultural and religious environment.

During the reconstruction process in Mozambique, the youth demographic could have emerged as a significant destabilizing factor. But although the country's youth today remain vulnerable, the reintegration program managed to quell any potential risk of their derailing the war-to-peace transition, and Mozambique has emerged as a relatively stable country (see table 2.6).

The outcome in Mozambique is largely explained through the constructive relationship between the UN program and NGO efforts. As tables 2.1 and 2.2 demonstrate, both the United Nations and NGOs were relatively successful in instituting their reconstruction programs. The UN mission ran several key programs, including DDR and refugee reintegration that included young people over 16 years of age. The DDR process essentially created a "negative peace" by providing just enough assistance with demobilization and reintegration to prevent the reemergence of violence in the short term. However, the United Nations did not design its policies to cater specifically to the needs of the youth demographic, thereby leaving a number of issues unresolved. Although the United Nations' programs did not explicitly address children and youth or go beyond violence prevention, its management of the overarching process allowed NGOs to dedicate their efforts specifically to meeting the critical youth needs left out of the overall UN mission. In addition, community-targeted humanitarian programs through the United Nations, such as the QIPs, were able to benefit multiple demographics, with a specific focus on youth and women. Thus, because key youth needs were met through the combined efforts of community-based programs and the efforts of a few youth-focused NGOs, the reconstruction effort in Mozambique succeeded in meeting initial youth needs despite its not having an overarching child and youth strategy or an abundance of youth programs.

Certain domestic policies and cultural factors also contributed positively by creating a constructive environment for the reintegration process. The government's retrospective blanket amnesty for all individuals involved in the conflict, while not aimed at youth specifically, contributed greatly to creating a culture of reconciliation after the conflict. Religion also added to this culture of reconciliation, with religious leaders and traditional healers working within the cultures to guide returnees back into their communities.

Today Mozambique is a relatively stable country politically and seems to have moved beyond the civil conflict without any serious or widespread reincitation of violence. While the reconstruction process was largely successful in stabilizing the country and achieving a negative peace, it is important to note that most of the programs, with the notable exception of ProPaz, focused on short- to medium-term relief rather than going on to provide long-term sociopolitical empowerment programs for the youth demographic.[119] As a result, youth in Mozambique continue to face inadequate opportunity and employment and remain a vulnerable population. In the transition to a peacetime environment, Mozambique, like many developing nations, has also struggled with economic reforms and development, and perhaps as a combined result of history, geography, and recent humanitarian crises—including devastating flooding in 2000 and 2001—Mozambique remains one of the more underdeveloped nations in the world.

---

119. This dichotomy between humanitarian programming during post-conflict reconstruction and longer-term development programming will be examined in further depth in the concluding chapter. The important thing to note here is that although the short- and medium-term reconstruction efforts in Mozambique upon the conclusion of the civil war were highly successful, the country was also faced with widespread poverty and development issues that have far outlasted the reconstruction period.

3

Democratic Republic of the Congo: Youth and the Perpetuation of Conflict

I n direct contrast to Mozambique, the post-conflict reconstruction process in the Democratic Republic of the Congo was riddled with ineffective policies and disorganized implementing agents. As a result, the reconstruction process has been unsuccessful as violence continues to destabilize the country, particularly in the eastern Kivu and Ituri provinces. Mozambique and the DRC faced similar circumstances with their youth demographics: both had a high proportion of youth in the population, and the DRC had an even higher proportion of child soldiers. In the DRC, however, the international community responded to the crisis on a much larger scale, both in the overarching reconstruction program and in youth- and child-specific policies. After the signing of the cease-fire and peace agreements, the DRC was inundated with international organizations and NGOs looking to provide humanitarian aid and transition assistance. The UN mission sent to manage the reconstruction process has become the largest peacekeeping mission in UN history. All the actors involved were acutely aware of the significance of the youth demographic and developed policies or programming specifically geared toward youth.

Despite the extremely high levels of participation, the reconstruction efforts and youth-specific policies have failed to produce a lasting positive impact. In fact, the DRC is the least stable of the three cases in this study, with high levels of postaccord violence and a continuation of the conflict in certain provinces. Elite actors have been able to continue their insurgency, in part due to ongoing youth participation and recruitment. The case of post-conflict reconstruction in the DRC is therefore particularly puzzling because, even with the prodigious level of effort from the international community and with the creation of numerous youth-specific policies and programs, children and youth in the DRC have emerged as a significant factor in the ongoing destabilization.

Several intervening factors and characteristics of the reconstruction program shaped the youth demographic's behavior and impeded reconstruction efforts. Even with the money and manpower behind the international operation in the

DRC, the mismanagement of the DDR program not only rendered the reconstruction process incomplete—with no significant reintegration programming—it also figured in the deterioration of the situation and in the ongoing violence. Consequently, NGOs were forced, often on an ad-hoc, emergency basis, to fill in for the failing DDR program in identifying, sheltering, feeding, and demobilizing children. Because these NGOs had to use their limited resources to compensate for the government's failing DDR program, they did not have the capacity to provide critical reintegration and follow-up programming, such as vocational education, health education, or conflict resolution programming. Also, extenuating circumstances, such as the DRC's extremely difficult geographic terrain, the ongoing violence, and the culture of impunity, must be taken into account as militating against the effectiveness of reconstruction efforts.

However, the failure of peacekeeping efforts in the DRC is not merely a case of an inhospitable environment. Rather, evidence suggests that because of the poor management of the DDR program, certain critical functions, such as reintegration programming and education opportunities, were left unmet, leaving thousands of former child and youth soldiers with little hope of a successful return to civilian society. As a result of the failure to facilitate young people's transition from war to peace, children and youth became a useful commodity for those wishing to destabilize the country. Children and youth with little hope of a better life in peacetime were easily recruited or rerecruited into rebel militias, or indirectly supported the conflict by laboring in the mines that finance rebel movements.

Background

The DRC occupies the heart of Africa, covering an area roughly the size of one quarter of the United States. It is home to nearly seventy ethnic groups, with significant regional and linguistic divisions. While the rugged terrain has plagued the process of development in the DRC (transportation is terribly difficult, and tropical diseases such as malaria, typhoid fever, sleeping sickness, and schistosomiasis are quite common), the environment is also one of the world's richest in natural resources. The DRC holds some of the world's largest deposits of diamonds, gold, timber, coltan, and casserite. To understand the depth of the world market for these resources, consider that coltan and casserite are vital components in nearly all modern electronic and cellular devices, including televisions, mobile telephones, and computers.

With these environmental factors in mind, an understanding of the current situation in the DRC, as in Mozambique, begins with an examination of the country's colonial roots. In the late 1800s, Belgium, under the rule of King Leopold II, established the Congo Free State in the region known today as the DRC. King Leopold II became infamous for the brutal tactics he used against the native people to convert the Congo Free State into an extremely profitable resource-extracting machine. Despite its profitability, the colonial enterprise left the colony politically underdeveloped, so that when the Congo was granted independence in 1960 and the Belgian civil servants left the country en masse, the nascent government institutions were extremely weak. Very few Congolese bureaucrats had any administrative experience, and most were preoccupied with capitalizing on resources to further their own personal wealth and influence.[1] This legacy of colonial extraction and self-serving elites led to decades of corrupt rule under the dictator Mobutu Sese Seko and remains a driving force in the modern Congolese political economy.

Although the war for independence led to the DRC's first civil conflict, in 1960–65, and to the first UN peacekeeping force to be deployed there, in 1961–64, the most recent conflict emerged directly in the aftermath of the 1994 Rwandan genocide. Amid the chaos following the ethnically charged civil war in Rwanda, in which Hutu-dominated government forces organized the mass murder of some 800,000 to 1.3 million Tutsi and "moderate" Hutu,[2] over one million predominantly Hutu Rwandan refugees fled to camps in the northeastern region of the DRC (then Zaire) known as the Kivus.[3] Intermixed among the civilian refugees were approximately 70,000 Hutu soldiers and militiamen, including both high-ranking leadership of the former Rwandan Armed Forces (ex-FAR) and common *génocidaires* of the Interahamwe (the paramilitary group whose members perpetrated the genocide).

The dire conditions in the camps (including a cholera epidemic) attracted the attention of international humanitarian organizations and saw the influx of nearly US$1.3 billion in humanitarian relief.[4] However, amid the UNHCR's lack of control over the situation, and with the tacit support of the Mobutu regime, the ex-FAR and Interahamwe members manipulated international humanitarian assistance to the refugee camps to reestablish their political and military system, soon to be known as the Forces Démocratiques de Libération du Rwanda (FDLR), which has used the camps in the DRC as bases for launching attacks against Rwanda. The presence of the ex-FAR/Interahamwe- and, later, FDLR-dominated camps in Zaire and Tanzania served as a catalyst for the civil unrest

---

1.　James Dobbins, *The UN's Role in Nation-Building: From the Congo to Iraq* (Santa Monica, Calif.: RAND, 2005).

2.　Sarah Kenyon Lischer, "Collateral Damage: Humanitarian Assistance as a Cause of Conflict," *International Security* 28, no. 1 (2003); Samantha Power, "Bystanders to Genocide," *Atlantic Monthly* 288, no. 2 (September 2001); BBC, "Rwanda: How the Genocide Happened," BBC News, December 18, 2008, http://news.bbc.co.uk/2/hi/africa/1288230.stm (accessed Sept. 1, 2009).

3.　Jane Boulden, *Dealing with Conflict in Africa: The United Nations and Regional Organizations* (New York: Palgrave Macmillan, 2003).

4.　Ibid.; Lischer, "Collateral Damage," 80. According to Lischer, while donors were willing to send billions of dollars in humanitarian relief to "tens of thousands of unrepentant genocide perpetrators," the same donors were unwilling to fund efforts to "disarm the militants, much less send peacekeeping troops to do so."

in Zaire (later the DRC) and for the broader instability that currently plagues the Great Lakes region.

In addition to creating tensions between the newly installed Rwandan government and Zaire, the influx of refugees began to exacerbate ethnic tensions in the Kivus. In the mid-1990s, local community leaders in the Kivus had begun a racially charged campaign against the Congolese Tutsi population, questioning their nationality status. In 1993 and again in 1996, local government leaders, with the support of the Mobutu regime, led violent campaigns to drive out and kill the Tutsi in the Masisi region of North Kivu, and the Banyamulenge (ethnically Tutsi) group in South Kivu.[5]

These actions, combined with the growing tensions in the refugee camps, led to increased instability and tension along the border. By September 1996, the First Congo War began, which pitted the Tutsi and Banyamulenge minority, backed by the Rwandan, Ugandan, and Angolan governments—which wanted to see an end to the Hutu militias' attacks on their territory—against the Zairian army and the ex-FAR/Interahamwe in the refugee camps. The foreign governments, in addition to sending their own troops, attempted to mask their acts of aggression before the international community by allying with indigenous anti-Mobutu movements[6] and supporting an alliance of Congolese revolutionary parties known as the Alliance des Forces Démocratiques pour la Libération du Congo (AFDL), led by Laurent Kabila. The international community, particularly the West, perceived the conflict as a civil war and anti-Mobutu revolution and focused instead on the unfolding humanitarian and refugee crisis rather than on the military conflict. Without international support, Mobutu was forced to flee the country in 1997. Kabila assumed power and renamed the country Democratic Republic of the Congo.

Kabila was in his new post for only fifteen months before war broke out again, in August 1998. During this time, Kabila had alienated the United Nations, the international community, and his Rwandan allies over a number of issues, including his refusal to allow a UN investigation of the massacre of thousands of the Hutu residents of the refugee camps. As a result, the second phase of the war saw a split among the former AFDL troops and in regional alliances: certain brigades within the AFDL rallied against Kabila and formed the Rassemblement Congolais pour la Démocratie (Congolese Rally for Democracy, or RCD) and, later, the Mouvement pour la Libération du Congo (MLC). Rwanda and Uganda broke with Angola to support the RCD[7] and other armed forces, such as the Mayi-Mayi, in their attempts to overthrow the newly installed government.

---

5. Boulden, *Dealing with Conflict in Africa*.

6. While there were a number of anti-Mobutu and revolutionary movements within Zaire, most adhered to nonviolent and nonmilitary strategies.

7. The RCD later split into the RCD-MLC (Mouvement de Libération du Congo), backed by Uganda, and the RCD-Goma, backed by Rwanda.

Angola continued to support Kabila's government, backed by the Congolese army and the governments of Namibia and Zimbabwe.

By July1999, after a year of regional interventions and negotiations, the parties succumbed to international pressures to put an end to the violence and signed the Lusaka Peace Accord (or Lusaka Cease-fire Agreement). However, it is important to note that unlike in Mozambique, not all the parties fully supported an end to the hostilities. Rather, signing the peace treaty was an opportunistic move for all those involved: the conflict had come to a stalemate, and greater scrutiny of all actors (along with the dire humanitarian and refugee situation) had increased the international community's desire to achieve a peaceful solution, leaving the parties no real alternative to the agreement. The Lusaka Cease-fire Agreement committed all parties, including representatives from the DRC and other regional actors (with the notable exception of the Mayi-Mayi), to a cessation of the violence and authorized a UN mission to the DRC to facilitate the peacekeeping process. The accord also called for an Inter-Congolese Dialogue to resolve the political disputes and facilitate national reconciliation in the DRC. But the reluctance of parties to commit fully to the peace process would continue to surface throughout the transition period as various factions actively avoided full compliance with peacemaking operations.

The Inter-Congolese Dialogue was supposed to last ninety days. In fact, it would take three years, several failed agreements, and multiple UN and international interventions in the negotiations to finally achieve an agreement. During this time, in 2001, Laurent Kabila was assassinated by one of his own men in a failed coup attempt. Ten days later, Kabila's son Joseph assumed power.

In December 2002, the government of the DRC, the RCD, the MLC, the political opposition, civil society, the Congolese Rally for Democracy/Liberation Movement, the Congolese Rally for Democracy/National, and the Mayi-Mayi signed the Global and All-Inclusive Agreement on the Transition in the DRC (sometimes called Pretoria II). The agreement renewed the parties' commitment to cease hostilities, established new government institutions and power-sharing agreements, and named Joseph Kabila head of the transition government.

While this agreement officially marked the beginning of the transition and reconstruction phase in the DRC, the northeastern regions remained largely unstable as armed groups continued to fight, and a former RCD general, Laurent Nkunda, waged an ethnically charged battle of instability against the transition government.

In October 2008, Nkunda's militia, the National Congress for the Defense of the People (CNDP), launched a large and brutal offensive to overtake the city of Goma, in Eastern Congo. After winning numerous battles and nearly taking control of the city, Nkunda declared a unilateral cease-fire, demanding negotiations with the government.

In a surprising turn of events, the CNDP split in early January 2009, as Nkunda's right-hand man, Brig. Gen. Bosco Ntaganda, declared a "failure in leadership" and formed his own faction of the militia.[8] On January 9, Rwandan officials (those allegedly backing the CNDP) arrested Nkunda on the DRC-Rwanda border. The arrest was the result of a deal between Rwanda and the DRC, which brokered Rwanda's withdrawal of support for the CNDP in exchange for the DRC government's allowing Rwanda to send troops into the DRC to eliminate the Hutu extremist FDLR. Members of the CNDP were integrated into the Congolese army. By late February, the joint Rwandan and Congolese forces claimed to have destroyed the command structure of the FDLR and other Hutu militias.[9]

The joint offensive, though ostensibly undertaken to impose order, reflects another episode in an ongoing cycle of violence, and many believe that its net result has been to imperil civilians rather than protect them.[10] In the war over Goma, the CNDP, FDLR, and government forces all committed horrific human rights abuses, including the killing and torture of civilians, use of civilians as human shields, use of child soldiers, and rape of countless women and children.[11] As of this writing, in September 2009, the DRC's future is unclear. Questions remain about the circumstances of Nkunda's arrest and detention, the joint offensive, the impact of any International Criminal Court (ICC) proceedings (Bosco Ntaganda and others have been charged by the ICC with war crimes, specifically for the recruitment and treatment of child soldiers), and the future stability of the eastern provinces.

The fifteen-year war in the DRC/Zaire has been characterized by extreme violence against civilians, resulting in more deaths than did the entire First World War, and producing what has been termed "one of the greatest humanitarian disasters in the world today."[12] By 2003, at least 3.3 million people had died as a direct or indirect result of the conflict, with an additional 2.7 million Congolese IDPs (90 percent of whom moved to the eastern regions) and 378,000 Congolese refugees seeking asylum in neighboring countries.[13] The DRC, meanwhile, has

8.   BBC, "Congo Rebels Back 'Ousted' Chief," BBC News, January 6, 2009, http://news.bbc.co.uk/2/hi/africa/7813235.stm (accessed Sept. 1, 2009).

9.   Peter Greste, "Nkunda's Spectacular Fall," BBC News, Nairobi, January 23, 2009, news.bbc.co.uk/2/hi/africa/7846940.stm (accessed Sept. 1, 2009).

10.   Human Rights Watch, "DRC: Groups Fear for Civilian Safety," www.hrw.org/en/news/2009/02/06/dr-congo-groups-fear-civilian-safety (accessed Sept. 1, 2009).

11.   Human Rights Watch, "DR Congo: Massive Increase in Attacks on Civilians," July 2, 2009, www.hrw.org/en/news/2009/07/02/dr-congo-massive-increase-attacks-civilians (accessed Sept. 1, 2009); BBC, "Hutu Rebels Killed in Congo Raid," BBC News, Feb. 13, 2009, http://news.bbc.co.uk/2/hi/africa/7888370.stm (accessed Sept. 1, 2009).

12.   Boulden, *Dealing with Conflict in Africa*.

13.   Mark Malan and João Gomes Porto, *Challenges of Peace Implementation: The UN Mission in the Democratic Republic of the Congo* (Pretoria: Institute for Security Studies, 2004).

received 330,000 foreign refugees.[14] While the situation in DRC—outside Kivu and Ituri provinces—improved to a considerable degree after 2003, by 2006 the death toll had reached 3.9 million, and 1,200 people continued to die each day from violence, preventable disease, or starvation as a result of the ongoing insecurity and lack of access to humanitarian and medical care.[15]

The conflict in the Congo has also become notorious internationally for its terrible effect on children and youth. Of the 3.9 million who died as a result of the conflict in the DRC, 45 percent were children (under 18).[16] As of 2006, 45 percent of the estimated 38,000 dying every month as a direct or indirect result of the ongoing violence were children. Also, the use of child soldiers has been a common practice throughout the conflict, with all sides recruiting children to serve in their ranks. Children associated with armed groups were particularly vulnerable both during and after the conflict. These children, often subjected to extreme brutality during recruitment, then participated in the widespread violence, often while under the influence of drugs. The young women and girls associated with armed groups were particularly at risk, since many not only fought on the front lines but also were regularly raped or were taken as "wives" and not later released by their male captors.

The education system also suffered terribly from the ongoing violence. Schools were the targets of numerous attacks and often were the sites of forced recruitment. By 2003, DRC was one of the five countries in the world with the largest number of children out of school, and a gross enrollment ratio of only 64 percent—less than the average in sub-Saharan Africa.[17]

Today the situation facing youth in the DRC has not significantly improved. Laurent Nkunda's arrest in January 2009 may prove to be a turning point, yet even if the violence decreases dramatically, the humanitarian crisis will still severely affect Congolese children and youth. Currently, the average life expectancy in the DRC is only 44 years, and 205 out of every 1,000 children will die before reaching age 5. Close to one-third of all children in the DRC are underweight, with malnutrition causing nearly half of all deaths among children under age 5.[18] In 2007, 37,000 to 52,000 children under age 15 were living with HIV/AIDS, and 270,000 to 380,000 children were orphaned, having lost one or

14. Watchlist on Children and Armed Conflict, "Struggling to Survive: Children in Armed Conflict in the Democratic Republic of the Congo," www.watchlist.org/reports/dr_congo.php (accessed Sept. 1, 2009).

15. Amnesty International, "Democratic Republic of the Congo: Children at War, Creating Hope for the Future," report, 2006, www.amnestyusa.org/document.php?id=ENGAFR620172006&lang=e (accessed Sept. 1, 2009).

16. Watchlist on Children and Armed Conflict, "Struggling to Survive," 5.

17. Sajitha Bashir, Democratic Republic of Congo: Country Status Report on Education, Priorities and Options for Regenerating the Education Sector, World Bank Report no. 30860-ZR, Nov. 15, 2004, www-wds.worldbank.org/external/default/WDSContentServer/WDSP/IB/2004/12/28/000012009_20041228095516/Rendered/PDF/308600ZR.pdf (accessed Sept. 23, 2009).

18. UNICEF, "Democratic Republic of the Congo," www.unicef.org/infobycountry/drcongo_636.html (accessed Sept. 1, 2009).

both parents to AIDS.[19] But despite the efforts of the international community, there is no good evidence that humanitarian aid is having a significant positive effect on the crisis in the DRC, and the prospects for youth development and empowerment are particularly bleak. In fact, two weeks after Nkunda's recent offensive in Goma, tens of thousands of civilians remained beyond the reach of humanitarian aid, and corridors that were previously safe for aid operations were closed off and under rebel control.[20]

This analysis explores the impact of international, domestic, and NGO policies on the reconstruction process. The evidence suggests that the reconstruction actors' failure to fully implement reintegration programs and education reform is directly connected to the ongoing instability. Without the resources necessary to make the transition into civilian life, many young people affected by the conflict have become increasingly vulnerable to (re)recruitment into armed groups and therefore have constituted an enduring resource for those wishing to prolong the conflict. Cultural and environmental issues, such as the inaccessible geographic terrain and the ongoing culture of impunity, also have hampered the implementation of reconstruction programs.

Variable Analysis: Impact on Youth and Stability

Youth Demographic Variables

As with Mozambique, it is important to understand the general situation facing youth in the DRC at the outset of the reconstruction period, including the proportion of youth in the population and how they were involved in or affected by the war, the status of the education system, and unemployment. These indicators give a general picture of the obstacles that youth must overcome to make a successful war-to-peace transition.

Youth Proportion of Population

In 2003, after the Global and All-Inclusive Agreement was signed, the DRC government estimated that approximately 60 percent of the 54.9 million people living in the DRC were under age 25, with only slightly more young men than young women.[21] According to U.S. State Department census data, from 2002 to 2007, 32 percent of the population was 10 to 24 years old, with a median age of

19. UNAIDS "Democratic Republic of the Congo," www.unaids.org/en/CountryResponses/Countries/democratic_republic_of_the_congo.asp (accessed Sept. 23, 2009).

20. UN Integrated Regional Information Networks, "Congo-Kinshasa: Agencies Cannot Reach Trapped Civilians," All-Africa News, Nov. 12, 2008, http://allafrica.com/stories/200811120821.html (accessed Sept. 1, 2009).

21. Government of Democratic Republic of the Congo, "Programme National de Désarmement, Démobilization et Réinsertion," 2003, www.unddr.org/documents.php?doc=852 (accessed Sept. 1, 2009); U.S. Census Bureau, "International Data Base," www.census.gov/ipc/www/idb/index.php (accessed Sept. 1, 2009).

16 across the population. In addition to the high proportion of young adults and adolescents, more than 45 percent of the 2007 population was under age 15, 35 percent was under age 10, and 19 percent was under age 5.[22] Because young children and youth formed such a high proportion of the population, they were also highly affected by the previous and ongoing violence.

Youth Refugees and Soldiers

In 2003, there were approximately 3.4 million internally displaced Congolese and another 350,000 Congolese refugees in Congo-Brazzaville, Zambia, and Tanzania, while 250,000 foreign refugees were residing in the DRC.[23] Over 80 percent of the internally displaced were women and children.

Perhaps the most significant demographic data is the numbers of children and youth serving in armed groups. In 2003, of the approximately 150,000 government troops and members of other armed forces, an estimated 30,000 were under 18, with children forming up to 40 percent of certain brigades.[24] Demonstrating just how fundamental youth and child soldiers were in the conflict, data from child demobilization programs conducted in 1999–2003 by Save the Children indicate that 82 percent of the children in these programs were over 15 at the time of demobilization yet had been involved in the conflict for over three years, often serving in more than one of the armed groups.[25] In fact, because such a large proportion of young children was serving in the armed forces, many of the older children quickly rose in the ranks, becoming noncommissioned or junior officers.[26]

While it is unclear how many of the children were forcibly recruited and how many volunteered, children have been associated with every armed group active in the DRC. Those most widely known for their egregious treatment and recruitment of children are the Mayi-Mayi and the RCD-Goma. Many children were kidnapped while working or on their way to school and were subjected to extremely harsh treatment, as attested by these two child soldiers:

> "We were on our way back from school when we met the rebels. They made us carry some luggage for them and then told us to go with them. . . . When we got to the camps, the

---

22. U.S. Census Bureau, International Data Base, Fund for Peace, Failed States Index, www.fundforpeace. org/web/index.php?option=com_content&task=view&id=99&Itemid=140 (accessed Sept. 1, 2009).

23. Malan and Gomes Porto, Challenges of Peace Implementation.

24. The common term used to describe those under 18 who serve in armed groups is "children associated with armed groups and forces." This category encompasses child soldiers as well as children serving in armed groups as cooks, spies, sexual slaves, or in other roles. The government of the DRC and other national and international organizations involved in peacekeeping, humanitarian, and reconstruction missions to the DRC use this term and definition in defining the scope of their policies focused on children. Amnesty International, "Democratic Republic of the Congo: Children at War."

25. Beth Verhey, "Going Home: Demobilising and Reintegrating Child Soldiers in the Democratic Republic of the Congo," Save the Children report, 2003, www.savethechildren.org.uk/en/54_5151.htm (accessed Sept. 1 2009), 11.

26. Amnesty International, "Democratic Republic of the Congo: Children at War."

rebels told [us] to join the military forces. They took us and threw us in a hole. We were given military outfits and told we had to wear them." (16-year-old boy)[27]

"Five CNDP soldiers stopped me on the road in the middle of the day. They sent me with a large group of other men and boys—some as young as 12, others as old as 40—to Murambi, where they said we would transport boxes of ammunition for the rebel soldiers. They beat us badly so we couldn't resist. When we got to Murambi, they didn't order us to transport boxes, but instead gave us military uniforms and taught us how to use weapons. Then after three days, they put us all in an underground prison. We stayed there for four days, and new recruits joined us every day." (Anthony, child soldier forcibly recruited outside a displaced-persons camp)[28]

As the evidence of child soldiering by all parties brought pressure from the international community, in 2003 the government pledged to end its recruitment and use of child soldiers. But the UN secretary-general reported that as of 2005, at least nine of the armed groups continued to recruit child soldiers, and in 2006, children were still associated with a number of integrated government brigades. Most notably, troops loyal to Laurent Nkunda were still actively recruiting child soldiers in 2007.

Interestingly, an estimated 40 percent of the children associated with armed groups were female. Young girls and women associated with armed groups are particularly vulnerable because sexual violence is rampant in the DRC and is used consciously as a weapon of war. In some cases, sexual violence is used as a tool to tear apart local communities, with soldiers raping mothers and daughters in front of their families.[29] Here are the accounts of two sisters who were raped and then rejected by their community:

"I was going to school and a soldier raped me while I was walking there. I was 14 years old. The men were from the Mai Mai [pro-Congolese government militia group]. I was very scared. I cried out for help but no one came because I was in the forest and no one heard me. Despite my cries, they carried on doing what they were doing to me.

"It's a habit here. Men in militias or in the military take women by force and no one talks to them about it, and no one stops them. It's commonplace.

"After being raped, my life became unbearable in my family. When I got home I told my family what happened. Directly afterwards they asked me how I could have accepted what had happened to me, and they drove me away. They refused to let me go back to school and they kicked me out. So I came here to my maternal aunt's house. I do not understand how they can treat me like this." (Zania, 16)[30]

"When I was going to buy manioc flour at the market, they caught me. I was on a dirt road in the bush. They took me by force and they raped me in the forest. They were [Congolese] government soldiers.

27. Peter Greste, "Congolese Children Forced to Fight," BBC News, Goma, Nov. 12, 2008, http://news.bbc.co.uk/2/hi/africa/7724088.stm (accessed Sept. 8, 2009).

28. Katie Paul, "The Bloodiest War: Civilians from the Eastern Congo Tell Their Stories," *Newsweek*, Nov. 25, 2008, www.newsweek.com/id/170763/page/1 (accessed Sept. 1, 2009).

29. Rebecca Freely and Colin Thomas-Jensen, "Getting Serious about Ending Conflict and Sexual Violence in Congo," ENOUGH! Strategy Paper no. 15, March 2008, www.enoughproject.org/publications/getting-serious-about-ending-conflict-and-sexual-violence-congo (accessed Sept. 1, 2009).

30. Matt Hobson, "Forgotten Casualties of War: Girls in Armed Conflict," Save the Children report, 2005, www.reliefweb.int/rw/lib.nsf/db900SID/EVIU-6BSFEG?OpenDocument (accessed Sept. 2009).

Then they let me go and I continued on my way. When I got to the house my family drove me away saying that if I stayed there and the military returned they could kill us all, so my parents chased me away. My sister and I live to this day with our aunt. We work very hard." (Vumilla, 15)[31]

Many young women and girls were also taken as "wives" by soldiers and were regularly raped by multiple soldiers in the camps. This girl's account of being a rebel "wife" is all too common:

"I was in the group for two years. I used a gun many times, in many battles. . . . The men took us as their 'wives'—they treated us badly. They didn't start to rape me at the beginning, for the first year. It was later on that it began. There were lots of little houses in the military camp. They put girls and men in the houses. Then, the military men took us as their women; they didn't consider the fact that we were still children. At any time they wanted they came and had sex with us. There were so many men. You could have one man who had sex with you and then he left. Then, a second came and talked to you and then had sex and went back to his home. Then a third would come to you, talk and have sex with you and go to his home. So they did what they wanted with me. We were only there to do what they wanted. Even if you refused, the men took you anyway—they would insist." (Aimerance, 17)[32]

Because of their precarious position as "wives" of soldiers, many of these girls were not included in the DDR process and, therefore, were not able to receive the potential benefits provided by demobilization and reintegration programs.

Education

Civil conflict inevitably damages infrastructure, but the DRC education system has suffered devastation beyond the norm. In 2003, the World Bank reported that the DRC was one of the five countries worldwide with the largest proportion of children out of school. One of the main reasons for the education system's poor functioning is "chronic underfunding," which the World Bank has cited as the "main factor that perpetuates low enrollment rates and the extreme degradation in the quality of services delivered."[33] As of 2005, the primary school completion rate was only 27 percent, with a pupil-to-teacher ratio of 70.3 to 1.[34] Over the course of the conflict, there were reports of armed groups (notably the Mayi-Mayi and RCD-Goma) systematically attacking, looting, and destroying schools. In some regions, particularly the Kivus, nearly every school had been seriously damaged if not destroyed.[35]

---

31. Ibid.

32. Ibid.

33. World Bank, "Project Appraisal Document on a Proposed Grant in the Amount of SDR 99.2 Million to the Democratic Republic of the Congo for an Education Sector Project," www-wds.worldbank.org/external/default/WDSContentServer/WDSP/IB/2007/05/14/000020953_20070514115336/Rendered/PDF/39704.pdf (accessed Aug. 1, 2009).

34. Mo Ibrahim Foundation, "Ibrahim Index of African Governance," www.moibrahimfoundation.org/the-index.asp (accessed Sept. 1, 2009).

35. For example, the UN assessment mission in November 2003 to the Walikale Territory "had found the territory's education system completely destroyed." All the schools had been damaged or "completely

In 2003, less than 1 percent of the national budget was allocated to education, and since then there has been little effort to make education a political and financial priority.[36] By 2006, although education funding had increased to almost 10 percent of the national budget, the UN secretary-general reported that at least 3.5 million primary-age children and 6 million adolescents remained out of school.[37] The secretary-general also reported ongoing targeting of schools by armed forces.[38] According to the *Small Arms Survey 2004*, armed confrontations resulted in the destruction of 211 of 228 schools in the town of Djugu, Ituri, since 1999. Only 10,620 of the 39,600 students and 701 of the 1,771 teachers remained.[39] As of 2004, the gross enrollment ratio (GER) was 64 percent, lower than the average for sub-Saharan Africa, and the primary completion rate was only 29 percent, with a general literacy rate of 63.5 percent.[40]

Unemployment

No reliable unemployment data or estimates are currently available for the DRC. This is in large part due to the dominance of the informal market. Years of corruption created a dual economy, in which formal businesses must operate at a much higher cost, and most economic transactions take place in the informal economy. Those who are salaried workers tend to be employed by the state or by mining companies, although a rising number work for telecommunications companies.[41] There is also ample evidence of youth and child labor, including forced labor by militias in natural resource mines and in sexual trafficking, although no statistics are available.[42]

Coding

The DRC is coded as having a high proportion of youth in the population. Although, at 33 percent, it is on par for sub-Saharan Africa, it is six percentage points higher than the average proportion of youth in the world population (27 percent in 2003) and much higher than the corresponding rate in developed

---

pillaged and destroyed," and of the eight schools visited by the team, none had a source of running water and only two had latrines. Forty percent of school-age children did not attend school. Watchlist on Children in Armed Conflict, "Struggling to Survive."

36. World Bank, Education in the Democratic Republic of the Congo: Priorities and Options for Regeneration (Washington, D.C.: World Bank, 2005).

37. United Nations, "S/2006/389: Report of the Secretary-General on Children and Armed Conflict in the Democratic Republic of Congo," http://daccess-ods.un.org/TMP/6174745.html (accessed Aug. 2009).

38. Ibid

39. Watchlist on Children and Armed Conflict, "Struggling to Survive"; Graduate Institute of International Studies, Geneva, Small Arms Survey 2004: Rights at Risk (Oxford: Oxford University Press, 2004).

40. Bashir, Democratic Republic of the Congo: Country Status Report.

41. Economist Intelligence Unit, "Country Profile 2008: Democratic Republic of the Congo," report, Sept. 19, 2008, www.eiu.com (subscription only, accessed Sept. 1, 2009).

42. Watchlist on Children and Armed Conflict, "Struggling to Survive."

countries (20 percent in 2003).[43] However, it should be noted that children under age 15 made up an ever greater proportion of the population—34.5 percent in 2003.[44] The DRC also saw extremely high levels of child and youth participation in the conflict. Despite the fact that the country is a signatory to international treaties forbidding the use of child soldiers, nearly one of every three soldiers was under age 18.[45]

International Policy's Impact on Youth and Stabilization

By the time the Lusaka Accord was signed, the conflict in the DRC had become the focal point of a regional crisis, involving up to nine foreign states with a military presence in the country, not counting the many domestic and foreign rebel groups. Consequently, the post-conflict reconstruction period in the DRC coincided with similar projects in neighboring countries and the involvement of many foreign governments in the peacebuilding process.

The largest international player in the peacekeeping and peacebuilding process was the United Nations. The United Nations Mission to the Democratic Republic of the Congo (MONUC), established in 1999 out of the Lusaka Agreement, is the largest and most expensive UN peacekeeping effort to date.[46] Included directly in the MONUC mandate, in addition to implementing the ceasefire and supporting the DDR program, was a specific instruction to address the humanitarian crisis facing children and child soldiers in the DRC. Specifically, MONUC's mandate required UN representatives to "facilitate humanitarian assistance and human rights monitoring, with particular attention to vulnerable groups including women, children and demobilized child soldiers, as MONUC deems within its capabilities and under acceptable security conditions, in close cooperation with other United Nations agencies, related organizations and nongovernmental organizations."[47]

Although the international actors involved, including the United Nations, were acutely aware of child and youth involvement in the conflict and took specific measures to address the problem, the programs and methods used were unsuccessful. However, in analyzing these variables, it is important to note that both

---

43. U.S. Census Bureau, International Data Base.

44. Ibid.

45. The DRC is a signatory to the Convention on the Rights of the Child (ratified 1990) and the Optional Protocol on the Involvement of Children in Armed Conflict (ratified 2001). In 2001, the DRC announced that it would sign on to the Optional Protocol on the Sale of Children, Child Prostitution and Child Pornography, but as of 2009, it had not completed the ratification. The DRC signed the Rome Statute of the International Criminal Court and attended the 2007 Paris Conference on Children in Armed Conflict.

46. United Nations, "Press Conference on the Democratic Republic of the Congo," 2005, www.un.org/News/briefings/docs/2005/051006_DRC_PC.doc.htm (accessed Sept. 1, 2009).

47. United Nations, "Democratic Republic of the Congo–MONUC–Mandate," www.un.org/Depts/dpko/missions/monuc/mandate.html (accessed Sept. 1, 2009).

the regional and the UN programs were highly coordinated with national actors and NGOs; therefore, the influence of the United Nations may not be easily separated from that of NGOs.

The Peace Accord

In 1999–2002, the DRC government, along with representatives of foreign governments and rebel groups, negotiated several agreements, including the Lusaka Cease-fire Agreement and the Global and All-Inclusive Agreement on the Transition in Democratic Republic of the Congo. The agreement that most explicitly addressed children and youth was the Lusaka Peace Accord. The agreement stipulated that all parties agree to stop recruiting child soldiers and cease all acts of violence against the civilian population, including all forms of sexual violence.[48] The Lusaka Accord also prescribed an active DDR program empowering the United Nations, in coordination with the national government, the Organization of African Unity, and the Joint Military Commission, to "track down and disarm armed groups" and facilitate humanitarian assistance as part of the peacekeeping mandate. While it is clear that the Lusaka Agreement envisaged forcible disarmament, MONUC's interpretation of the mandate differed significantly. (See the section on United Nations involvement, below.) Finally, while the agreement acknowledged that the extremely high numbers of child soldiers constituted a humanitarian issue, the agreement did not reference in any way how this would be handled within the DDR process.[49]

The series of talks following Lusaka was largely unsuccessful and did not add significantly to the conditions of the cease-fire. For instance, the Pretoria agreements, reached between the DRC and Rwanda in 2002 on the withdrawal of Rwandan troops from DRC territory and the dismantling of the ex-FAR and Interahamwe forces, left the official protocol for DDR unchanged and, if anything, more muddled than as stipulated in the Lusaka Cease-fire. The most relevant addition to the agreements concerning youth was the dialogue at Sun City, South Africa, in April 2002, in which signatories agreed to establish several institutions supporting democracy, including a national observatory for human rights, potentially including advocacy for children's rights. This was later reiterated in December, in the Global and All-Inclusive Agreement, in which it was decided that the members of the civil society, or *forces vivres*, would take on the responsibility of establishing these institutions.

---

48. Lusaka Cease-fire Agreement, article I, section 3c, www.usip.org/files/file/resources/collections/peace_agreements/drc_07101999.pdf (accessed Sept. 1, 2009).

49. The Lusaka Agreement's acknowledgment of child soldiers implies that parties were aware of the gravity of the situation and that these child soldiers would need specialized care during the reconstruction process. However it is unclear whether the omission of how to deal with the issue represents a missed opportunity or whether including details on implementation would have impeded getting a peace treaty signed.

Foreign Government Involvement

Many neighboring governments remained highly involved in the DRC's transition period. Most notably, these governments were signatories to the various treaties regarding the situation in the DRC (including Angola, Namibia, Rwanda, Uganda, Zambia, and Zimbabwe).

Several Western governments are active donors of humanitarian aid, particularly for programs related to children and youth. For example, the U.S. government gives $200 million annually to the UN peacekeeping operation in the Congo, in addition to supporting USAID, which finances and facilitates a number of programs directly involving youth in the DRC. In 1997–2001 and 2002–6, USAID's Transition Initiatives program carried out several projects intended to help war-affected youth reintegrate into host communities and to increase understanding of issues key to the transition process.[50] For instance, a large part of the Transition Initiatives budget went to implementing the Synergie d'Education Communautaire et d'Appui à la Transition (SE*CA), an initiative coordinated with the International Rescue Committee (IRC). It included a six-month training program for youth affected by the conflict (including ex-combatants, IDPs, victims of sexual violence, and others). The program provided vocational training, basic living skills education and psycho-social assistance, a small-grants program to support community-driven activities, and media programs to help communities get accurate information about the transition process and to serve as a forum for discussion and participation.[51]

As part of the SE*CA program, USAID carried out a Youth Empowerment and Skills (YES) module, which, by October 2005, had trained 10,164 people in 280 communities in Orientale and Maniema provinces. For example, through the SE*CA program's YES module, ex-combatants in the Sukisa neighborhood of Bunia participated in workshops on peace, reconciliation, and conflict management, and one group chose to do a building activity to help its community overcome one of its biggest problems: lack of access to education.[52] These former combatants were able to earn an income while building six classrooms, an office, and four latrines at a local school. Many of the participants, who ranged in age from early twenties to mid-forties, had joined militia groups as teenagers.[53]

SE*CA also sponsored several emergency initiatives to deal with youth issues.[54] For example, as the 2005 elections were drawing near, political parties

---

50. USAID Transition Initiatives, "Country Programs: Democratic Republic of the Congo," www.usaid.gov/our_work/cross-cutting_programs/transition_initiatives/country/congo/progdesc_en.html (accessed Sept. 1, 2009).

51. Ibid.

52. USAID, "USAID/OTI DROC Success Story," www.usaid.gov/our_work/cross-cutting_programs/transition_initiatives/country/congo/topic0206a.html (accessed Sept. 1, 2009).

53. Ibid.

54. USAID, "USAID/OTI DRC Field Report," Oct. 2005, www.usaid.gov/our_work/cross-cutting_programs/transition_initiatives/country/congo/rpt1005.html (accessed Sept. 1, 2009).

were manipulating youth gangs to destabilize and violently intimidate civilians in the Kisangani region. In response, SE*CA launched an emergency program that successfully stabilized the situation by providing the youths "with conflict management and democracy and governance training so that they could understand their role in creating conflict, as well as the proper role of political parties. In addition, the youths were involved in paid rehabilitation work on one of the roads so that they would be less enticed by the political parties' payments."[55]

USAID also contracted with the Commission Nationale de Désarmement, Démobilization et Réinsertion (CONADER), the national agency in charge of the DDR process, to carry out reintegration programs for ex-combatants in Ituri province. As part of the Ituri reintegration program, the ex-combatants, along with 5,040 community members, received the YES training. These community members were then offered the choice of being paid to work on rehabilitation projects or receiving basic vocational training with a corresponding resources kit. According to the 2005 annual reports, this program was highly successful, especially with its Conflict Management and Reaffirmation of Values module, which was instituted in 213 communities in Ituri province. Further, the program reported that the ex-combatants were highly satisfied with the training and that as a result, word had spread, producing a large demand for the program.[56]

Although these programs specifically targeting youth were relatively successful and created a positive impact, as part of the Office of Transition Initiatives (OTI) they were only for the short term and ended in March 2006, when the OTI closed its portfolio in the DRC. OTI provides only short-term programs, generally in the immediate aftermath of a crisis or during windows of opportunity for democratic change. Although USAID continues to operate in the DRC, it maintains less of an emphasis on youth programming. Its focus on short-term programming reflects a larger trend that is hindering the success of reconstruction measures in the DRC: NGOs and other aid agencies depend on funders that demand immediate results in the form of emergency and short-term programming, and this keeps them from pursuing programs with a longer-term focus. Currently, the USAID programs in the DRC focus on health, food security and agriculture, democracy and governance, education, protecting biodiversity in the Congo Basin, and reintegrating former combatants and victims.

United Nations Involvement
The MONUC mission and mandate: The establishment of MONUC directly followed the provisions of the Lusaka Accord to bring in the United Nations as the enforcing agent. MONOC originated in 1999 under a Chapter VI peacekeeping mandate (which allows the United Nations to intervene and support the pacific

---

55. Ibid.
56. Ibid.

settlement of disputes), with an authorization for up to 500 military observers and 5,537 military personnel. Because of the ongoing violence and crisis in the eastern regions, in 2003 the UN Security Council approved a Chapter VII status for MO-NUC, thereby authorizing the use of "all necessary means," including coercion and force, to fulfill its mandate, and increased authorized troop levels to 16,700 by 2004. While these troop numbers are extremely high for a UN mission, there were fewer than 3 UN troops for every 10,000 citizens. In fact, the secretary-general had recommended deploying 23,900 troops to improve the mission's operational capabilities.[57] As of November 2007, there were 18,407 MONUC uniformed personnel, including 16,661 troops, 735 military observers, and 1,011 police, as well as 931 international civilian personnel, 2,062 local civilian staff, and 585 UN volunteers.[58]

The MONUC mission encompasses five core programs: peace and security, facilitating the transition to democracy, supporting the establishment of rule of law and human rights, improving human conditions for sustainable peace, and supporting the International Criminal Court and the establishment of a truth and reconciliation commission. These core programs included ensuring and coordinating the DDR and disarmament, demobilization, repatriation, resettlement, and reintegration (DDRRR) process; providing strong advocacy to fight the "culture of impunity" that enables the practice of recruiting children into militias; and providing support for the reintegration of child soldiers.[59] UN Security Council Resolution 1565, adopted in 2004, also established within MONUC's mandate the responsibility to "assist in the promotion and protection of human rights, with particular attention to women, children and vulnerable persons."[60]

To carry out its mandate to protect children and child soldiers, MONUC established a Child Protection Unit, the largest such unit in any UN peacekeeping operation yet and the first to include child protection advisers (CPAs), who have been deployed in the field since 2006.[61] The unit's main goal is to protect children's interests by integrating a "child-conscious approach within MONUC in all its activities," predominantly through monitoring and reporting violations against children, promoting advocacy for children's rights, and supporting children's DDR programs.[62]

---

57. United Nations, "S/2004/650: Third special report of the Secretary General on the United Nations Organization Mission in the Democratic Republic of the Congo," http://daccessdds.un.org/doc/UNDOC/GEN/N04/457/42/IMG/N0445742.pdf?OpenElement (accessed Sept. 1, 2009).

58. United Nations, "MONUC: Facts and Figures," www.un.org/Depts/dpko/missions/monuc/facts.html (accessed Sept. 1, 2009).

59. "DDRRR" refers to the process of demobilizing combatants who were fighting outside their home country. Therefore, it is not enough to reintegrate these combatants; there is also a repatriation and resettlement process. Malan and Gomes Porto, Challenges of Peace Implementation.

60. United Nations, United Nations Security Council Resolution 1565, http://daccessdds.un.org/doc/UNDOC/GEN/N04/531/89/PDF/N0453189.pdf?OpenElement (accessed Sept. 1, 2009).

61. Watchlist on Children and Armed Conflict, "Struggling to Survive."

62. Ibid.

The United Nations and children's DDR: In 2003–04, an interagency group co-ordinated by UNICEF, including the MONUC Child Protection Unit and representatives from the transitional government and various iNGOs, developed the Operational Framework for the Disarmament, Demobilization and Reintegration of Children (le Cadre Opérationnel pour les Enfants Associés aux Forces et Groupes Armés), which outlined specific guidelines and procedures for CONADER to use in the national DDR process. (For details of the CONADER DDR/DDRR program, see the "Domestic Policy" section of this chapter.) The goals outlined in the Operational Framework include removing all children from armed forces and groups, facilitating reintegration through reinsertion programs, using community mechanisms to reinforce "sustainable conditions for the protection of children," developing specific strategies to reintegrate girls associated with armed forces, and preventing child recruitment by armed forces.[63]

While CONADER had the official responsibility for establishing the adult and child DDR programs, it lacked staff with expertise to begin supporting children's demobilization right away. Instead, MONUC and UNICEF held most of the responsibility for implementing the child DDR programs and coordinating the work of other international NGOs. As of 2006, CONADER and UNICEF were working in coordination with nine iNGOs (including Save the Children, CARE International, and the IRC) and thirty-five national NGOs to implement children's DDR.[64] Although the DDR program had seen to the official demobilization of about 31,000 children by mid-2007, this number does not necessarily point to success.[65] The figure represents the total number of demobilized children who were reported to be associated with armed forces. But the actual number of child soldiers is likely higher, because there are many cases of self-demobilization, in which children and youth simply left the forces. Also, many girls and young women were left out of the process because they had become "wives" or domestic and sexual servants during the war and were never released by the armed groups. As discussed in detail in the "Domestic Policy" section of this chapter, the overall DDR process, including children's DDR, was riddled with delays, inefficiency, and corruption. Most significantly, the official demobilization of children did not begin in earnest until 2005, and there was a severe lack of funding for reintegration programs. As a result, UNICEF and Save the Children were often forced to organize DDR and relief programs on an emergency, ad-hoc basis, and many of the officially demobilized children received no reintegration support whatsoever.

---

63. Ibid., 47.

64. United Nations, "S/2006/389," paragraph 48.

65. Coalition to Stop the Use of Child Soldiers, "Democratic Republic of the Congo: Priorities for Children Associated with Armed Forces and Groups," 2007, www.reliefweb.int/rw/RWB.NSF/db900SID/TBRL-75QQQX?OpenDocument (accessed Sept. 1, 2009).

MONUC's role in adult DDR: In addition to UNICEF's work in children's DDR, MONUC worked with UNDP (considered the lead UN agency) to organize the national adult DDR/DDRRR program. However, MONUC's mandate did not allow it to carry out the DDR/DDRRR program in full, but only to provide "advice and assistance to the Government of Transition" in facilitating the DDR process. The full responsibility of carrying out the DDR fell instead on the national commission for DDR (CONADER), with aid from the Multi-Country Demobilization and Reintegration Program (MDRP), a multiagency body supporting and funding demobilization and reintegration of ex-combatants throughout the Great Lakes region.

Although MONUC's mandate to assist the DDR efforts came directly from the stipulations of the Lusaka Agreement, the nature of MONUC's DDR program was distinctly different from the program envisaged by the Lusaka signatories. According to the wording of the cease-fire, the United Nations was not only to "supervise disengagement of forces" but was also responsible for "tracking down and disarming all armed groups."[66] While it is clear that the Lusaka Accord sanctioned a forcible demobilization program, in practice the secretary-general and the Security Council required that the UN-administered DDRRR program be based on voluntary participation.[67] There were a number of logistical and political reasons for pursuing a voluntary program, not the least of which was that the United Nations did not expect to be able to rally the necessary number of troops for a long-drawn-out military campaign that was likely to suffer significant casualties.[68] Further complicating things, the demobilization program in the DRC was distinctly different from other UN-facilitated DDR programs in that it (a) involved both domestic and foreign troops and (b) was sent to disarm groups that had "signed no agreement with MONUC or with any other party, still considering themselves at war."[69] It was therefore politically and logistically infeasible for MONUC to lead a forced and all-inclusive demobilization program. As explored later in the chapter, this decision, though perhaps the only option available, led to the formation of parallel chains of command as different armed groups volunteered for the demobilization program but maintained a degree of loyalty to their previous commanders once they were demobilized and redeployed as part of the new national army—most notably in the case of troops loyal to Laurent Nkunda. This formation of parallel structures within the newly operational mixed brigades opened the door for the rerecruitment of many child soldiers who had already been demobilized.

---

66. Lusaka Cease-fire Agreement, Annex A, Chapter 8, sections 8.2.1.d and 8.2.2.a.

67. Peter Swarbrick, "DDRRR: Political Dynamics and Linkages," in Malan and Gomes Porto, *Challenges of Peace Implementation*, 166.

68. Ibid.

69. Ibid., 167.

The United Nations and Emergency Humanitarian Relief

Finally, the UN mission also had a significant impact on emergency humanitarian relief projects, particularly for the large population of IDPs. For instance, attacks on schools were a common practice among militias as a mechanism of terrorism and recruitment. In response, starting in 2004, UNICEF and the United Nations' DRC Office for the Coordination of Humanitarian Affairs (OCHA) managed a rapid-response mechanism that provided immediate assistance to schools, including rehabilitating buildings and classrooms or providing temporary school facilities along with replacing school materials. These repairs are estimated to have provided temporary education benefits to at least 12,000 displaced schoolchildren.[70] By 2006, as the displacement crisis continued, the rapid-response mechanism was aiding 120,000 new IDPs per month.[71] However, because emergency conditions have continued over such a long time, the United Nations has not been able to sustain the necessary programming. Despite that MONUC was one of the largest-funded UN missions to date, by June 2006 OCHA had received donations to cover only a third of the requested funding for the year's consolidated humanitarian action plan.[72]

UN-NGO and intra-UN cooperation: Despite the money and manpower behind MONUC's humanitarian programs and its strong advocacy for children's rights, the mission has been largely ineffective in carrying out its peacekeeping mission. To be fair, circumstances outside MONUC's control have hindered its success: the political climate enabled rebel groups to operate despite the ceasefire, and the difficult natural terrain presented serious obstacles. But the mission was also plagued by competition and scandal within its ranks. For example, before the Operational Framework was instituted, UNICEF, Save the Children, and MONUC's Child Protection Unit were all working to demobilize child soldiers. But UNICEF and Save the Children took opposite approaches, with Save the Children engaging local communities to improve child protection, while UNICEF worked with the RCD-Goma political leadership to stop the ongoing recruitment. Whereas these different approaches could have been coordinated to attack the problem in concert from different directions, instead competition created tension between the two organizations, hindering both efforts.[73]

The UN child abuse scandal: In 2004, news broke that amid the ongoing chaos in the DRC, MONUC was also adding to the problem, as allegations surfaced of UN peacekeepers' prostitution and sexual abuse of female children. Some 150 cases involved "severe and ongoing" sexual exploitation and abuse by UN military and civilian personal.[74] Most of the cases involved girls from 14 to 18

---

70. United Nations, "S/2006/389."

71. Ibid.

72. Ibid.

73. Verhey, "Going Home."

74. Amnesty International, "Struggling to Survive."

years old, although some victims were as young as 11. MONUC took legal action against the perpetrators, calling in the UN Office of Internal Oversight (OIOS) to carry out investigations and dismiss the personnel involved. The investigation resulted in new, stricter regulations, in a Code of Conduct on Sexual Exploitation and Sexual Abuse for all MONUC personnel.

The sexual abuse scandal is particularly tragic in light of the rampant use of sexual violence, especially against women and children, as a weapon in the DRC conflict. The irony that MONUC's policy was specifically focused on aiding and protecting children, when in fact it was exploiting many of the very children it was there to protect, is all too clear. Although the MONUC administration reacted swiftly, the scandal was symptomatic of a failing and ineffective mission that had lost control over its team and, instead, became part of the culture of impunity it was sent to fight against.

Coding

The international efforts in the DRC are coded as having a low-level positive impact. The positive impact refers to the movement away from conflict as a result of the UN intervention, demobilization, advocacy, and democratization efforts. The efforts are rated as having a low-level impact because the programs did not adequately meet the demands of the situation and because the negative aspects of the mission (especially the cases of sexual abuse) detracted from the overall positive impact.

Domestic Policy: Impact on Youth and Stability

With the United Nations providing the logistical and technical support for the peacekeeping efforts (as agreed in the Lusaka Cease-fire Agreement in 1999), when the Global and All-Inclusive Agreement was signed in 2002, the transitional government took on the responsibility to organize and implement reconstruction efforts "writ large." Specifically, its responsibilities included "(1) reunification, the re-establishment of peace, reconstruction of the country, restoration of territorial integrity and the re-establishment of the state's authority over the whole national territory; (2) national reconciliation; (3) the formation of a restructured and integrated national army; (4) the organization of free and transparent elections at all levels with a view to the establishment of a democratic constitutional regime; and (5) the establishment of structures aimed at creating a new political order."[75] This meant that the transitional government was responsible for the DDR/DDRRR process and the creation of the new national forces, the Forces Armées de la République Démocratique du Congo (FARDC). (However,

---

75. Amnesty International, "Democratic Republic of the Congo: Disarmament, Demobilization and Reintegration (DDR) and the Reform of the Army," 2007, www.amnesty.org/en/library/info/AFR62/001/2007 (accessed Sept. 1, 2009).

as noted earlier, the government relied on MONUC and iNGOs for the expertise, technical support, and staff to actually implement the DDR programs.) The domestic management of the DDR process, along with the restructuring of state institutions such as the education and justice systems, is essential to meeting the needs of the youth demographic and enabling the overall stability and future development of the country. However, because of poor coordination, lengthy delays, bureaucratic competition, corruption, and mismanagement of funds, the national government was instead an impediment to the implementation of these programs. As a result, the ineffective programming contributed directly and indirectly to the ongoing instability.

DDR/DDRRR

Perhaps the most significant of the government-managed reconstruction programs to the immediate reconstruction requirements was the DDR/DDRRR program. From the outset, the magnitude and complexity of the situation in the DRC demanded that the DDR program overcome several environmental and political obstacles. The sheer size of the conflict in the DRC, both in numbers of combatants and geographic area, meant that the DDR process was going to require massive manpower, funding, and coordination. There were an estimated 300,000 to 330,000 fighters on DRC soil, including 150,000 troops linked with government forces and domestic armed groups, and an estimated 30,000 to 33,000 children associated with the armed groups.[76] The presence of thousands of foreign troops further complicated the process because these combatants, once demobilized, required repatriation, resettlement, and reintegration rather than mere reinsertion into the domestic society. Demobilization and reintegration were critical for the DRC's many child and youth soldiers, who, like the young man quoted below, desperately wanted to find a way out of the war and return home.

> "Since the AFDL in 1996, at nine years old, I enrolled voluntarily with my friends. We fought a long time on the front lines . . . In May 2002 I fell ill and our commander sent me to Bukavu for care. I took advantage of being in Bukavu to ask to be demobilized. I was taken to Save the children/DIVAS [Division of Social Affairs] transit center where I received food, lodging and health care. Despite this, my greatest hope is to go home." (Patrik, DRC)[77]

The DDR/DDRRR program design: To facilitate the DDR and DDRRR processes, CONADER was established in December 2003 by presidential decree to manage and implement both the adult and the child DDR programs. A number of governmental ministries were established to facilitate the process, including the Inter-Ministerial Steering Committee on DDR and the DDR Financial Management Committee (CGFDR). The MDRP funded the process

---

76. Ibid.

77. Verhey, "Going Home."

with $272 million in grants from the World Bank and direct contributions from bilateral donors. By March 2004, CONADER had published a National Plan for DDR (PN-DDR), but relied on UNDP, MONUC, and NGO partners to implement interim disarmament and reinsertion programs before the official launch of the program.[78] This plan later included as an addendum an Operational Framework on Children in Armed Conflict, outlining the specific mechanisms for the children's DDR program.

The scheme outlined by the PN-DDR addressed both the demobilization of troops and the reformation of the national army under a *tronc commun*, or common path of disarmament. Under this program, units of the various armed groups who volunteered to disarm would gather at regroupment centers, operated by the military, where they would be disarmed. The disarmed troops would then be transported to orientation centers (COs) operated by CONADER. (However, the troops were often forced to wait for several weeks before the transfer.) At the COs, adults and children would be separated, and adults given the choice of demobilization or entry into the FARDC. Adults choosing to continue military service would then undergo *brassage*, the military reconstruction process whereby troops from government and non-government forces were combined into integrated brigades and then redeployed to provinces outside their previous base. Those adults choosing demobilization would be given information and guidance on returning to civilian life, along with a demobilization kit of various living essentials such as clothes, shoes, soap, seeds, and cooking utensils.[79] They would also receive an initial monetary payment of $110 to cover transportation and living expenses, along with the promise of an additional $25 per month for one year, and vocational training or other reintegration support.[80]

Children to be demobilized, once identified, were to be taken to separate children's spaces operated by child protection personnel within the COs, and transferred within forty-eight hours to transit care facilities (SETs) operated by partnering child protection NGOs. At the SETs, NGOs were responsible for providing education, vocational training, and recreational activities. After sheltering a child for about three months, the NGOs would arrange for family reunification. Under the Operational Framework, upon leaving the program, children were also to receive a reinsertion kit consisting of "essential tools or equipment to enable them to pursue their chosen trade," along with an official certificate of release, and the guarantee of either one year of schooling (for those under age 15) or three to nine months of vocational training in their hometowns.[81] In addition, CONADER was supposed to finance and

---

78. Ibid.

79. The demobilization kits were to include all these items and more. However, in practice, the composition of the kits depended on what the implementing agencies chose to include.

80. Amnesty International, "Democratic Republic of the Congo: Children at War."

81. Ibid.

implement community-based reintegration projects for all children upon return to their communities.[82]

DDR/DDRRR implementation: While the DDR program envisaged by the Operational Framework and the PN-DDR was developed with the specific needs of children and youth in mind, it was largely unsuccessful, especially in the reintegration of children and youth. These failures were quite evident, both to the international community and to the young ex-combatants themselves, as shown by their keen observations on going through the demobilization process:

> "Currently it's destabilization; what I want to say, it's that in the army, I suffered, but I had a home, a place to stay; I could organize myself, I ate. It's not like where we are now . . . I would like to flee you know, some children fled so as not to be demobilized . . . some stay a month here, and then they run away." (Michel, young soldier in the DRC)

> "At least in the army, we had money, we received wages. But since we're here, nothing." (Christine, young soldier in the DRC)[83]

From the beginning, CONADER's mishandling of the management and coordination mechanisms, along with interministerial battles with CGFDR, led to lengthy delays in approving and implementing programs. Although CONADER was established in 2003 and the PN-DDR was published in early 2004, official DDR programs and army reunification through CONADER did not begin in earnest until mid-2005, and most reintegration programs did not begin until 2006. Just a few months later, in July 2006, CONADER had spent (or lost) nearly all of the $200 million World Bank trust, forcing the program to temporarily suspend all activity and leaving the DDR process incomplete.[84] The funds that were not lost or stolen were spent almost entirely on disarmament and demobilization programs, leaving little or no money for reintegration programming for children or adults. While the MDRP was working in 2007 to acquire additional funding for the reintegration programs, it refused to hand over the money until the DRC government agreed to abolish CONADER and reimburse the MDRP for $6.8 million in misspent funds.[85]

Moreover, CONADER's poor management meant that most of the DDR programs, instead of being carried out in an organized and consistent fashion, were implemented by NGOs that were forced to negotiate directly with armed groups on an emergency, ad-hoc basis as each commander volunteered for demobilization.[86] As a result, the plans for disarmament and demobilization outlined in the PN-DDR and the Operational Framework existed mostly in theory, while the

---

82. Ibid.

83. Brett and Specht, Young Soldiers: Why They Choose to Fight.

84. Multi-Country Demobilization and Reintegration Program (MDRP), "Status of the MDRP in the Democratic Republic of the Congo," www.mdrp.org/PDFs/N&N_10_07.pdf (accessed Sept. 1, 2009).

85. Ibid.

86. United Nations, "S/2007/391: Report of the Secretary-General on Children and Armed Conflict in the Democratic Republic of the Congo," paragraph 65, www.un.org/Docs/sc/sgrep07.htm (accessed Aug. 1, 2009).

actual programs implemented, particularly children's DDR, were inconsistent and incomplete.

For example, although the Operational Framework established that children were supposed to be identified and housed separately from adults, in practice there were large inconsistencies, and physical separation from the adults was problematic at best. The Operational Framework also stated that children were to receive reinsertion kits rather than monetary payments. However, it failed to specify the contents of the kits, and different NGOs included different items in the kits, causing the demobilized children to complain that they were not receiving equal opportunities. As a result, children often tried to play one NGO against another to obtain better kits or else abandoned the orientation sites altogether, thinking that they could receive a better package with a different organization. The process was so fraught with problems that eventually, many NGOs stopped the practice of providing kits altogether.[87]

There was also much frustration among the children because they could not receive a monetary stipend, which, many of them said, would have helped them start income-generating projects when they returned home. Although giving children a monetary payment could have caused additional problems upon reintegration, it became a disincentive to participate in the process and created tension among the children who did volunteer for demobilization, many of whom attempted (or were instructed by their commanders) to pass as adults so they would receive the demobilization payment.[88]

Finally, the high-profile arrests of several high-ranking officers for the recruitment of child soldiers also became an obstacle to NGOs trying to negotiate with commanders to release children. Many of the commanders, unaware of the details of the DDR process, feared they would be prosecuted for war crimes if they revealed the children in their ranks, making it difficult for NGOs to gain access to the children.[89]

The DDR program claims to have officially demobilized over 157,583 combatants, including 31,000 children, by mid-2007.[90] However, it was later revealed that at least 45 percent of the "children" demobilized were actually over age 18, while many younger children remained in the armed forces.[91] Also, less than 2 percent of the children demobilized were girls (although 40 percent of child soldiers were known to be female), and less than 30 percent of all demobilized

87. Amnesty International, "Democratic Republic of the Congo: Children at War."

88. Ibid.; Amnesty International, "Democratic Republic of the Congo: Disarmament, Demobilization and Reintegration."

89. Amnesty International, "Democratic Republic of the Congo: Disarmament, Demobilization and Reintegration."

90. Coalition to Stop the Use of Child Soldiers, "Democratic Republic of the Congo: Priorities for Children Associated with Armed Forces and Groups"; MDRP, "Status of the MDRP in the Democratic Republic of the Congo."

91. Watchlist on Children and Armed Conflict, "Struggling to Survive."

ex-combatants (45,000) had received any type of reintegration programming.[92] By 2007, CONADER had not approved and implemented a single economic-reintegration program for children. In fact, NGOs reported that in eastern DRC, even general reintegration programs were entirely absent.[93]

Consequences of incomplete DDR/DDRRR: As a result of the incomplete reintegration, many of the children were harassed upon their return to their home communities and were highly vulnerable to both forced and voluntary rerecruitment. In the absence of any substantial reintegration programming, the official certificate of release from the DDR program often served as the only real protection against rerecruitment. However, as we see in the testimonies of rerecruited youth, the certificates were often destroyed or simply disregarded by armed groups, which in many cases went back to the homes of former child soldiers to force them back into the group.

> "It was two years ago when the RCD passed through our village and gathered many youth. As I was only 13, a commander with good will took me as a guard at his house. I was relieved by this because before I was incapable of doing the military work and was whipped.... Happily in early 2002, the military authorities from Goma demobilised a number of children. Some children returned home on their own. I was taken by the military to Sake and then walked home.... But later at home I was harassed by other members of the RCD. Fortunately, I saw some agents from ICRC in our area. The took me to Goma to protect me and to request the military authorities to give me my demobilization order." (Faustin, DRC)[94]

Claude's Story: "Claude was forcibly recruited by the RCD-Goma in his village at age 15. He fought in many battles. When his group was finally in Bukavu, he was demobilized by his commander. Two months later, he was reunified with his mother. But a few days later, local military officials forcibly rerecruited him and sent him to the front. Fortunately his group was sent through Bukavu where military commanders remembered him and resent him to the Save the Children-DIVAS centre."[95]

The consequences of an incomplete and inconsistent DDR process are especially evident in the case of DDR among troops loyal to rebel leader Laurent Nkunda in eastern DRC. Nkunda's troops were allowed to undergo a unique *brassage* process, whereby the newly formed mixed brigades were not redeployed to different provinces but were restationed in their previous locations. As a result, Nkunda was able to keep a parallel chain of command over many of the brigades.[96] While these brigades were technically part of the national army, the United Nations and a number of NGOs reported that the mixed brigades have "contributed to rising insecurity, ethnic tension and human rights

---

92. Amnesty International, "Democratic Republic of the Congo: Children at War."

93. Coalition to Stop the Use of Child Soldiers, "Democratic Republic of the Congo: Priorities for Children Associated with Armed Forces and Groups."

94. Verhey, "Going Home."

95. Ibid.

96. Ibid.

abuses in the province" and that they "certainly contributed to ongoing child soldier recruitment and use in both mixed army brigades and armed groups."[97] By 2007, it was estimated that from 300 to 500 children continued to serve in the mixed brigades loyal to Nkunda in North Kivu, and thousands more were in imminent danger of (re)recruitment.[98] Indeed, recruitment and rerecruitment of children had been actively ongoing throughout the *brassage* process.[99]

In this case, it is clear that the incomplete and makeshift DDR process was perhaps just as detrimental as the ongoing violence. Where consistent demobilization procedures and successful reintegration programming might have been able to protect children from rerecruitment, instead, "children in the DRC remain a reservoir of potential strength" for armed forces, which, trained and rearmed by the official demobilization process, continue to wage a war of terrorism and instability.[100]

Education

In addition to taking on the responsibility of the DDR/DDRRR process, the transitional government was also responsible for rebuilding infrastructure, including the repair and reform of educational institutions. Even though the conflict took an enormous toll on the education system, leaving almost half the school-age population out of school in 2003, the government did not make the education system a priority in the reconstruction process, thus leaving schools and schoolchildren especially vulnerable. Despite its promise to provide free and compulsory education to all children up to age 14, the Congolese government has not given adequate funding to keep schools running. Without government funding, the main financial burden for education falls on families, who typically provide 80 to 90 percent of the money spent on schools, through direct fee payments.[101] But most Congolese families cannot afford these costs, leaving millions of children out of school.[102]

Violence also entered the classroom as many of the children and youth active in armed groups during the conflict destroyed schools and forced the students to join their forces, as a means of "taking revenge on 'normal' children."[103]

---

97. Ibid.

98. Ibid; United Nations, "S/2007/391."

99. Coalition to Stop the Use of Child Soldiers, "Democratic Republic of the Congo: Priorities for Children Associated with Armed Forces and Groups."

100. Amnesty International, "Democratic Republic of the Congo: Children at War."

101. Ibid.

102. In 2006, there were 3.5 million primary school-age Congolese children out of school, and at least 6 million unschooled Congolese adolescents. United Nations, "S/2006/389."

103. Michel Kassa, "Humanitarian Assistance in the DRC," in Malan and Gomes Porto, Challenges of Peace Implementation.

For example, MLC and RCD-National militiamen used the slogan "Wipe out the blackboard" during their attacks on Mambasa (southern Ituri) in December 2002.[104] This targeting of schools has continued throughout the reconstruction process.

The lack of educational opportunities is both a detriment to long-term development and a concrete advantage for armed groups looking to recruit child soldiers. Many children, including former combatants, have joined or returned voluntarily to armed groups out of a lack of meaningful educational or economic opportunities.[105] Several examples illustrate this dynamic. In one case, Aimerance, a 17-year-old from North Kivu who participated in one of Save the Children's reintegration programs, told Save the Children that she was in her third year of primary school when she was forced to leave because her father did not have enough money to pay for school. After Aimerance left school, a friend convinced her that she would be better off if she joined a Congolese rebel army. Aimerance volunteered and served in the group for two years before eventually fleeing. However, because she was not officially demobilized, she has no official papers, and rebel groups continue to come to her house and harass her and her family.[106]

Another example is John (quoted in chapter 1), a 15-year-old who was demobilized in May 2006 after serving five years with the Mayi-Mayi. In an interview with Amnesty International, John commented on his experience in the demobilization process:

> Now, I have been demobilized and I am with my family. It is good to be home, but I have nothing to do. I would like to study or work, but I have no money, there is no training and there is no work. I feel sad, because I feel unhelpful to my family. I am at home but I am worthless. During the day I try not to think of my life as a fighter, because it makes me cry, but sometimes I think maybe I should go back to the armed groups.[107]

Aimerance's and John's stories are typical of many children's experiences during the DDR and reconstruction process and demonstrate how the incomplete DDR and lack of education opportunities increase their vulnerability to rerecruitment into armed groups.

This link between the failed DDR program and increased instability is especially important for understanding young people's potential impact on post-conflict reconstruction. In this case, without reintegration support or access to education, children and youth affected by armed conflict became even more vulnerable to (re)recruitment. While these young people may not have actively sought to destabilize the situation, they are directly linked to the ongoing instability by serving as a resource for rebel leaders.

---

104. Ibid.

105. Amnesty International, "Democratic Republic of the Congo: Children at War."

106. Hobson, "Forgotten Casualties of War: Girls in Armed Conflict."

107. Amnesty International, "Democratic Republic of the Congo: Children at War."

Juvenile Justice System

Finally, the justice system has not been able to deal adequately with the issues resulting from the conflict—either in prosecuting crimes against children or in dealing with crimes committed by child soldiers. Child soldiers have been arrested and tried before military courts for offenses such as desertion, and since 2003, at least nine child soldiers have been sentenced to death for alleged crimes committed while serving in armed groups.[108] These actions are not only in direct violation of the Convention on the Rights of the Child but also serve as a disincentive for children to flee armed groups voluntarily, for fear of prosecution.

Coding

Domestic policy in the DRC is rated as having a high-level negative impact. The coding is negative because failed and incomplete programming contributed to the ongoing violence. The high-level coding reflects the severity of the negative impact, particularly on the youth demographic, since the poor policy negatively affected both international and NGO activity and also enabled the youth demographic to play a destabilizing role.

NGO Involvement: Impact on Youth and Stability

The conflict in the DRC has attracted numerous NGOs and humanitarian workers ever since the aftermath of the Rwandan genocide. Despite the number of NGOs actively involved in the reconstruction process, the humanitarian effort has been largely unsuccessful, particularly in addressing the needs of Congolese children and youth. The inefficacy of NGO programming is largely due to

- dependency on a funding base with donors focused on emergency relief rather than medium- or long-term development,
- the need to compensate for local government shortcomings, particularly with the DDR and education programs, and
- an almost exclusive focus on "children" and "child soldiers" to the exclusion of older adolescents and needy young people not associated with armed groups.[109]

The combination of an emergency relief focus, the cumbersome geographic terrain, the culture of impunity, and the obstinate transition government stifled NGOs' effectiveness, particularly in executing reintegration programs for demobilized child soldiers.

---

108. Coalition to Stop the Use of Child Soldiers, "Democratic Republic of the Congo: Priorities for Children Associated with Armed Forces and Groups."

109. Amnesty International, "Democratic Republic of the Congo: Children at War."

Emergency Humanitarian Relief: Funding Dictates Programming

The humanitarian crisis in the DRC was one of the top priorities for international emergency relief donors. In 2004, the DRC was receiving, on average, US$30 million per year from the European Community Humanitarian Office and the Office of U.S. Foreign Disaster Assistance (OFDA), the emergency funding wing of USAID.[110] (Yet even this funding was woefully insufficient to meet the needs and was often unmatched by other donors.)[111] Donors' focus on emergency humanitarian relief was due in part to the continued environment of human insecurity, armed violence, and absence of respect for universal human rights.[112] While emergency humanitarian relief was unquestionably necessary, the reliance on such funding dictated the nature of the programming: emergency assistance is, by definition, short-term and often focuses on specific categories such as health, nutrition, and shelter. NGOs receiving grants from these donors have therefore been expected to focus their efforts on short-term rapid-response projects that can show their funders immediate results.

The lack of any medium- or long-term vision among donor agencies has stifled NGOs' potential impact on children and youth. While children and youth represent a large percentage of the population in need of immediate humanitarian assistance, there is a distinct difference between giving them emergency relief and facilitating their transition to long-term peace. Children and youth also constitute a significant proportion of the population in need of medium-term development programming, such as community reintegration programs, conflict resolution training, education, and income-generating activities.

Dynamics among NGOs, the United Nations, and Local Communities

To make it easier to monitor its money, the donor community has shown a distinct preference for funding only a few well-known international programs, including UNDP and UNOPS, rather than local NGOs. According to Michel Kassa, former head of OCHA, this tendency to fund only outside actors exacerbated tensions between the United Nations and local NGOs:

> An atmosphere of resentment, frustration and mistrust has often characterized the working relationship (if any) between local and international non-governmental or UN organizations. This also applies to local state structures, tempted or forced to see in humanitarian structures their only possible source of income to compensate for the decade-long absence of any decent and regular salary. Frequent and uneasy exchanges punctuate the daily work of relief organizations, forced to explain to frustrated civil servants and local

---

110. Kassa, "Humanitarian Assistance in the DRC."

111. Also, whereas in other crises there has been a swell in political momentum to provide relief (such as in Kosovo, Sierra Leone, and Afghanistan), there was no real political momentum driving international relief in the DRC. Thus, whereas the few international donors dedicated funds to emergency operations, there was not enough international support to sustain the humanitarian strategy as proposed. Ibid.

112. Ibid.

actors that their families do not constitute the primary target groups to benefit from emergency relief.[113]

This dynamic of resentment between NGOs and the United Nations, combined with insufficient and inefficiently used humanitarian funds, creates a situation where, despite the "high level of engagement" from NGO and UN actors, there is a lack of real, consistent, operational access and impact.[114] Indeed, part of the fault for the inefficacy of the humanitarian program must be attributed to the ongoing violence, which has prevented many humanitarian organizations from operating at anywhere near their capacity or progressing with more developmental programming. However, with donors focused on emergency relief, and the high volume of funds dedicated to short-term projects funneled through international rather than local initiatives, there is little opportunity or funding for any medium- or long-term projects. The influx of international funds has also created an environment of dependency on emergency funds, which resulted in a number of corrupt NGOs' seeking to benefit from one of the few sources of money coming into the country.[115]

NGO Coordination with CONADER for DDR

As previously discussed, the ease and efficiency with which NGOs are able to implement and coordinate their programs has a direct impact on the quality and success of youth programming. In the DRC, NGOs ran into a number of funding and logistical obstacles while trying to coordinate DDR programming with CONADER. As a result of the bureaucratic stagnation, interministerial competition, and corruption that plagued CONADER, the agency was extremely slow in approving the NGO-based reintegration projects. By March 2006, of fourteen reintegration projects for children under review, none had received final approval from CONADER. By June, CONADER still had not implemented one community-based economic reintegration program for children.[116] These delays forced NGOs to fill in for the missing programming that CONADER failed to provide. Any education and vocational reintegration activities that were under way were run entirely by NGOs. However, these programs had nowhere near the capacity or funds to completely fulfill the nationwide commitments of the CONADER program.[117]

---

113. Ibid.

114. Kassa argues that the lack of impact may be a misconception of the international community due to extremely high expectations and the "lure of treating 20 million." Ibid. Indeed, it is impossible to expect that the humanitarian relief effort could cure the crisis. However, in this case, not only was the effort failing to cure the crisis, it perhaps worsened the situation by heightening tensions and focusing only on emergency relief.

115. For example, Save the Children reported encountering several illegitimate NGOs, including one that "sold the humanitarian assistance which they were supposed to distribute to displaced families." Verhey, "Going Home."

116. Amnesty International, "Democratic Republic of the Congo: Children at War."

117. Ibid.; Coalition to Stop the Use of Child Soldiers, "Democratic Republic of the Congo: Priorities for Children Associated with Armed Forces and Groups."

Although the UN secretary-general reported in June 2006 that nine iNGOs and thirty-five national NGOs were implementing a range of children's DDR activities in coordination with UNICEF and CONADER, most of this programming consisted of NGOs responding on an emergency basis to identify, transport, shelter, and feed children associated with armed groups.[118] Few resources were left for preparing and carrying out reintegration projects. Moreover, the programs were exclusively for children under age 18, thus excluding from specialized reintegration support any child who had come of age while serving in an armed group.[119]

Save the Children was one of the most active NGOs focused on children's issues in the DRC, and it ran a number of child orientation and transit centers as a part of the national DDR program. However, most of Save the Children's efforts were focused on advocacy and family reunification. And it did indeed reunite many former child soldiers with their families, but it did not always have the capacity to follow up with adequate support for education or other reintegration programs.

Coordination within the NGO Community

Coordination among NGOs was considerably more successful than with CONADER. Several positive relationships emerged among coordinating partners, for example, among Save the Children, DIVAS, and the ICRC, in organizing reunification programs for demobilized and separated children. However, as the work expanded (both in the numbers of children needing aid and in the number of locations), the number of actors increased and coordination became more of a challenge.[120] As of 2003, several different networks and child protection commissions were actively trying to coordinate efforts, including a network for local NGOs for "children in especially difficult circumstances," child protection councils, and a child soldier task force in the Kivu provinces.[121] But their effectiveness was limited by competition among local organizations and by the NGOs' tendency to collaborate with other organizations only as dictated by funding.[122]

NGO Community and Reintegration Programming

Despite the lack of funding, a few organizations tried to implement community-based reintegration programming for youth. For example, although most of its programming was centered on the demobilization process, Save the Children also implemented some community-oriented reintegration programs, such as its

---

118. United Nations, "S/2006/389," paragraph 48.

119. Amnesty International, "Democratic Republic of the Congo: Children at War."

120. Watchlist on Children and Armed Conflict, "Struggling to Survive."

121. Provincial "child protection commissions" included international, governmental, and civil society representatives focused on humanitarian issues, along with "child protection councils," led by DIVAS and DIVIFAM, with UNICEF and Save the Children as supporters and observers. Save the Children organized the Child Soldier Task Force in the Kivus, and the Coalition to Stop the Use of Child Soldiers ran a forum of eighty-seven organizations focused on advocacy and awareness campaigns. Ibid.

122. Ibid.

community child protection networks (CCPNs). The overall goal of each CCPN was to improve physical security for children in their communities, along with boosting grassroots participation in child protection and children's rights advocacy, thereby easing children's reintegration into community life. The networks were essentially a forum for local authorities, religious leaders, representatives from economic and service sectors, and the children themselves, to discuss and resolve child protection issues. While Save the Children reported that the CCPNs were relatively successful in generating awareness, it saw no significant participation by children. Also, the CCPNs' advocacy framework limited their usefulness as a reintegration program.

Awareness campaigns are unquestionably important, especially in the DRC, where there has been little respect for children's rights during conflict. But advocacy and reunification programs cannot serve as a substitute for social and economic reintegration programs that provide young people with opportunities for active participation. Without these programs, children may be inclined to see rejoining the armed groups as their best option, or they may become increasingly vulnerable to forced recruitment.

One NGO that has been particularly successful in implementing reintegration and empowerment programming for children and youth in the DRC is Search for Common Ground, an international NGO that operates in conflict zones around the world to promote conflict prevention, resolution, and transformation, with a particular emphasis on the youth demographic. The organization began working in the DRC in 2001 and has organized a variety of different programs, including participatory theater, to promote conflict transformation techniques, "football for peace" soccer matches to bring together opposing groups in a spirit of peace and healthy competition, and the launch of a private radio station that included journalism training programs for youth.[123]

Search for Common Ground's *Sisi Watoto* radio program has been especially successful in addressing youth issues. The show, whose programming is developed in coordination with child protection and child DDR organizations including Save the Children and UNICEF, is dedicated to discussing "issues faced by young people in the context of armed conflict."[124] Each broadcast provides information and discussion about the dangers of recruitment and gives up-to-date information on the demobilization program, encouraging child soldiers to participate in the process.

---

123.   Search for Common Ground, "Search for Common Ground in the Democratic Republic of the Congo: Programme Overview," www.sfcg.org/programmes/drcongo/programmes_drcongo.html (accessed Sept. 1, 2009).

124.   Mary Myers and Judy El-Bushra, "Mid-Term Evaluation of Search for Common Ground (Centre Lokolé) 'Supporting Congo's Transition towards Sustainable Peace' Programme in Democratic Republic of the Congo (DRC)," program evaluation final report, March 2006, www.sfcg.org/sfcg/evaluations/drc2006.pdf (accessed Sept. 1, 2009).

In addition to generating awareness among its listeners, the *Sisi Watoto* program successfully bridges the gap between advocacy and reintegration programming by training young reporters in journalism and production techniques.[125] In 2004, *Sisi Watoto* won first prize in UNICEF and OneWorld's competition for radio programs by children for children, and there is anecdotal evidence from interviewing former child soldiers that the program helped "give voice" to ex-combatants and provided practical information to parents and children on where to find programs and locate family members.[126]

Search for Common Ground is still working in the DRC, but it faces a number of obstacles, particularly in gathering sufficient funding, since USAID, one of its major donors, suspended funding to all DRC programs in 2006. The organization was seeking alternative funding through CONADER, UNHCR, the Belgian government, and the Swedish International Development Cooperation Agency (all pending approval), and it continued to sponsor activities in 2007.[127] However, its struggle to maintain adequate funding is representative of the problem that many NGOs in the DRC are facing. While Search for Common Ground has been able to continue with its programming, many other programs, particularly local reintegration programs such as those doing vocational training, have been forced to shut down due to lack of funding.

Coding

NGO involvement in the DRC is rated as having a low-level positive impact. The variable is coded as positive since, on the whole, the presence of the NGO community contributed to moving the trajectory of the reconstruction process toward stability. The impact was only low level, however, because coordination and time-frame issues and funding freezes limited the programs' impact. Also, NGO efforts were overwhelmingly for children. Given the large number of child soldiers and the prevalence human rights violations against children, attention was justifiably focused on children's needs. But as a result, programming was more advocacy based, limiting impact for youth too old to qualify as children and excluding a demographic of young people age 18 and over. The level of effort, though high, was not nearly enough to meet the demands of the situation.

Impact of Cultural and Environmental Factors

As in any conflict, the cultural and environmental context has had a significant impact on the reconstruction process. In the DRC, several extenuating factors

---

125. Ibid.

126. Ibid.

127. Ibid; Search for Common Ground, "DR Congo Update," www.sfcg.org/programmes/drcongo/archive/march2007.pdf (accessed Sept. 1, 2009).

contributed to the continuation of the conflict and are key to understanding the transition period.

First, the type of violence that characterized the conflict in the DRC—that of armed groups using terror against civilians as a way to create instability and oust the government—is particularly significant. Often referred to as a "culture of impunity," the level of violence against civilians and ignorance of basic human rights doctrine has become a major obstacle for reconstruction and peacebuilding actors, hindering their ability to work in certain areas and also demanding the immediate programmatic attention of those NGOs able to operate. Instead of working on active and participatory programming with a focus on the long term, most of the humanitarian effort was focused on advocacy and awareness building, particularly for children.

One element that is considered a part of this culture of impunity is the sexual violence that was rampant throughout the conflict and has continued to be "consciously deployed as a weapon of war . . . to humiliate, intimidate and tear apart families and entire communities or even force them in an alliance" during the transition period.[128] Gender-motivated violence has affected the lives of thousands of Congolese women and girls, with over 30,000 survivors of sexual violence identified since 2005.[129] The epidemic of sexual violence is not only a human rights concern; it deeply affects the ethos of the society by breeding terror and ripping apart communities, as women who have been raped are often rejected by their communities.

Second, the cultural and religious beliefs of many communities in the DRC limited many former child soldiers' ability to reintegrate back into their communities. For example, children, especially girls, are often accused of witchcraft or sorcery and forced to leave their homes. As one 13-year-old girl noted, "My father did not want to see me at home. He chased me to go and get rid of sorcery. I was beaten up and tortured. The situation became such that I ran away to protect myself."[130]

As of 2006, nearly half the children living in shelters in Kinshasa reported that they had fled their homes after being accused of sorcery.[131]

Upon leaving their homes, children have very few opportunities, and many choose (or are forced) to volunteer in armed forces as a way to survive. For instance, Angelique, a young girl demobilized by Save the Children, and some of her friends had refused the sexual advances of a young man in her town. Later the boy announced to the community that the girls were planning acts of sorcery against him, and the girls were forced to leave. They joined the RCD-Goma

---

128. Martin Bell, "Child Alert: Democratic Republic of the Congo," UNICEF report, July 2006, www.unicef.org/childalert/drc/ (accessed Sept. 8, 2009).

129. United Nations, "S/2006/389," paragraph 510.

130. Watchlist on Children and Armed Conflict, "Struggling to Survive."

131. Ibid.

with the goal of seeking revenge.[132] Although Angelique was later demobilized and eventually reintegrated back into her community, her story shows how the cultural inclination to accuse girls of witchcraft provides armed groups with new recruits.

Finally, the DRC's geography—both its sheer size and its dense rain forest terrain—also had a negative effect on the reconstruction process. In addition to dealing with the ongoing violence, NGOs and other implementing agencies also had to navigate the DRC's relatively inaccessible natural environment, often without adequate transportation infrastructure. Thus, environmental factors became a structural hindrance to the reconstruction process.

Whereas in Mozambique the cultural environment, and religious practices in particular, supported the reconstruction process, cultural and environmental factors in the DRC had the extreme opposite effect and have been a serious obstacle for all reconstruction actors. While it is difficult to quantify how much each of these extenuating environmental and cultural factors influenced the overall conflict, it is clear that each presents a significant problem for the peacebuilding effort and a potential source of strength for rebel groups to continue their operations.

Coding

The cultural and environmental factors in the DRC are coded as having a high-level, negative impact. The negative rating reflects that certain cultural and environmental factors have been major obstacles to establishing stability and operating the reconstruction program. The high-level rating reflects the extent to which cultural and environmental factors, from the disregard of human rights to the inaccessibility of the terrain, were felt across the board by all actors involved, exerting a systemic detrimental influence on the reconstruction process.

Dependent Variable: Level of Stability as Related to Youth

Renewed Conflict

Despite the domestic and UN efforts to control the violence in the DRC, the overall level of instability since 2003 has remained extremely high in the northeastern provinces, at some points escalating to renewed conflict. While the day-to-day violence in Kinshasa and other parts of the country declined significantly since wartime, the rebellion led primarily by former RCD general Laurent Nkunda persisted into 2009, destabilizing the region and subjecting the civilian population to unconscionable brutality.

Nkunda and his commanding officers were especially adept at recruiting new forces by using the large population of youth to their advantage. For example,

132. Verhey, "Going Home."

linked to the Nkunda army is the Association des Jeunes Réfugiés Congolais (Association of Congolese Youth Refugees), which actively recruited Congolese ethnic Tutsi children and youth from various refugee camps to join Nkunda's forces.[133]

Protests and Riots

The DRC has also experienced high levels of instability due to widespread violence and protests that flared across the country in 2005 and 2006 during the transitional elections. While it is common for violence to reemerge during an election year, the fact that the DDR program had not been completed before the elections were held may well have contributed to the high level of insecurity during that time.

Illicit Trade of Weapons and Natural Resources

Similar to the experience in Mozambique, the ease of access to small arms that is symptomatic of the Great Lakes region continues to fuel ongoing violence and regional conflict.[134] A number of reasons may explain why the arms trade continues to flourish, including the mismanagement of the DDR program and the lack of independent verification of the disarmament process. Because there was no independent verification, many groups left large caches of arms behind, stockpiled for future use, before going to the orientation centers. As of 2005, nearly 70 percent of the weapons turned in were defective, indicating that the forces were hanging on to operational weapons.[135]

The small-arms trade is also linked to the illicit sales of natural resources controlled by rebel groups. The DRC's vast supply of natural resources has been a significant factor in prolonging the conflict, as rebel groups use profits from the sale of coltan, diamonds, and other resources to purchase weapons for their troops and fund their insurgency. One of the ways that rebel groups have been so successful in exploiting the natural resources is by using child labor. The high proportion of youth in the population, combined with inadequate education and reintegration programming, has made children and youth a "key component in the illicit exploitation of natural resources."[136] Approximately 60,000 young men

---

133. Human Rights Watch, "DR Congo: Army Should Stop Use of Child Soldiers," Human Rights Watch News, April 19, 2007, www.hrw.org/en/news/2007/04/19/dr-congo-army-should-stop-use-child-soldiers (accessed Sept. 1, 2009).

134. Economist Intelligence Unit, "Country Report: Democratic Republic of Congo," March 2004, www.eiu.com (subscription only, accessed Sept. 1, 2009). Additionally, the EIU reported that in 2007 all sides were rearming in the Kivus. The FARDC received arms shipments from China and Ukraine, and some of the weapons have been making their way into the hands of the FDLR and progovernment ethnic Mayi-Mayi militias. Laurent Nkunda was also receiving arms supplies via Rwanda. Economist Intelligence Unit, "Country Report: Democratic Republic of the Congo," December 2007, www.eiu.com (subscription only, accessed Sept. 1, 2009).

135. Amnesty International, "Democratic Republic of the Congo: Disarmament, Demobilization and Reintegration."

136. Watchlist on Children and Armed Conflict, "Struggling to Survive."

and boys work in appalling conditions in mines, often as stone crushers or in narrow, hard-to-reach mine tunnels.[137]

Children and youth with meager income-generating alternatives have also contributed to the ongoing insurgency as entrepreneurs in their own illicit trade activities. For instance, the OPEC Boys are a group of unemployed youth and ex-combatants from the Ugandan Lord's Resistance Army (LRA) and the Allied Democratic Forces (AFDL) in the DRC, who make a profit smuggling fuel from the DRC to Uganda.[138] In tapping into a trade that is profitable for them, these young men actively contribute to the ongoing violence and regional conflict because they often sell fuel to various rebel and government forces in Uganda that are also active in the DRC.

Outside Indicators of Stability

Various indicators show that the level of instability in the DRC remained at medium to high levels during 2003–07:

- In 2005, the DRC earned a 69.4 out of 100 on the 2008 Ibrahim Index of African Governance's rating for Safety and Security (with 0 representing least safe and secure, and 100 most safe and secure). While this is an improvement over its score of 49.8 in 2002, only ten countries ranked lower than 69.4 in 2005. Also, the DRC scored only 25 out of 100 in both 2002 and 2005 for physical human rights.

- On the Failed States Index for 2005–07, the DRC rated "alert"—the highest level of risk. In 2007, the DRC was the seventh most "critical" and likely to fail out of 177 states (although this was an improvement from 2005 and 2006, when the country ranked second in the world, after Côte d'Ivoire in 2005 and Sudan in 2006). One of the main subcategories affecting the DRC's "alert" ranking is the social demographics indicator, in which the DRC received a score of 9.4 (with 10 being the worst possible score) for demographic pressures due to the country's large youth bulge, high population growth, and high infant mortality rate.

- RiskMap 2008 puts the DRC's political risk for business at medium, and its security risk as medium (in Kinshasa and Southern Katanga) to high (in eastern Ituri and North Kivu).

- The EIU country reports from 2002 to 2007 indicate a relatively high level of violence and instability, especially in the eastern provinces, despite the effects of the peacekeeping efforts and the increased stability in other regions.

---

137. Ibid.

138. Els Lecoutere and Kristof Titeca, "Les Opec Boys en Ouganda, Trafiquants de Petrole et Acteurs Politiques," *Politique Africaine* 103 (2006).

These analyses confirm that despite the peacekeeping efforts, high levels of instability have continued to plague the DRC throughout the postaccord reconstruction phase. One of the most salient aspects of this ongoing instability is that actors in the DRC consciously and successfully manipulated the youth demographic to their advantage in perpetuating the conflict.

Coding

The DRC is coded as having an extreme level of instability. The extreme rating reflects the level of politically motivated violence and a reincitation of the conflict in the northeastern regions. While the level of security improved in other areas, the ongoing instability in the east took a toll on the entire peace process, and the effects were felt throughout the country.

Summary of Variables' Impact

Tables 3.1 through 3.7 summarize the information in this chapter, synthesizing the details in each variable and showing the variable's impact on the youth demographic and the general level of stability in the DRC. Tables 3.1 through 3.5 address independent variables, and tables 3.6 and 3.7 address dependent variables.

Conclusions

Across the board in the DRC, reconstruction actors were acutely aware of the importance of children's issues and of the need for distinct policies on children and youth. But despite the high level of international and NGO efforts focused on children, the situation has remained highly unstable. In fact, children and youth helped perpetuate the instability in three major ways:

- A failed DDR program provided little support for youth reintegration and opened the door to young people's recruitment and rerecruitment into armed groups.
- Youth were manipulated by militia leaders to serve as soldiers and to support the natural resource extraction that financed the rebel movements.
- Unemployed entrepreneurial youth with little support have entered into the informal market, in some instances helping sustain internal and cross-border conflict.

Although the high concentration of money and manpower that was mobilized for reconstruction programs in the DRC should have improved stability, the mismanagement of the reconstruction programs, specifically the DDR/DDRRR process, has helped perpetuate the violence in which youth played a direct role.

Table 3.1. DRC: International Involvement

Variables	Program Specifics	Impact
Treaty	• Establishes DDR program to be carried out through UN • Calls for end to recruitment of child soldiers • Neither provision is effectively implemented	Low positive impact
Foreign Governments	• Involvement in negotiation process • High level of humanitarian aid, with some transition programs focused specifically on youth	Medium positive impact
United Nations	• Assists with DDR • Emergency humanitarian relief, reintegration of IDPs and refugees • Child Protection Unit, advocacy • Works with national government to develop operational framework for children's DDR • UN personnel involved in prostitution, rape, and abuse of young women	Overall medium positive impact despite instances where program detracted from stability (negative impact)
Overall Effectiveness		**Medium positive impact**

Table 3.2. DRC: NGO Involvement

Variables	Program Specifics	Impact
Coordination	• Coordination among NGOs relatively smooth, although marked by high levels of competition and donor-driven programming • Coordination between NGOs and national government poorly executed	Medium negative impact
Types of Programming	• Emergency humanitarian relief • Children's DDR • Advocacy and awareness campaigns • Very few youth empowerment or reintegration programs	Low positive impact despite high level of efforts
Level of Efforts (number of NGOs or international personnel)	• High level of efforts • Relative lack of success in meeting demand	Low positive impact
Time Frame	• Short-term emergency focus is a significant obstacle to instituting development-oriented programs	Medium negative impact
Overall Effectiveness		**Medium positive impact**

Table 3.3. DRC: Domestic Policy

Variables	Program Specifics	Impact
Focus on Youth	• Identifies children's issues, especially within the DDR/DDRRR program • Despite policies' focus on children, the policies are not effectively implemented	Low positive impact
Types of Programming	• DDR/DRRR—lack of effective reintegration programming • Education reform • Juvenile justice	High negative impact
Overall Effectiveness		**High negative impact**

Table 3.4. DRC: Cultural and Environmental Factors

Variables	Role	Impact
"Culture of Impunity"	• Contributes to ongoing violence, breaking down communities and preventing NGOs from operating effectively • Significant obstacle for development programming; instead of development initiatives aimed at the long term, most international and NGO programming must focus on immediate humanitarian support to victims and human rights awareness campaigns in response to ongoing impunity	High negative impact
Terrain	• Lack of transportation infrastructure, dense rainforest, and vast size of the country complicate logistics of providing humanitarian aid	High negative impact
Natural Resources	• Rebels sell diamonds, oil, coltan, and other natural resources to continue financing their movement • A significant number of youth work in natural resource extraction	High negative impact
Religion and Religious Practices	• Obstacle to reintegration because many young people, especially young women, are accused of sorcery and shunned from their communities	Low negative impact
Overall Effectiveness		**High negative impact**

Table 3.5. DRC: Demographic and Objective Statistics

Population age 10–24	• 32% of population age 10–24 • 45% of population under age 15 • Total population (2003): 57,722,115
	Baseline • Average for sub-Saharan Africa: 32% in 2003 • Average for more developed countries: 20% in 2003
Level of Youth Participation	• Over 30,000 of 150,000 armed combatants were under age 18 (up to 40% of certain brigades in 2003)
Unemployment	• Unemployment statistics unavailable
GNI per Capita	• US$120 (2005)
	Baseline • Average for sub-Saharan Africa: US$1,082.00 (2008)
Overall Coding	• **High proportion of youth in the population** • **Extremely high level of youth involvement in the conflict**

Baseline population statistics taken from U.S. Census Bureau, "International Data Base"; baseline for GNI per capita taken from World Bank, "Key Development Data and Statistics."

Table 3.6. DRC: Level of Instability

Overall Description of Stability	• While violence declines in Kinshasa and other areas, violence at warfare intensity persists in the eastern provinces • Ongoing human rights violations and sexual violence are used as a tool to perpetuate conflict • Protests and rioting around 2005–06 election
Youth Involvement	• Recruitment and rerecruitment of youth into armed groups throughout reconstruction process • Young soldiers recruiting others into armed groups • Youth participation in resource extraction/black market
Youth's Effects on Overall Level of Instability	Extreme instability, ongoing violence throughout the country, and instability to the point of reincitation of conflict in the eastern provinces Youth involvement helps perpetuate the conflict via recruitment and rerecruitment into armed groups, resource extraction, and black market activities that fund rebel movements

Table 3.7. DRC: Supporting Indicators of Level of Instability

Ibrahim Index of African Governance	• Safety and Security: 69.4 out of 100 (100 = most secure)
Failed States Index	• "Alert" level • Out of 177 states, 7th most vulnerable to collapse or conflict in 2007
RiskMap2008	• Medium political risk • Medium security risk in Kinshasa, high security risk in eastern Ituri and North Kivu

Indeed, the failing DDR/DDRRR process has been one of the main factors impeding the establishment of durable stability. The inability of the local government to follow through from the initial demobilization to reintegration took a huge toll (see table 3.3) and forced NGOs to use their limited resources to compensate for the government's failings. As tables 3.1 and 3.2 suggest, despite the international community's relatively high degree of involvement addressing children's needs, poor coordination and programming driven by short-term emergency funding hindered their ability to have a significant positive impact. Extenuating situational circumstances (see table 3.4) also had a significant negative impact, inhibiting international actors' ability to administer humanitarian and development programming.

The deficient reconstruction process created an environment where serving in the armed forces was one of the few opportunities for youth to find food, power, and community. Many young people voluntarily returned to armed groups or were forcibly rerecruited, remaining a resource for the armed groups still operating. Successful reintegration programs could have provided former combatants with various forms of educational or vocational training to ease the transition to civilian life. But instead, youth participation in the ongoing conflict as members of rebel groups and illegal traders of natural resources was fundamental to the rebel groups' ability to prolong the conflict and was a significant hindrance to reconstruction efforts.

While it is clear that the DRC has been highly unstable since 2003, it is arguable that the violence, at least in the eastern regions, represents a chronic conflict rather than a reincitation of violence. However, the failings of the transition and reconstruction process played a major role in prolonging the violence in the east and made it easier for those elites determined to continue fighting to destabilize the country.

Drawing comparisons between the DRC and Mozambique helps elucidate this issue. For example, whereas in Mozambique the entire country was markedly war weary and most elites were willing to reach a resolution, in the DRC a number of armed groups in the eastern region were determined to carry on the conflict. The rest of the DRC dedicated itself to a transition from war to peace and embarked on a transitional plan including demobilization, institution building, and elections. Certainly, these programs have been much less successful there than in Mozambique, but what would the situation have looked like had the reconstruction actors successfully implemented the DDR process and seen it through to the finish? Had CONADER coordinated with the United Nations and NGOs to effectively facilitate the DDR programs according to the Operational Framework, children and youth might not have been caught in a situation where they perceived themselves better off joining armed groups than making the transition to civilian life. If these actors had effectively provided reintegration and education and empowerment opportunities, young people may not have become such an easily manipulated resource for those few elites set on prolonging the conflict. As a result, the ineffective international, domestic, and NGO efforts have not only been unable to foster stability but have actually *promoted* instability by failing to meet these critical youth needs.

With the arrest of Laurent Nkunda in 2009, the DRC is at a potentially crucial turning point, and the youth demographic remains a significant factor in determining the country's future development. Because of the failing reconstruction program, many children remain out of school, and former youth soldiers lack any real economic or educational opportunities. As a result, children and youth represent a central contributing factor in the ongoing instability. Without more effective policies and programming, as this population ages, Congolese youth may have the potential to exert increasing influence and agency in destabilizing the country.

4

Kosovo: Youth as Agents of Change in an Unstable Environment

The aftermath of the 1998–99 conflict in Kosovo presented the international community with several daunting challenges. Although Kosovo is only a small republic, the civil war and intervening NATO air campaign had created a regional refugee and humanitarian crisis and destroyed the province's physical infrastructure. To further complicate matters, Kosovo has one of the largest proportions of youth population in the world and an extremely high rate of youth unemployment.

To meet these challenges, numerous international, regional, and non-governmental organizations flooded the reconstruction scene with an unprecedented level of involvement relative to the size of the conflict. The immediate efforts paid off, and these actors were able to prevent any serious spoiling of the peace and begin the process of building a stable national infrastructure. But because of the emergency nature of the international involvement, the reconstruction process has yet to establish a stable foundation for long-term peace. While the immediate post-conflict reconstruction efforts were able to contain most of the violence and prevent a reincitation of hostilities, there remains great potential for instability in the ongoing and pervasive sense of tension between Kosovar Albanians and Kosovar Serbs.

A number of intervening factors, both positive and negative, have contributed to this tenuous balance between hostile tension and constructive peace-building that has characterized both the sentiments of the youth population and the discourse of the post-conflict reconstruction process. Immediately following the NATO intervention, which ended the war and stopped the Serbian ethnic cleansing campaign, NGOs, international organizations, and regional security groups flooded into Kosovo and the refugee camps in Albania. NGOs and international actors, acutely aware of the potentially destabilizing power of the youth demographic, provided a broad range of programming specifically focused on youth.[1] With the humanitarian crisis resolved relatively quickly, international

---

1. UNDP, the World Bank, and the European Union were all aware of the importance of supporting Kosovo's youth during the reconstruction process. According to UNDP, there was a great need to help

actors were able to satisfy the youth population's immediate and critical needs, such as psychosocial support and family reunification, and also implement various types of youth development programming that covered the spectrum of political, social, and (to a lesser extent) economic empowerment. As a result, these organizations were able to defuse any destabilizing potential and also empower the youth demographic to contribute actively to the reconstruction process.

This initial onslaught of international actors also had several detrimental effects. While Kosovo once had a strong tradition of community participation and volunteerism, the surge of emergency relief allowed international actors to dominate the scene, creating dependence on the international community while inadvertently eroding existing community structures.[2] As the international interest and funding waned, the newly established programs and reforms began to suffer. Five years after the NATO intervention, unemployment rates remained high, and the struggling education system and continued uncertainty over the status of independence created a situation in Kosovo in which the destabilizing potential of the youth population remained a central factor in determining the country's future.

The following analysis will explore the intervening factors that have created this precarious balance between stability and instability, between youth building peace and youth participating in violence. The reconstruction process in Kosovo is particularly important for this study because it serves as an analytic foil for the previous cases. Both the DRC and Mozambique were countries grappling specifically with the issue of child and youth soldiers. While Kosovo's large youth population was also active during the conflict, these young people were not necessarily child soldiers—allowing for the analysis of other types of youth involvement. Also, both the previous cases had a more or less decisive outcome: one reaching a relatively stable resolution to the conflict, the other falling back into a pattern of violence. Kosovo, on the other hand, serves as the "in-between" case, where the country's future stability remains unclear. With these factors in mind, analyzing the type, quality, and effectiveness of the reconstruction programming in Kosovo may elucidate how these programs shape the youth population's influence on the post-conflict reconstruction environment.

Kosovo's youth become constructive actors in their communities because "Kosovo has the youngest population in Europe, with roughly 60% of the population being under the age of 25. . . . Papers by the World Bank and the European Union presented at the Brussels conference in November 1999 identified young people between the ages of 15–20 as the greatest potential source of civil unrest in Kosovo." UNDP, "UNDP in Kosovo: Youth Post-conflict Participation Project," UNDP Project Summaries, www.kosovo.undp.org/Projects/YPCPP/ypcpp.htm (accessed April 1, 2008).

2.   Julie Mertus, "Improving International Peacebuilding Efforts: The Example of Human Rights Culture in Kosovo," *Global Governance* 10, no. 3 (2004): 333–51.

Background

While the origins of the conflicts in Mozambique and the DRC were intrinsically tied to their colonial heritage, the conflict in Kosovo is best understood through the development of competing nationalist claims.[3] Although it is home to an Albanian majority, both Serbs and Albanians have historic claims to Kosovo that are deeply integrated into their ethnic, national, and religious identities. Serbian nationalist myths treat Kosovo as the cultural and religious heart of the historically Serbian nation, brutally wrested away by the Ottoman Empire in the battle of Fushë Kosovë/Kosovo Polje in the twelfth century. For Serbs, Kosovo represents centuries of oppression at the hands of the Ottoman Empire (and its collaborators, the Albanians). Albanians, for their part, have similar claims on Kosovo as an integral part of the Albanian national and cultural state. Centuries later, in the early 1900s, the Ottoman Empire collapsed and fighting broke out across the Balkans. During the Balkan Wars of 1912–13, Albanians fought desperately but unsuccessfully to resist Serbian nationalist forces from claiming most of the territory of Kosovo. Integral to Albanian national myths that persist today is the story of the suffering of Albanian civilians at the hands of the Serbian-Montenegrin army during that time.

When Albania declared independence in 1912, the leaders had imagined a state that would include Kosovo. However, claims on the territory were caught up in the battle between the great regional powers of Austria-Hungary and Russia, and in the 1913 Protocol of Florence, Kosovo was assigned to Serbia. While none of the Balkan states were satisfied with the terms of the Florence Protocol, Albania had received one of the worst lots, for the treaty drew the borders so that half the Albanian population was now living outside the new state of Albania.[4]

With the 1980 death of President Josip Broz Tito of the Socialist Federal Republic of Yugoslavia, the question of Kosovo's independence once again came to the forefront. Although Kosovar Albanians had endured decades of oppression and institutionalized prejudice under Tito, Kosovo was also given a large degree of independence as an autonomous province of Serbia. As an autonomous province, Kosovo had its own administration and civic structures, similar to the construction of the Yugoslav republics, though it did not have the right to secede from the Federation of Yugoslavia.[5] The independence allowed under Tito's reforms was symbolically embodied in the Kosovar Albanian culture in

---

3. Note on language: The use of dual language markers for cities is a symbol of nationalist sentiment that is a constant reminder of claims on space and territory. In this case, "Kosova" is the Albanian pronunciation, and "Kosovo" the Serbian. For simplicity's sake, this chapter will use "Kosovo," the name used in most references by the international community. City names will appear with the Albanian pronunciation followed by the Serbian pronunciation (e.g., "Prishtinë/Priština").

4. Dick A. Leurdijk and Dick Zandee, *Kosovo: From Crisis to Crisis* (Aldershot, UK: Ashgate, 2000), 4–13.

5. Ibid.

the establishment of an independent education system in Kosovo, centered in the University of Prishtinë/Priština.

Tito's death left a power vacuum in Yugoslavia, and the reforms began to unravel. Whereas Tito had managed to keep ethnic tensions at bay in the interest of maintaining a unified republic, Slobodon Milošević began his rise to power on an agenda of Serbian nationalism, which he outwardly proclaimed in a speech at Fushë Kosovë/Kosovo Polje. Milošević's mission to prevent the disintegration of Yugoslavia centered on a strategy of removing minority power, including the Albanian social and cultural presence in Kosovo.[6] In 1990, a series of policies aimed at reconstructing the ethnic composition of Kosovo culminated in Milošević's dissolving the Kosovo parliament, revoking Kosovo's autonomy, and marking the end of the 1974 constitution and the Federation of Yugoslavia.[7] The abolition of Kosovo's autonomy coincided with a renewal of human rights abuses and discriminatory policies aimed to "Serbianize" the province, including discriminatory language policies and the imposition of a new curriculum for the education system. During this period, Serbian forces arbitrarily arrested, detained, and tortured Kosovar Albanians on a regular basis, and thousands, including more than 180,000 teachers and staff of Albanian-language schools, were purged from their public office positions.[8]

The Kosovar Albanian community responded by organizing a campaign of nonviolent resistance. The movement soon established a "voluntary" tax system to finance the formation of a parallel structure of government for Albanians in Kosovo, and in 1991 the Kosovar government held a referendum on independence. Though Kosovar Serbs boycotted the election, 99 percent of the vote was in favor of independence. It is important to note that for many citizens, the system of parallel government was the primary form of resistance against Serbian oppression, and that resistance was symbolically represented not only in the government structures but particularly in the maintenance of the Albanian education system. By 1993, the parallel education system comprised 20,000 teachers and administrative staff, over 317,000 preschool and elementary school students, 65 secondary schools with 56,920 students, 20 faculties and colleges with 12,000 students, two schools for disabled children, and several other educational institutions.[9] While most of the primary schools remained in their previous buildings, the rest of the 204 facilities that housed the education system were homes or garages donated by Kosovar Albanians.

Throughout the 1990s, the situation in Kosovo deteriorated. When the Kosovo issue was ignored in the 1995 Dayton Agreement over Bosnia, it seemed

---

6. Stephen Schwartz, *Kosovo: Background to a War* (London: Anthem, 2000).

7. Independent International Commission on Kosovo, *The Kosovo Report: Conflict, International Response, Lessons Learned* (Oxford: Oxford University Press, 2000).

8. Ibid., 41–42.

9. Ibid., 46.

evident to many Kosovar Albanians that the peaceful resistance had failed. In 1996, the Albanian Kosovo Liberation Army (KLA) emerged, dedicated to using all means necessary to achieve Kosovo's independence, and began to take over the cause of resistance from the nonviolent Lidhja Demokratike Kosovës (Democratic League of Kosovo). What began as a series of terrorist attacks by the KLA on Serb/Federal Republic of Yugoslavia (FRY) targets in 1996 started a cycle of retaliatory massacres committed by both sides. (The Federal Republic of Yugoslavia [1992–2003] consisted of the two remaining states from the former Soviet Federal Republic of Yugoslavia: Serbia and Montenegro.) By 1998, the situation had escalated into a state of war, with KLA militias fighting FRY/Serbian military forces.

As news of the increasing violence and mass atrocities spread in the international media, pressure developed for international authorities to take action. While both the KLA and FRY/Serb Forces committed egregious attacks against civilians, the Serb violations of human rights far exceeded those of the KLA, and the Western media portrayed the violence as predominantly Serbian aggression against Albanian victims. The Reçak/Račak massacre, in which Serbian forces brutalized and killed more than 40 Kosovar Albanians in January 1999, drew extensive news coverage in the West, increasing the pressure on foreign governments to intervene. It became the widespread belief among Western leaders and, increasingly, of the U.S. general public that Milošević was planning, if not already perpetrating, an ethnic cleansing campaign to rid Kosovo of Albanians.[10]

Based on the fear that without an intervention Milošević would continue his ethnic cleansing, and for a number of political reasons, the United States and NATO took the lead role in mediating an end to the violence. The humanitarian motivations were clear: thousands of refugees were flooding out of Kosovo, and NATO members justified their actions as preventing the "massacre and displacement of the Kosovar Albanians."[11] On the political front, the United States and NATO had previously negotiated with Milošević during the Bosnian conflict; therefore, the emergence of violence by Milošević in Kosovo had the potential to shatter NATO's image as an effective security force in post–Cold War Europe. After a series of failed negotiation attempts, Serbian and Albanian leaders convened for one last attempt at dialogue, sponsored by the Contact Group in Rambouillet, France. Representatives of the KLA agreed to the proposal, put

10. Jan Repa, "Ethnic Cleansing: Revival of an Old Tradition," BBC News, March 29, 1999, http://news.bbc.co.uk/2/hi/special_report/1998/kosovo2/307261.stm (accessed Sept. 1, 2009); Steven Erlanger, "U.S. Ready to Resume Sanctions against Serbs over Kosovo Strife," New York Times, June 6, 1998, www.nytimes.com/1998/06/06/world/us-ready-to-resume-sanctions-against-serbs-over-kosovo-strife.html?pagewanted=all (accessed Sept. 1, 2009); Katharine Q. Seelye, "Crisis in the Balkans: Washington; Clinton Blames Milosevic, Not Fate, for Bloodshed," New York Times, May 14, 1999, www.nytimes.com/1999/05/14/world/crisis-in-the-balkans-washington-clinton-blames-milosevic-not-fate-for-bloodshed.html?pagewanted=all (accessed Sept. 1, 2009).

11. Repa, "Ethnic Cleansing: Revival of an Old Tradition."

forth at Rambouillet, that would restore Kosovar autonomy but leave the future status of full independence for reconsideration. But the Serbian forces refused to agree, and the negotiations failed.

In March 1999, NATO, with its reputation on the line after the failed negotiations at Rambouillet, authorized an air campaign against the FRY/Serb forces. Whether NATO acted to prevent a humanitarian crisis or to protect its credibility remains the subject of debate. NATO claimed to be protecting the Albanian population, and yet, its own bombing campaign caused more displacement and destruction. The bombing drove many civilians from their homes and destroyed much of the physical infrastructure. Worse yet, immediately after the bombing began, the FRY military and paramilitary units began an ethnic cleansing campaign to expel Kosovo's Albanian population.[12] However, by proclaiming a humanitarian mission to prevent further crisis in Kosovo, NATO would become a dominant actor in Kosovo's reconstruction.

The NATO bombings lasted for seventy-eight days before the parties finally reached an agreement for an immediate cessation of the violence, the withdrawal of FRY forces from Kosovo, and reestablishment of Kosovo's autonomy, though still under the umbrella of the Serbian government. In reality, Kosovo turned into a UN and NATO protectorate. On the same day that the air campaign ended, the UN Security Council passed Resolution 1244, authorizing the United Nations to act as the civilian administrator for the republic, through the establishment of the United Nations Interim Administration Mission in Kosovo (UNMIK). The UN mandate also authorized NATO-led peacekeeping forces, the Kosovo International Security Force (KFOR), to facilitate the safe return of refugees and "contribute to a secure environment for the international civil implementation presence."[13] Despite the cessation of the violence, the issue of Kosovo's independence remained unresolved.

The conflict in Kosovo during 1998–99 resulted in over 10,000 deaths and displaced over 1.5 million people, predominantly Kosovar Albanians, either internally or as refugees to neighboring countries. The years of violence and the final three months of air campaigns had also led to the widespread destruction of physical infrastructure in both Kosovo and greater Serbia.

Particularly significant for the purposes of this case study is the role played by student activists throughout the conflict. Students were symbolic members of

---

12. There is still debate in the international community regarding the origins of the ethnic cleansing campaign (so-called Operation Horseshoe) and whether the NATO air campaign may actually have provoked the violence and consequently created a humanitarian disaster instead of stopping one. According to *The Kosovo Report*, "The issue is still open, but it is very clear that there was a deliberate organized effort to expel a huge part of the Kosovar Albanian population and such a massive operation cannot be implemented without planning and preparation." Whether NATO caused the humanitarian disaster is harder to assess, although it is clear that the campaign "created an internal environment that made such an operation feasible." Independent Commission on Kosovo, *The Kosovo Report*.

13. Ibid.

the resistance through their participation in the parallel system of education, and they also served as an active and driving force in promoting the cause of full independence. Massive student protests in 1981 and 1997 paralleled turning points in the conflict, reflecting the community's sentiments, drawing international attention, and fueling the independence movement. The tradition of student protests has continued throughout the transition process as a dominant symbol and mechanism for the Albanian independence movement in modern Kosovo.

Today ethnic tensions remain a part of daily life in Kosovo, and uncertainty over the status of independence has hindered Kosovo's economic and social development. But in February 2008, the Kosovo Assembly officially declared its independence from Serbia. With this declaration of independence, the future of Kosovo seems open to many possibilities, with the potential for either peaceful development or renewed violence and conflict.

The following analysis shows that despite the dedicated international effort to rebuild the war-torn province, the impact of the post-conflict reconstruction process in Kosovo remains unclear. While international actors, including the United Nations, regional security groups, and NGOs, took on the bulk of the responsibility for governing Kosovo and provided a wide range of programming specifically focused on youth issues, the exclusion of domestic actors in the reconstruction process inadvertently eroded the existing ethos of community involvement.[14] Also, NGOs' dependence on, and competition for, emergency grant funding diminished their ability to provide long-term support for Kosovo's youth. Consequently, even with the concentration of international efforts aimed at helping young people become constructive community actors, the youth demographic remains a source of potential destabilization (or peace) for the newly independent country.

Variable Analysis: Impact on Youth and Stability

Demographic Variables

The obstacles facing youth in post-conflict Kosovo can be better understood through analysis of certain demographic variables. Although these variables are inextricably linked, it is useful to group them in the following broad categories: the proportion of youth in the Kosovar population, youth participation in the conflict, availability of employment opportunities, and education.

Youth Population
Kosovo has the youngest population in Europe, and one of the highest proportions of youth in the world. Over half of Kosovo's two million people are under

---

14. Mertus, "Improving International Peacebuilding Efforts."

age 25, with 21 percent between ages 15 and 25, and 65 percent under age 30.[15] As a result, since 1999, Kosovar leaders have been grappling with how to deal with youth-related issues and include a youth perspective in political, economic, and social policies.

Children and youth were also greatly affected by the conflict, comprising over half the 600,000 internally displaced Kosovars and the 860,000 refugees who fled to neighboring countries in 1998–99.[16] An estimated 23 percent of the persons remaining on the International Committee of the Red Cross's missing-persons list for Kosovo in 2001 were under age 25—most of them Albanian young men. This percentage is probably actually much higher, since a large number of missing-persons cases, especially of young women, go unreported.[17]

Youth Refugees and Soldiers

Unlike in the cases of Mozambique and the DRC, it is unclear to what extent children and adolescents under 18 participated as soldiers or militia members during the Kosovo conflict. Although the KLA officially claimed that it did not accept "under 18s" in its ranks, it is likely that at least 10 to 20 percent of the KLA forces were under 18 (mostly 16- and 17-year-olds), with some estimates as high as 30 percent.[18] Only 2 percent were children under 16—mostly girls recruited to cook for the soldiers, not to fight.[19] Another marked difference between Kosovo and the two African cases is that while the KLA did some forced conscription, most of its underage members were volunteers.[20] As we learn from the young KLA fighters quoted below, many young Albanians idealized the KLA fighters and their cause, often dressing up in their uniforms and trying to enlist, though often these volunteers were turned away until they reached 18.[21]

> "The reason why I joined the KLA was the terror that happened to my people from the Serbs. Especially after the massacre in Prekaz, where people were massacred so bad, women, children, and old people. I just felt that I had to do something for my people." (J., 18)[22]

15. Sokol Ferizi and Novi Sad, "Youth Despair of Decent Future in Kosovo," Balkan Investigative Reporting Network, Nov. 15, 2007, www.birn.eu.com/en/113/10/5821/ (accessed Sept. 8, 2009); UNDP, "Youth: A New Generation for a New Kosovo," report, 2006," www.ks.undp.org/repository/docs/hdr_eng.pdf (accessed Sept. 1, 2009).

16. Jane Lowicki and Allison A. Pillsbury, "Making the Choice for a Better Life: Promoting the Protection and Capacity of Kosovo's Youth," Women's Commission report, 2001, www.womenscommission.org/pdf/yu_adol.pdf (accessed Sept. 1, 2009).

17. Ibid.

18. Ibid.

19. Coalition to Stop the Use of Child Soldiers, "Child Soldiers Global Report 2001—Federal Republic of Yugoslavia," www.unhcr.org/refworld/docid/498805fbc.html (accessed Sept. 1, 2009).

20. Ibid.

21. It is unclear exactly why the KLA turned many "under 18s" away. In some cases, this may have resulted from a culture of not wanting young children to fight. There is also speculation that the KLA was actively trying to garner international support and, therefore, did not want to have any overt policy, such as the blatant use of child soldiers, that would weaken its international image.

22. PBS, "Frontline: War in Europe—NATO's 1999 war against Serbia over Kosovo. Interviews: Three KLA Soldiers," www.pbs.org/wgbh/pages/frontline/shows/kosovo/interviews/kla.html (accessed Sept. 1, 2009).

"The first time I tried to join was in 1998, and they didn't accept me. I tried again early in 1999, and that time I told them, 'Either you take me, or I'm going to kill myself.' I started in a guard position at night, and very slowly I worked my way up to the front line. . . . At night, sometimes I still dream that a live grenade has been thrown just meters from me, and I wake up yelling. But I know this is normal, and anyway, I don't care for my dreams. I'm willing to give my young life for the land that belongs to my grandparents. I didn't fight for glory, I fought for our freedom." (Bashkim H., 16, from Gjakova/Djakovica)[23]

Although children's involvement in the militias was relatively low, young adults and adolescents made up much of the KLA fighting force: 40.09 percent of ex-KLA combatants surveyed by the IOM were age 14 to 24.[24]

Unemployment

Unemployment is perhaps the most significant issue facing young people in Kosovo today. The unemployment rate (35–44 percent in 2005) is nearly 5.5 times the average rate in European Union (EU) countries and nearly twice as high as the estimated 21 percent unemployment in Mozambique in 1997. Kosovar Albanians, comprising over 91.4 percent of those unemployed in 2005, are the group most affected by unemployment.[25] While unemployment in Kosovo is high across all demographics, the youth population is disproportionately affected: youth unemployment in 2004 was estimated at 63 percent and has remained at least 10 percent higher than the overall unemployment rate.[26] Moreover, as of 2004 there was a significant gender gap among youth, with 74 percent of young women age 15 to 24 unemployed, compared to 56 percent of young men.[27]

The high unemployment rate is the predominant concern of most young Kosovars, who believe that they do not have a chance to succeed if they remain in Kosovo. Nearly 70 percent of young Kosovars surveyed in 2004 responded that they were "very preoccupied" with unemployment, and in a December 2008 survey, unemployment remained the top concern for most citizens.[28] However, while many youth are searching for jobs, their frustration has not necessarily turned to protest. Instead, most youth look to opportunities outside Kosovo as their way to succeed: according to the 2007 UNDP report, because of the

---

23. Lowicki and Pillsbury, "Making the Choice for a Better Life."

24. Dmitry Pozhidaev and Ravza Andzhelich, "Beating Swords to Ploughshares: Reintegration of Former Combatants in Kosovo," Center for Political and Social Research paper, Pristina, Kosovo, 2005, http://un-ddr.org/docs/Beating%20Swords%20Into%20Plowshares.pdf (accessed Sept. 1, 2009).

25. UNDP, "Youth: A New Generation for a New Kosovo." Youth unemployment is defined as unemployment among those over age 15 and under 25.

26. UNICEF, "Youth in Kosovo," report, 2004, www.unicef.org/kosovo/kosovo_media_pub_youth.010.04.pdf (accessed Aug. 1, 2009).

27. Ibid; UNDP, "Human Development Report Kosovo 2004," www.ks.undp.org/repository/docs/KHDR2004.pdf (accessed Sept. 1, 2009).

28. UNICEF, "Youth in Kosovo"; UNDP and USAID, "Fast Facts: Early Warning Report 23 December 2008," www.kosovo.undp.org/repository/docs/Fast_Facts_23_EnglishFINAL.pdf (accessed Sept. 1, 2009).

unavailability of good jobs and education, nearly half the population age 15 to 24 would emigrate if they could.[29]

Education

The parallel Albanian education system had a strong symbolic role throughout the conflict. But such efforts, forced to operate underground and without adequate funding or space, could not compensate for the lack of a regular school system. In addition to the disruption of normal school operations, the educational infrastructure also suffered a high degree of physical damage as a result of the violence. By the end of the 1999 NATO campaign, nearly 45 percent of schools were completely destroyed, and only 17 percent emerged undamaged. (However, even the areas around many of these schools were planted with land mines to prevent children from returning to school.)[30] Immediately after the NATO bombings, there was a strong campaign to rebuild the educational infrastructure, and from 1999 to 2001, 1,000 school buildings were rebuilt or repaired.[31]

While enrollment, especially across the mandatory levels of education, has been largely restored since 2000, the quality of education, attendance, and access to secondary- and university-level programs remains poor by European standards. (In 2003–04 only 75.2 percent of the secondary school-age population was enrolled).[32] Also, as discussed later in this chapter, curriculum reform and the restructuring of the Kosovar education systems remains a highly contentious topic that is far from being fully resolved.

Coding

The proportion of youth in the population in Kosovo is rated as high. With over half the population under age 25, and 21 percent age 15 to 24, Kosovo has one of the highest proportions of youth anywhere in the world.[33] Youth participation in the conflict is also coded as high, with 40.09 percent of the KLA age 14 to 24. Finally, the youth unemployment rate in Kosovo is coded as extremely high, because not only is the rate much higher than in other European countries, but the proportion of unemployed youth exceeds the overall unemployment rate by 10 percent.

---

29. Ferizi and Sad, "Youth Despair of Decent Future in Kosovo."

30. UNDP, "Youth: A New Generation for a New Kosovo."

31. Ibid.

32. Ibid. This level of enrollment is far higher than the corresponding rate for sub-Saharan Africa (31.7 percent in 2005) but considerably less than the average for Eastern Europe and Central Asia (89.2 percent in 2005).

33. The average proportion of youth in Eastern Europe's population is 34.5 percent (age 0–24), and 15.9 percent (age 15–24). The corresponding world averages are 47.6 percent (age 0–24) and 17.7 percent (age 15–24). However, the rates in Kosovo correspond with the average rates for sub-Saharan Africa, with 63.9 percent (age 0–24) and 20.1 percent (age 15–24). U.S. Census Bureau, "International Data Base," www.census.gov/ipc/www/idb/index.php (accessed Sept. 1, 2009).

International Policy's Impact on Youth and Stabilization

International and regional organizations took over the reconstruction efforts in Kosovo to a degree unparalleled in similar operations elsewhere. With Kosovo's status as an international protectorate, UNMIK took on the responsibility of governing the province, while NATO and Civilian Police/KFOR remained in the area as peacekeeping and policing forces. The international actors involved were highly aware of Kosovo's large youth population and the potential dangers of ignoring youth needs, and representatives from both the World Bank and the European Union identified young people age 15 to 20 as "the greatest potential source of civil unrest in Kosovo."[34] As a result, in the aftermath of the 1999 NATO mission, a flood of youth-specific programming poured in from the international community. Many of these programs were highly effective in meeting the immediate needs of youth affected by the conflict, and many also strove to help Kosovo's youth become a productive force in peacebuilding efforts. But after the initial deluge of international humanitarian aid, the continued predominance of the international actors over local efforts had the indirect effect of stifling the local culture of volunteerism and community service, thereby lessening the long-term benefits of youth empowerment programming.

UN Policy

UNMIK was established in 1999 immediately following the NATO-led campaign to stop the ongoing ethnic violence in Kosovo. UNMIK's first task was to coordinate disaster relief and ensure the safe return of the thousands of refugees and IDPs. It also took direct control of all essential civil administrative tasks for the province, including the police and justice system. And it coordinated the efforts of regional organizations to begin the process of democratization and institution building (led by the Organization for Security and Co-operation in Europe [OSCE]) and to facilitate the reconstruction and economic development of the province (under the leadership of the EU).

UNMIK's youth programs: From the outset, the United Nations took the lead in providing youth-oriented programming in the refugee camps. UNMIK worked with UNICEF and its NGO partners to implement the Child Friendly Spaces program, through which each camp dedicated a certain area for women and children to benefit from educational and health programs, participate in recreational activities, receive psychosocial support, and get up-to-date information on protection issues specific to their needs. UNICEF also administered capacity-building and empowerment programs with its Youth to Youth approach. The Youth to Youth programs not only provided psychological relief resources to adolescents but also sought to mobilize youth participation in the refugee camps through empowering young adults and adolescents to support and counsel their

---

34. UNDP, "Youth Post-conflict Participation Project."

younger peers. Under this program, UNICEF worked with the Albanian Youth Council in organizing weekly meetings to discuss and resolve problems in the camps, such as the lack of activities for young people. The participants then developed and implemented various community service programs, such as organizing sports tournaments and concerts in the camps, setting up camp schools, fund-raising for the poorest families, improving security in the camps, distributing information about land mines, and providing psychosocial activities for the younger children.[35]

UN support for youth civil society: In the months following the conflict, Kosovar youth had, "spontaneously and with institutional support," mobilized on the "path to becoming a force for sustainable development and peace in Kosovo."[36] With youth-run community programs emerging throughout the refugee camps, the United Nations and its partner NGOs attempted to tap into the youth potential and help these young people organize as an effective voice. For instance, UNDP and the IRC sponsored a youth empowerment program called the Youth Post-conflict Participation Project (YPCPP) in 2000–01. The YPCPP supported the emerging yet highly fragmented youth civil society movement by providing the necessary resources to form a more cohesive youth participation system and integrate youth programming into the overall recovery processes.[37] Through the YPCPP, the UNDP helped youth movements in the refugee camps organize into five regional working groups, which were then trained in how to research and initiate development subprojects. In 2001, YPCPP established the Kosovo Youth Congress to serve as a non-governmental body, run by youth, to advocate for youth issues and advise policymakers on issues relevant to the youth demographic.[38] The first meeting of the Kosovo Youth Congress laid the groundwork for the foundation of the Kosovo Youth Network, which has become a highly effective network of NGOs and youth centers throughout Kosovo, all dedicated to youth empowerment and community development. The Kosovo Youth Congress continues to meet annually to give voice to youth concerns and maintain an updated Youth Action Plan, which decides priorities and provides possible solutions to youth issues.

The YPCPP was widely successful in channeling the initial outpouring of youth activism. However, while the Kosovo Youth Congress still operates, the YPCPP project was funded only as an emergency program and ended in 2001.

UNDP did implement another project during 2003–04—Effective Youth Empowerment Strategy (EYES)—to build on previous youth empowerment efforts.

---

35. Lowicki and Pillsbury, "Making the Choice for a Better Life."
36. UNDP, "Youth Post-conflict Participation Project."
37. Ibid.
38. Ibid.

But the program got only one-third the funding that YPCPP had received.[39] The EYES project represents the trend in Kosovo of a massive influx of initial money and programs, followed by a steady decline in funding and interest. For youth participation to continue to be effective and popular, capacity-building programs needed to remain a long-term priority rather than stopgap emergency efforts.

While programs like the YPCPP and EYES were relatively short-lived, UNMIK did recognize that youth issues needed to be made a priority in the interim administration. With this view, UNMIK created the Department of Youth to take the lead in coordinating the ongoing youth activities, supporting youth initiatives such as the annual Youth Week, and making policies that would benefit the youth demographic, such as education programming to prepare youth for employment opportunities.[40]

The UN role in rebuilding Kosovo's education system: International actors also helped with education programming in Kosovo. UNICEF, with the UNMIK Department of Education, UNESCO, and the World Bank, led the rehabilitation and reform of Kosovo's education system. As previously discussed, during Milošević's tenure, Kosovar Albanians sent their children to a parallel education system alongside the Serbian system. As the conflict intensified, both Albanian and Serbian schools in parts of Kosovo shut down, and as a result, by the time UNMIK and international NGOs set about restoring the education system, they faced two devastated school infrastructures and management systems.[41] The UNMIK Department of Education and Science, under donor pressure to achieve immediate results, acted quickly and effectively to mobilize funds and help communities rebuild school buildings and get the system up and running again, and within three months after the NATO campaign, 80 percent of primary and junior secondary school students were back in school.[42]

Despite the rebuilding of the physical infrastructure, curriculum reform and the organization of the education system remained highly contentious issues throughout the reconstruction process and have not been resolved to date. Due to the brutally enforced segregation of the previous decades, the state-run school curriculum served as a tool to fuel ethnic tensions. The curriculum was highly politicized and lacking in overall quality, often teaching biased versions of historic events and civil structures. The fight for control over the new curriculum has remained an ethnic-nationalist rallying cause for hard-line politicians and has been a significant obstacle to reform. As Denisa Kostovicova explains,

---

39. The YPCPP had initial funding of $300,000, while EYES received only a little over $100,000. UNDP, "Effective Youth Empowerment Strategy (Kos/02/005)," www.kosovo.undp.org/Projects/YEP/yep.htm (accessed April 1, 2008); UNDP, "Youth Post-conflict Participation Project."

40. Lowicki and Pillsbury, "Making the Choice for a Better Life."

41. Marc Sommers and Peter Buckland, "Negotiating Kosovo's Educational Minefield," *Forced Migration Review*, no. 22 (2005).

42. Ibid.

"Both Serbs and Albanians equated the fate of their national education systems with the prospects for realizing their respective national visions in Kosovo."[43]

Without solutions to these issues, the education system put in place just three months after the NATO campaign basically reestablished the previous parallel system. As a 24-year-old student from Prizren said, "Reforms may be on paper, but we do not see them."[44] While the international actors charged with implementing educational reforms agreed that segregation of Albanians and Serbs was unacceptable and that the new education system should be a single, inclusive organization that respected students' language and cultural rights, the reality on the ground made it extremely difficult to combine the segregated schools. Security issues alone prevented schools from consolidating, as UNMIK protection forces were often required for buses escorting Serbian children from their villages to consolidated schools. As a result, separate schooling became the effective reality.[45] In 2008, some of Kosovo's Serbian communities continue to keep their children out of the "multiethnic" schools. For instance, in the villages of Brestovik, Cige/Siga, and Levoshe/Ljevosa, many Serbian children study in private homes using the Serbian Ministry of Education's curriculum.[46]

Despite the domestic resistance, international actors remained determined to reform the system. To facilitate these organizational and curricular reforms, UNMIK adopted a "lead agency" approach, giving certain international agencies near-total authority in reforming the education structures. For example, UNICEF was the lead agency in managing children's return to school, while UNMIK was the lead agency for establishing a civil administration for education.[47] UNICEF was also the lead agency in curriculum reform, working closely with UNESCO. Driven by donors that required the UNMIK Department of Education to keep its structure "lean," the agency excluded domestic actors from the reform process. With the internationals' heavy hand quickly implementing reforms and new programs, the new system "retained little from Kosovo's educational heritage."[48] Not only did the United Nations miss an opportunity to involve local experts, students, and teachers in a community effort to reform the system, but local actors were so marginalized from the reform process that many withdrew from any direct involvement in reconstruction or else looked to NGOs for the opportunity to contribute.[49]

---

43. Denisa Kostovicova, *Kosovo: The Politics of Identity and Space* (New York: Routledge, 2005), 209.

44. UNICEF, "Youth in Kosovo."

45. Marc Sommers and Peter Buckland, "Parallel Worlds: Rebuilding the Education System in Kosovo," UNESCO International Institute for Educational Planning, working document, 2004, www.unesco.org/iiep/PDF/pubs/kosovo.pdf (accessed Sept. 1, 2009).

46. Ilir Osmanaj, "Kosovo Serb Children Boycott Multiethnic School in Pec," BBC Monitoring Europe, June 13, 2008.

47. Ibid.

48. Sommers and Buckland, "Negotiating Kosovo's Educational Minefield."

49. Ibid.

Although the education reform process did eventually establish a new singular curriculum for Kosovo, the process was widely perceived as closed and disrespectful of local opinion, fueling distrust and tension between the international actors and local educators. The new curriculum called for 80 percent of content to be the same in corresponding grade levels across Kosovo, with individual schools having autonomy over 10 to 20 percent of content.[50] However, to date, the education system continues to suffer from a lack of objectivity in subjects taught—an issue that is particularly important for a province where ethnic divisions remain one of the most significant obstacles to enduring peace.

Foreign Government Involvement

Because NATO led the military campaign against the Serbian forces,[51] it was forced to take on a substantial role in the humanitarian efforts after the crisis. However, NATO wasn't the only foreign government agency interested in restoring stability to Kosovo. As an international protectorate, the province had a number of regional security groups and individual foreign governments actively involved in its administration.

NATO's relief programs, military versus humanitarian intervention: Although NATO is a military organization, it was forced to take on both military and humanitarian responsibilities to control the situation and secure its future role as the leading European security organization.[52] The intervention had set the organization's reputation on the line for its future significance in Western Europe: should NATO's efforts against Milošević fail for a second time and the humanitarian crisis remain unresolved, its preeminence as a security force in the post–Cold War era was likely to fade away.

Consequently, NATO's efforts during the post-conflict reconstruction period were initially focused on coordinating humanitarian relief for the refugee population. NATO's key role in providing humanitarian assistance was underlined when UNHCR was caught unprepared to deal with the massive influx of refugees. Calling on NATO for support, UNHCR worked under the authority of NATO planners and engineers to set up camps for Albanian refugees. With children and youth making up over half the refugee population, NATO's effectiveness in providing and coordinating humanitarian aid would have a direct impact on many young Kosovars' lives.

Although, by many accounts, NATO provided effective emergency relief, its role as the coordinating body for humanitarian aid angered many of the other hu-

---

50. UNDP, "Youth: A New Generation for a New Kosovo."

51. The NATO-led international peacekeeping force entered Kosovo in June 1999, with 48,000 troops on the ground by 2001. Lowicki and Pillsbury, "Making the Choice for a Better Life."

52. Jef Huysmans, "Shape-Shifting NATO: Humanitarian Action and the Kosovo Refugee Crisis," *Review of International Studies* 28, no. 3 (July 2002).

manitarian organizations. These organizations argued that UNHCR and international NGOs essentially served as "subcontractors" in the NATO humanitarian effort and that this blurred the distinction between military and humanitarian intervention.[53] Many of these organizations felt that a NATO-led humanitarian effort biased humanitarian support against Serbians, forcing organizations essentially to "take sides" in the conflict. As a result, agencies with the resources to function independently, such as Doctors without Borders, tried to distance themselves from the NATO operation.

NATO's military campaign and role as humanitarian-aid coordinator, while not specifically related to youth, had a striking effect on the overall perception of humanitarian aid at the local level. Instead of seeing the humanitarian effort as providing equal assistance to all those in need, Kosovars were decisively split along ethnic lines. There are many anecdotes of Serbian fighters telling Albanian families driven from their homes such things as "You wanted NATO? Let NATO protect you." In this sense, NATO's presence heightened ongoing ethnic tensions.[54]

In addition to the backlash against NATO's role as a humanitarian coordinator, in 2004, the presence of NATO and UN personnel was linked to the growing sex-trafficking trade in Kosovo. UN peacekeepers, NATO forces, and Western aid workers were the main clientele increasing the demand for the sex industry following the international occupation of the province in 1999. The trafficking industry has grown drastically as young women from neighboring countries were brought to Kosovo and forced to work as sex slaves. Kidnappings of Kosovar women domestically were also increasing. Both the United Nations and NATO operate on a zero-tolerance policy regarding sexual abuse, and both dealt with the issues internally. However, the abuse of authority and the proliferation of the sex trade is a severe impediment to Kosovo's development and horrific for those personally affected, many of them underage girls who were regularly raped and tortured. Moreover, news of the scandal intensified the perception that NATO and the United Nations were illegitimate as the security force for Kosovo.

OSCE and other regional security groups' youth programming: Whereas NATO's role was largely confined to emergency humanitarian assistance and security issues, a number of other regional security groups were highly engaged in the reconstruction and development efforts and had specific policies addressing youth issues. For instance, OSCE, the European Agency for Reconstruction, and the Stability Pact on South Eastern Europe were all directly involved in youth programming. OSCE in particular was an integral partner in the UNMIK mission and has been on the ground in Kosovo since 1999, working closely with UNHCR, NATO/KFOR forces, and the EU to support the

---

53. Sarah Kenyon Lischer, "Military Intervention and the Humanitarian 'Force Multiplier,'" *Global Governance* 13, no. 1 (2007): 99.

54. Lowicki and Pillsbury, "Making the Choice for a Better Life," 11.

development of democratic institutions, human rights and good governance practices, and ongoing public safety and security. As a part of this mandate, OSCE has helped establish municipal youth assemblies throughout Kosovo, through its Youth Assemblies for Community Development project. The assemblies promote youth capacity building through various educational and vocational training activities and encourage youth participation in local government.

In addition, OSCE partnered with UNMIK's Department of Youth to engage the youth demographic in the ongoing elections activities. "Register Now/ Win Now" concerts, similar to MTV's "Rock the Vote," were held throughout Kosovo to attract attention and increase awareness about the ongoing political events. In 2006, the OSCE mission established a Youth and Education Support Unit, which sponsors programs that promote institution building for higher education, youth employment, civic participation, and empowerment. The Stability Pact for South Eastern Europe has also been actively involved in similar education programming in Kosovo, through its Task Force on Education and Youth.

Foreign aid programs: Western governments, too, paid particular attention to the humanitarian crisis facing Kosovo in the aftermath of the NATO campaign. The United States, with its leading role in NATO, was one of the largest contributors of humanitarian aid in the years immediately after the bombing. The United States and other foreign governments and government organizations, including Canada and the EU, not only donated large sums in humanitarian aid but also sponsored several youth-specific programs during the transition phase. For example, the U.S. State Department Bureau for Population, Refugees, and Migration granted over $3 million to programs dealing with at-risk children and youth during 1999–2000. The bulk of the grants supported the IRC's and the International Medical Corps' efforts to establish youth centers throughout Kosovo and provide psychosocial support to those in need.[55] The USAID Office of Transition Initiatives was also involved in the reconstruction process, providing more than $70,000 to youth-related activities and $750,000 toward establishing a Displaced Children and Orphans Fund. During 1999–2000, the Canadian International Development Agency and the European Community Humanitarian Office each donated between $8 million and $9 million to education programs, including distributing school equipment and textbooks and facilitating the emergency rehabilitation of primary and secondary schools.[56]

But even with the rush to stem the immediate humanitarian crisis following the NATO intervention, international funding, especially for education

---

55. Ibid. The BPRM granted an additional $10 million to the Kosovo Women's Initiative, which supported "women's self-reliance and economic stability," thereby indirectly benefiting children.

56. Ibid.

programming, dwindled after 2002.[57] Whereas USAID committed over $12 million in 1999 and $8.5 million in 2000, the budget was just $75,000 in 2006 and $79,000 in 2007.

Coding

International involvement in Kosovo is rated as having a high-level positive impact. Overall, the international community's various interventions and relief efforts helped stabilize the situation. Also, the degree of involvement by foreign governments and the United Nations was high relative to the situation and successfully met the demands of the situation (at least in the short term). It should be noted that the level of youth programming has not been maintained to the same degree since 2004. But even though the level of funding has declined, the international community remains highly involved in Kosovo's internal affairs.

NGO Involvement: Impact on Youth and Stability

Considering the degree of attention that the crisis in Kosovo received in the Western media, it is not surprising that during 1999–2002, the scene was inundated with international NGOs and donors. This flood of NGOs was able to tap into the already burgeoning youth civil participation and establish a wide range of successful youth programs that cut across political, social, and economic divides. The relatively quick resolution to the violence and the rapid return of refugees to their homes allowed humanitarian workers to take on more development-oriented programming rather than devote most of their time and money to immediate needs such as food, shelter, and medical assistance. However, the culture established in the NGO environment was driven by competition to win grants and attract donors, and as a result, the massive influx of competing international actors unintentionally eroded the existing community structures.[58] While international actors replaced local actors in providing critical community service in the immediate aftermath of the crisis, when the international fund-raising fervor inevitably died down, many of the newly implanted international civil society programs could not sustain their operations, leaving the local structure unable to support the needed programs.

Although the eventual decline in NGO commitment served as a significant setback to the long-term impact of youth empowerment programs, the high degree of attention in the initial years was highly successful, compared to other post-conflict efforts, in addressing the youth population's immediate physical and psychosocial needs and facilitating active youth participation in the

---

57. USAID Transition Initiatives, "Kosovo Program Description," www.usaid.gov/our_work/cross-cutting_programs/transition_initiatives/country/kosovo/kos2000.html (accessed Sept. 1, 2009); USAID, "USAID: Kosovo Budget," www.usaid.gov/policy/budget/cbj2007/ee/ko.html (accessed Sept. 1, 2009).
58. Mertus, "Improving International Peacebuilding Efforts."

reconstruction and peacebuilding process. Despite setbacks in coordination, and competition among NGOs for financing, in the first few months of the refugee crisis a number of successful programs emerged that focused directly on addressing youth needs.[59]

NGO Family Tracing and Psychosocial Programs

Initially, many of the NGOs in the refugee camps set about establishing programs to help families, adolescents, and children reconnect with lost loved ones, cope with the trauma of war, and find things to do in the camps. For example, UNICEF's Child-Friendly Spaces program provided educational and recreational activities, health and psychological care, and information networks to track family members. The Red Cross (ICRC) created the Balkan Family News Network, which helped refugees locate lost family members. And the IRC sponsored the Child Connect and Kosovar Family Finder projects, which contained databases of 20,000 families (approximately 120,000 individuals) and coordinated with Save the Children to provide satellite phone access to children and youth seeking to get in touch with their families.[60] The IRC also implemented a psychosocial support program for refugee youth, which trained young people in how to assist their peers, by hosting workshops and providing information on the common reactions to crisis that so many members of their communities were experiencing.[61] Also, Save the Children began a number of support programs for young people in the Albanian refugee camps, including creative activities such as art and drawing programs. Expositions of the artwork were then held both in the camps and in the International Center of Culture, Albania's contemporary art museum.[62]

NGO Support for Youth-Generated Initiatives

While NGOs provided direct care for children and youth through programs such as Child-Friendly Spaces, many of the youth in the camps were mobilizing on their own to help their communities. Recognizing this potential, NGOs supported these youth-generated initiatives by providing funding and helping young people organize a variety of youth-to-youth community service, education, and reconciliation initiatives.

Community service: One example of youth-driven initiatives is the work of the Albanian Youth Council. Enlisting young refugees looking for an outlet from the boredom and depression in the camps, the Albanian Youth Council mobilized an

---

59. Lowicki and Pillsbury, "Making the Choice for a Better Life."

60. Ibid.

61. Ibid.

62. Ibid.

emergency network of youth groups. The groups were active in the camps, taking responsibility for different projects ranging from organizing concerts and sports tournaments to setting up information tents, providing language courses and hygiene kits for their peers, and starting aid programs for youth with special needs. With organizational support from the IRC, the network grew to include groups in over forty-five camps and cities throughout Kosovo and Albania and would eventually become the Kosovo Youth Council (KYC). The KYC also worked with the UN volunteers to organize the Kosovo Youth Volunteers, to encourage young people to participate in social development and reconciliation programs.[63] Here is one teen's account:

> "The research team I was on [with the Kosovo Youth Council] took action. We did an anti-hate graffiti campaign and painted over hateful ethnic slurs still left written on walls since the war. We helped secondary school students organize student governments. We ran creative classes for Roma girls to try to increase their interest in education; even after we stopped, they showed up every day, wanting more and bringing their sisters along. We worked with the Serb young people on a youth advocacy project. We pushed youth issues with government officials, who were not used to young people taking action or having opinions about their work." (Dafina, 16, on her work with the KYC and the Women's Commission in 1999)[64]

The KYC has continued to operate throughout Kosovo as a voice for the youth demographic and as a coordinating body for youth community service, civil society, and empowerment initiatives. One of the reasons that the KYC has been so successful is that it has striven to include youth representation from all ethnic backgrounds and has become a hub for youth-led tolerance-building activities by providing a space for young adults from different communities to discuss relevant issues, find solutions, and take action in their communities.

Local youth clubs and informal education: Several other youth-generated initiatives emerged after the conflict and partnered with international donors or NGOs. In 2001, Kosovo had 280 youth organizations and clubs, with over 20,000 participants, mostly in the Albanian community.[65] Activities in these organizations included youth-run radio programs, awareness campaigns, and roundtable forums to promote dialogue about current events, youth participation, and tolerance. The IRC and International Medical Corps also established nine youth centers across Kosovo with funding from the U.S. State Department's Bureau for Population, Refugees, and Migration. These youth centers work to promote interethnic contact and serve as an educational and recreational base for many children and young adults, providing a diversity of programs including vocational education and English classes.

Youth-led interethnic dialogue: With ethnic and nationalistic tensions remaining high throughout the post-conflict period, there was a dire need for positive

---

63. Ibid.

64. Women's Commission for Refugee Women and Children, "Youth Speak Out."

65. Ibid.

interaction and dialogue between youth from various ethnic communities. In 2005, students from the University of Pristina, in Kosovo, and the University of Novi Sad, in Serbia, founded the Youth Dialogue Programme (YDP) to promote partnerships among Serbs and Albanians and "build towards the normalization of relations, restoration of trust and reconciliation among young people from Serbia and Kosovo."[66] YDP emphasizes that by being an organization developed by youth, it has a direct perspective on the issues youth face and on the ways young people can help promote reconciliation and cooperation.

Since 2005, over 500 young people have participated in YDP's cooperative activities, ranging from dialogue workshops to concerts and regional conferences on such themes as the position of minority communities in Kosovo and the role of media and interethnic intolerance in the region. YDP also takes an active role in lobbying national and international organizations to promote a better understanding of the problems facing young people in the region and to advocate for a sustainable multiethnic Kosovar society. Most recently, YDP has brought together young people from Kosovo and Serbia to discuss issues related to Kosovo's declaration of independence.[67]

Another example of youth-led interethnic dialogue is the *Graffiti* program on Prishtinë/Priština's Contact Radio, an independent radio station founded by the Prishtinë/Priština based NGO, Civic House. The station offers programming in Albanian, Serbian, and Turkish to "bridg[e] information exchange across ethnic communities."[68] Young people from different ethnic backgrounds work together to organize the *Graffiti* program, both serving as the show's on-air broadcasters (taking turns presenting the show in different languages) and participating "at the highest level of decision-making about programming for the station."[69]

Youth Political and Economic Empowerment

There have also been a number of initiatives aimed at youth political and economic empowerment. For instance, in addition to the UN- and OSCE-sponsored political participation programs such as the Youth Congress and Youth Week, the IRC implemented the Civil Participation Initiative (CPI) to address social and economic recovery for youth. The CPI mobilized youth "corps" to identify problems facing young people in their communities, and then put people in contact with government officials and other community representatives who could help get responses to the identified issues.

---

66. Youth Dialogue Programme, "About Us," http://ydprogramme.org/onamae.htm (accessed Sept. 1, 2009).

67. Youth Dialogue Programme, "YDP Newsletter" 4th ed., July 2008, http://ydprogramme.org/downloads/YDP%20Newsletter%20July%2008.pdf (accessed Sept. 1, 2009).

68. Lowicki and Pillsbury, "Making the Choice for a Better Life."

69. Ibid.

The Kosovo Youth Council is also an active advocate for youth involvement in local decision-making processes and has worked with the Women's Commission for Refugee Women and Children to research and raise awareness about youth issues and the importance of youth participation and consultation in the reconstruction and development process. With youth and children representing over half the population in Kosovo, initiating dialogue between young people and local leaders so that they may consider youth perspectives on legislation and local policy may prove essential for Kosovo's future.

Continued community engagement and dialogue between young people of different ethnicities and religions is essential to the long-term reconstruction and reconciliation process. As these examples demonstrate, young people have been a driving force behind reconstruction efforts, implementing community service, education, media, political advocacy, and reconciliation programs. These programs and organizations are not solely for the benefit of young people. They extend also to the greater community and directly affect the overarching reconstruction and reconciliation process by promoting mutual cooperation and advocating that youth voices be consulted in national and regional policy.

NGO Impact and the Decline of Volunteerism

The broad range of youth programming had tremendous success in the years immediately after the 1999 crisis, helping provide many youth refugees with both the support they needed and the opportunity to participate in projects beneficial to the entire community. But most of these programs were funded with emergency humanitarian funds and couldn't survive when international interest and funding dried up. For example, in 1999, thirty-one youth centers sprang up all over the province, supported by various international donors. But within a few years, the international enthusiasm to fund reconstruction efforts died down, so that by 2006, nearly all these youth centers had closed due to lack of funding or were completely dysfunctional.[70]

Youth participation and volunteerism has also declined. Whereas youth participation was very high in 1999 and 2000, especially in initiating peacebuilding and community-building programs, in 2006 only 6.3 percent of youth surveyed reported that they were participating in NGO projects or youth initiatives. However, more than three times as many of the youth surveyed, 21.7 percent, reported having participated in protests.

The decline in the ethos of volunteerism and community development that was so prevalent throughout the 1990s and in the immediate aftermath of the 1999 crisis was due in part to the atmosphere created by international organizations and NGOs. The community participation that had flourished as part of the Kosovar Albanian resistance evolved into an institutionalized culture of volun-

---

70. UNDP, "Youth: A New Generation for a New Kosovo."

teerism that functioned with the support of only a few NGOs. But as the 1998–99 crisis gained attention in the international media, many NGOs saw Kosovo as an opportunity to gain humanitarian market share. The tide of international organizations and NGOs into the region created an intensely competitive atmosphere as organizations fought each other to win grants from the dominant international donors. The donors' preference to sponsor iNGOs or a few well-established local agencies created an imbalance in the labor market, favoring the international NGOs over the existing community networks and structures. As these international agencies and NGOs took over the reins in providing the resources that volunteer structures were previously responsible for, they removed the need for grassroots efforts. As a result, the NGOs not only created tension between local and international actors but also inadvertently eroded the social structures that had supported an ethos of community service and "effectively ended the period of institutional volunteerism."[71]

Other factors also contributed to the decline in participation. The spirit of volunteerism was primarily a solidarity movement against the discrimination suffered under the Milošević regime. With the immediate threat removed, it is not surprising to see a drop in volunteer activities. Still the role of NGOs in contributing to this steep decline should not be discounted. In addition to taking over the role that the volunteer community had filled during the conflict, a significant part of the population was discouraged by the lack of transparency in NGO operations or felt that their contributions were no longer valued during the reconstruction efforts. Most notably, many teachers and educators who had been highly active and were even considered heroes during the conflict felt ignored by the international organizations and NGOs, because they were rarely consulted in developing the reconstruction policies and programs.[72]

According to the 2006 Human Development Report in Kosovo, this apparent change in the spirit of civic and community participation is especially evident in the level of youth participation. Among many Kosovar youth today there is a marked sense of apathy, and most youth report that they believe they do not have any real power to effect positive changes in their communities.[73] While the decline in Kosovo's youth participation corresponds with similar trends in neighboring transitional democracies, the impact of the international community is especially distinct in Kosovo.

Coding

NGO involvement in Kosovo is rated as having a low-level positive impact. The positive rating reflects that NGOs were largely helpful in establishing a secure

---

71. Ibid.

72. Sommers and Buckland, "Negotiating Kosovo's Educational Minefield."

73. Ferizi and Sad, "Youth Despair of Decent Future in Kosovo"; UNDP, "Youth: A New Generation for a New Kosovo."

environment and catering to youth needs. However, the low level of impact reflects both the degree to which coordination and competition issues detracted from the overall success and the relatively short-term nature of the funding or operation of NGOs.

Domestic Policy: Education Reform and Combating Youth Unemployment

With the ongoing transfer of power from the UNMIK operation to the Kosovar Assembly, local decision makers are faced with the ongoing dilemma of how to address the needs of Kosovo's disproportionately large youth demographic. In particular, local politicians have emphasized the importance of solving the widespread trend of youth unemployment. Education also remains a priority, but the groundswell to resolve curriculum and quality-of-education issues, especially on the university level, has turned into a proxy battle of ethnic nationalism. While international organizations are working with domestic policymakers to strengthen the education program, the reduction in international funding and the politicization of education issues continue to hamper the growth of educational institutions.

Kosovo's Struggle with Youth Unemployment

The stagnant economy and alarming levels of unemployment in Kosovo have kept local politicians occupied, and the disproportionately large number of youth affected is especially worrisome. With increased rates of youth criminality following the war, there is a significant fear among elites that a large population of unemployed youth could militate against efforts toward peace and reignite the ethnic tensions of the past decade.[74] Employment is not simply a way for youth to earn a living and keep out of mischief. Having a job can provide a sense of purpose—a sense that one has a place in society, and the opportunity to grow within it. Without the prospect of employment, many young people may feel marginalized from a society that appears to be making decisions for them, and they may turn to other methods for inclusion. This may mean finding other ways to earn money, such as crime, drugs, and the black market. But in Kosovo's case, ethnic, religious, and national identity provides a particularly strong way to find that missing sense of inclusion and community.

Despite the international community's efforts to stimulate Kosovo's economy, unemployment across the board has continued to rise in recent years, especially among youth. While economic growth has been lagging across the nation, there are a number of reasons why youth are particularly affected. A majority of university graduates in Kosovo aspire to work in public administration, since

---

74. UNDP, "Youth: A New Generation for a New Kosovo"; Lowicki and Pillsbury, "Making the Choice for a Better Life."

public-sector jobs are seen as one of the few promising career avenues, and many young Kosovars see the opportunity as a way to become involved in the process of creating a modern Kosovo.[75] However, the current administration has shown a degree of conservatism and distrust toward the youth demographic, indicating that it is not yet ready for the younger generation to become a major force in public administration.[76] Also, most entry-level positions require English language proficiency and computer skills, which, thanks to the poor quality of education, most Kosovar youth do not have.[77] As a result, many young people have withdrawn from attempts to seek employment in Kosovo and see their futures as dependent on getting out of Kosovo, at least temporarily.[78] (For more on the broad impact of the "exit option," see the following section, "Cultural Context.") This frustration was evident in a roundtable discussion with youth from Rahovec/Orahovac:

> Public employment services do not perform any concrete and useful function for facilitating youth employment. There is little information available that could guide us in regards to possible occupations, qualification level, and geographical distribution. Also, training capacity is limited at most of them, which in turn limits the number of young people who can benefit.[79]

To address the chronic youth unemployment, in 2006 local policymakers collaborated with the ILO to create the Youth Employment Action Plan in Kosovo for 2007–10. The Action Plan identifies obstacles to youth employment and sets key priorities for improvement. These include decreasing the primary school dropout rate; increasing the span of vocational education curriculum and opportunities to participate in vocational education programs; improving access to information, education, and career guidance; increasing entrepreneurship and startup businesses; decreasing the number of youth in the informal economy; and increasing the number of youth registered in public employment services.[80] The total cost of the plan for programs addressing these priorities is $17.1 million. While the government of Kosovo has committed to cover one-third of these costs, international donations must cover the rest.[81] The Kosovo Youth Action Plan, a similar measure intended to address a number of issues facing young Kosovars, also dedicates the majority of its $13.9 million budget to measures stimulating youth employment.

---

75. UNDP, "Youth: A New Generation for a New Kosovo."

76. Ibid.

77. Ibid.

78. Ferizi and Sad, "Youth Despair of Decent Future in Kosovo."

79. UNDP, "Youth: A New Generation for a New Kosovo."

80. Ibid.

81. Ibid.

Vocational Education

Kosovo's leaders have acknowledged that improving the education system, particularly the quality and availability of vocational education, is integral to improving the quality of the workforce and combating the ongoing trend of youth unemployment. However, a drastic reduction in the level of international funding jeopardizes the prospects for continued improvements in the education system. International funding for education in 2004 (approximately US$2.8 million) was only one-twentieth the funding committed in 2000.[82] While the Kosovo Assembly has tried to compensate by increasing gross spending on education from the Consolidated Budget, the percentage of the national budget spent on education actually *decreased* from 20 percent to 14 percent during 2000–4. Although this proportion of education spending is par for nations that entered the EU before 2007, the education systems in those other countries were already well established and also receive significant funding from other public and private sources. In Kosovo, the funding from the Consolidated Budget is essentially the only funding provided to rebuild the entire education system. Moreover, because Kosovo has the highest proportion of schoolchildren in Europe, the shortfall is even more severe.[83] Kosovo's leaders have committed to increasing the percentage of the national budget spent on education to 16 percent by 2009, but funding remains a significant obstacle to the quality of education and to alleviating the unemployment crisis.

Reforming Institutions of Higher Education

The quality and accessibility of higher education also remains a significant issue facing young Kosovars, since the university system has become central to the ongoing nationalist rivalries between Kosovar Serbs and Kosovar Albanians. Kosovo has one main university, the University of Prishtinë/Priština, in the city of Prishtinë/Priština, where the official language of education is Albanian (although, legally, classes may be taught in other languages). In 2001, another university was established, in the predominantly Kosovar-Serb town of Mitrocië/Mitrovica, where all instruction is in Serbian. The university was immediately caught up in interethnic politics and the issue of unresolved national status. For Serbs, the university was a source of pride and a show of Serbian authority in the government administration. For Albanians, the establishment of the University, with UNMIK's backing, was an infringement on Kosovo's national territory, and a clear demonstration that UNMIK supported Serbian parallel institutions.[84] Consequently, the draft statute of the university—essentially the university's application for incorporation into the Kosovar education system—was rejected in 2004, and the university continues to rely on the Serbian gov-

---

82. Ibid.

83. UNDP, "Youth: A New Generation for a New Kosovo."

84. Kostovicova, *Kosovo: The Politics of Identity and Space* (London: Routledge, 2005).

ernment for most of its funding.[85] The ethnic division between the universities not only perpetuates community tensions by using the parallel education systems as a political battleground for nationalist agendas, it also reduces the possibility for successful reform to improve the quality of higher education in the near future.[86]

The poor quality and inaccessibility of higher education is an immediate obstacle to youth employment and empowerment. The same lack of funding and resources that hinders curriculum reform on the mandatory levels of education also plagues higher education, where the quality of instruction is particularly poor by European standards. Only 12 percent of university-age students are enrolled in higher education—a rate one-quarter the average for OECD countries.[87] This is largely due to the insufficient capacity of the institutions to admit students. The University of Prishtinë/Priština can admit only one-third of applicants.[88] A number of local and international actors have developed plans to improve the capacity of higher education, with at least seven different education reform strategies introduced for 2005–17.[89] But none of these multiple efforts were coordinated to maximize the impact, and little is being done to measure their success.[90]

Coding

Domestic policy in Kosovo is coded as having a low-level positive impact. Overall, the domestic policy's orientation toward addressing issues such as youth unemployment and education reform has helped create an environment more conducive to stability. However, the low level of success reflects the domestic policy's relative impact on the reconstruction process and the overall lack of success in addressing these issues.

Cultural Context: Youth's "Exit Option"

One of the most important differences between the sub-Saharan African cases and Kosovo is the perceived possibility of leaving one's country to find a better life. Because of the ongoing uncertainty over Kosovo's status, the poor quality of education, and rampant unemployment, many young Kosovars have withdrawn

---

85. Ibid.

86. Ibid.

87. UNDP, "Youth: A New Generation for a New Kosovo."

88. Ibid.

89. These include the Pre-university Education Strategy, 2007–2017; Planning Strategy for the Development of Education, Science and Technology, 2007–2013; High Education Development Strategy in Kosovo, 2005–2015; Strategy for the Education of Rural Population; Gender Strategy; Youth Policy of Kosovo; and Kosovo Development Strategy Plan, 2007–2013. Ibid.

90. Ibid.

from the political scene, expressing apathy toward their country's future development. These young people feel that their future success depends on leaving home.[91] In fact, half of Kosovo's youth (across all ethnic groups) have stated that they would emigrate if they could.[92] Most of those responding said they wanted to leave because of their economic situation (41 percent) or to create a better life for themselves (38 percent), while 10 percent said they wanted to find a better education.[93] While EU visa restrictions have limited freedom of movement, making moving abroad difficult for youth in Kosovo and other Eastern European transition states, the possibility of moving abroad remains an option that many young people believe is available.[94] The following comments give a sense of young Kosovars' frustrations over the lack of educational and economic opportunity:

> "I can't take this anymore! I have simply stopped thinking about what's around me. . . . I definitely need to move away for five years." (Eremire Krasniquq, 22, sociology student)[95]

> "Now I am back, I want to make use of the quality education I got and which in Kosovo I lacked ever since primary school." (Arber Dormi, master's graduate from the London School of Economics)[96]

> "For the moment I'm thinking I want to stay and build my future in Kosovo, but I definitely feel isolated." (Miodrag Pantović, student)[97]

> "People in our municipality—men and women, in particular young ones—have traditionally been zealous workers. But unemployment has now touched everyone. We, the youth, are the most affected by it. In these conditions, the only solution is that instead of being unemployed in Kosovo, it is better to emigrate to the West." (Member of roundtable discussion in Rahovec/Orahovac)[98]

This "exit option" is especially important in understanding the rise of youth apathy toward the current situation in Kosovo. Whereas in post-conflict situations in sub-Saharan Africa or other more isolated regions, youth typically may not see leaving the country as the main avenue or realistic alternative to better their lives, for youth in Kosovo the option to emigrate as a strategy for success is quite tangible. The unresolved status of Kosovo's independence for the eight years following the conflict may also have added to these feelings of stagnation and apathy, since the frustration that young people felt observing the slow transition

---

91. Ferizi and Sad, "Youth Despair of Decent Future in Kosovo"; UNDP, "Youth: A New Generation for a New Kosovo."

92. UNDP, "Youth: A New Generation for a New Kosovo."

93. Ibid.

94. For more information on freedom of movement, see International Crisis Group, "EU Visas and the Western Balkans," *Europe Report*, no. 168 (2005), www.crisisgroup.org/home/index.cfm?id=3809 (accessed Sept. 1, 2009).

95. Ferizi and Sad, "Youth Despair of Decent Future in Kosovo."

96. Ibid.

97. Ibid.

98. UNDP, "Youth: A New Generation for a New Kosovo."

to independence is integrally related to their frustrations in the everyday experiences of transition into adult life in Kosovo. While Kosovo was in statehood limbo, many of its young people were unable to begin their transition into adult life through the usual mechanisms, such as going to university or getting a job and supporting their families. However, with Kosovo's declaration of independence in February 2008, these sentiments may change. Whether they change for better or worse, however, remains unclear. Independence may increase freedom of movement, allowing more young people to emigrate, and it may also support Kosovo's developing economy, increasing the availability of jobs and education opportunities.

Coding
Cultural and environmental factors are coded as having a low-level positive impact on youth and stability. The "exit option"—that is, fleeing Kosovo—seems to have suppressed some of the potential youth aggression that could have adversely affected stability. However, the beneficial effect is coded as low-level, because the "exit option" has also contributed to the apathy that has eroded youth community participation.

Dependent Variable: Level of Stability as Related to Youth

After the 1999 NATO air campaign, there was a relatively quick end to the violence in Kosovo. Refugees and internally displaced persons returned quickly to their homes, and NATO/KFOR forces took on the responsibility of policing the international protectorate. While violence has not climbed back to the level that consumed Kosovo during the period leading up to the NATO bombing, ethnic tensions remain markedly high in the region. These tensions were largely due to Kosovo's uncertain status following the NATO campaign. When Kosovo was made an international protectorate temporarily under UN control, the question of independence at the heart of the conflict was left unresolved. Keeping Kosovo as an international protectorate for longer than necessary was intolerable for both sides because the vast majority of Kosovar Albanians were unsatisfied without a declaration of full independence from Serbia, whereas Kosovar Serbs remained loyal to their home country, refusing to accept the possibility of Kosovo's secession.

Ethnic Tension
The dynamics between the Kosovar Albanians, Kosovar Serbs, and other ethnic minorities have remained tense in the years following the conflict, as the following comments attest:

"Can we live with the Serbs? Never!"
"But some of them helped us get to safety."
"No, no, you can't trust any of them." (Albanian youth focus group discussion, Tirana, Albania, June 1999)[99]

"Never can we live together with Albanians."
"Why not? We were friends before, we could be friends again."
"They killed and raped us; how can we live with them?"
"It is difficult now, but perhaps for future generations, yes. If it happens it will be the youth who will make it possible." (Adolescent-led Serbian youth focus group discussions, Kosovo, June 2000)[100]

While there have been instances of isolated violence, most of the tension has emerged through largely peaceful protests. Despite the sense of apathy among youth as a result of the political and economic stagnation,[101] a number of these protests over Kosovo's political status were led by university students seeking to draw the attention of international actors. For instance, in 2006, students protested against plans to decentralize Kosovo, which would include forming two municipalities in the ethnically divided town of Mitrocië/Mitrovica.[102] In October 2007, students at the University of Prishtinë/Priština gathered to protest the delays to Kosovo's independence. In a peaceful rally, the leader of the student union that organized the event said, "We must inform the local and international opinion that Kosova cannot wait anymore, that students cannot wait anymore."[103]

Riots

While these protests were largely peaceful, there has been one major exception: the violent riots that broke out in March 2004. Sensationalistic media coverage falsely reporting that Serbs were responsible for the drowning of three ethnically Albanian boys is largely acknowledged to be the spark that ignited the riots.[104] The tragic events and the following biased media coverage reignited ethnic tensions still boiling beneath the surface.

The 2004 riots took place over forty-eight hours beginning on March 17. At least twenty-two riots broke out with an estimated 51,000 protestors. Over

---

99. Lowicki and Pillsbury, "Making the Choice for a Better Life."

100. Ibid.

101. Ferizi and Sad, "Youth Despair of Decent Future in Kosovo."

102. Mina News Agency, "Pristina Students Protest against Decentralization of Kosovo," BBC Monitoring Worldwide, May 3, 2006.

103. KosovaLive, "Kosovo Albanian Students Rally in Support of Independence," BBC Worldwide Monitoring, Oct. 10, 2007.

104. Other circumstances also contributed to the frustration. In the weeks leading up to the riots, many Kosovar Albanians were angry because Kosovar Serbs, who were protesting the murder of a Serb teenager by an unknown attacker, had blocked off the main Prishtinë/Priština–Skopje road. And on March 16, KLA veterans held a demonstration to protest the arrest of former KLA leaders on charges of war crimes. Human Rights Watch, "Kosovo: Failure of NATO, U.N. to Protect Minorities," *Human Rights Watch News*, July 26, 2004, www.hrw.org/en/news/2004/07/26/kosovo-failure-nato-un-protect-minorities (accessed Aug. 1, 2009).

the course of the violence, 19 people died and 900 were wounded. At least 550 homes and 27 orthodox churches were burned, mostly in Kosovar Serb communities, and 4,100 persons from minority communities were displaced from their homes.[105] KFOR and UNMIK were unable to handle the situation and lost much credibility due to their weak and disorganized response to the violence. The explosiveness of the riots demonstrates the high degree of latent tension that has continued to affect daily life in Kosovo and the potential that tension has to flare into mob violence.

Crime and Sex Trafficking

With the exception of the 2004 riots, there has been no widespread reincitation of the conflict. However, ongoing insecurity remains a significant issue. Since 1999, Kosovo has seen an increase in both sex trafficking and crime. In the years directly following the 1999 campaign, the refugee and minority populations were especially vulnerable to crime and kidnapping, and youth criminality, particularly in the Albanian community, has become an increasing problem. From January to August 2000, youth age 10 to 25 were responsible for 27.6 percent of a total 24,338 offenses ranging from theft and criminal traffic violations to rape and murder.[106] Many youth admit to carrying weapons for self-defense purposes, such as protecting themselves against gangs or kidnappers.

Kidnapping and sex trafficking has also become a significant security concern facing young women in Kosovo. The majority of women subject to sex trafficking are brought into Kosovo from surrounding countries. However, increasing numbers of Kosovar women and young girls are internally trafficked, and cases have been documented of girls as young as 11 being sold into sexual slavery in Kosovo. Below, a young girl shares her fears of being kidnapped:

> "I was near my house on my way to school, which is about 100 meters from my home. Suddenly, a black car appeared, and three men wearing black masks opened the door and tried to pull me into the car. I screamed for help, and my neighbors and parents stepped outside. The men got away, even though KFOR soldiers were not far away. . . . The car with the masked men came back again another day, outside my friend's house. . . . I didn't report what happened to the police. I was afraid to. I am afraid of the kidnappers and afraid of what Albanians might do if I report such an incident." (Egyptian adolescent girl living in Gjilan/Gnjilane)[107]

The growth of the market in Kosovo for prostitution and sex trafficking has been linked to the large international population, particularly NATO and UN personnel.[108] Amnesty International reported in 2004 that international personnel

---

105. Ibid.

106. Lowicki and Pillsbury, "Making the Choice for a Better Life."

107. Ibid.

108. Amnesty International, "Kosovo (Serbia and Montenegro): "So Does It Mean That We Have Rights?" Protecting the Human Rights of Women and Girls Trafficked for Forced Prostitution in Kosovo,"

make up 20 percent of the people exploiting trafficked women and girls, even though the international demographic makes up only 2 percent of Kosovo's population.[109] While many of the alleged perpetrators have been dismissed from their positions in UNMIK, UN personnel are immune from prosecution in Kosovo, and many have escaped criminal proceedings in their home countries.[110]

Outside Indicators of Stability

The uncertainty of the situation in Kosovo is reflected in the mixed ratings it receives for various stability indicators. While the level of violence is relatively low, with widespread ethnic and political tensions and increased crime, insecurity in Kosovo has remained a fact of daily life.

- On the 2007 Global Peace Index, Serbia received an overall score of 2.181 on a scale of 1 to 5 (1 being most peaceful), ranking 88th most peaceful of 121 countries.[111] While Serbia received, on the same scale, a 2 for level of organized internal conflict, it earned 3s across the board for political instability, likelihood of violent demonstration, level of violent crime, potential for terrorist acts, and citizens' level of distrust in other citizens.[112]
- On the Failed States Index, Serbia is rated at "warning" level for 2005–07, largely due to the situation in Kosovo. In 2007, Serbia ranked 66th most likely to fail of 177 countries; in 2006, it ranked 55th of 146 countries. According to the Failed States Index country profile, tensions between ethnic Albanians and Serbs in Kosovo remain high, and the tension between Albanian and Serbian political parties contributed to the high risk subscore for "factionalized elites." In addition, the subscores for corruption and unemployment, along with the high risk of unrest should Kosovo declare independence, were significant factors in Serbia's "warning" rating.[113]
- RiskMap 2008 rates Kosovo as a high political risk and a medium security risk.[114]

May 5, 2004, www.amnesty.org/en/library/info/EUR70/010/2004 (accessed Sept. 9, 2009); BBC, "Kosovo UN Troops 'Fuel Sex Trade,'" BBC News, May 6, 2004.

109. Amnesty International, "So Does It Mean That We Have Rights?"

110. Ibid.

111. Because Kosovo was not officially declared a country until February 2008, most of the data examining peace and stability there is couched within the context of Serbia.

112. All the Global Peace Indexes cited are ranked on a scale of (1) very low to (5) very high by Economist Intelligence Unit analysts. Each index is a qualitative assessment of the intensity or level of the specific attribute being measured. The GPI adds, "The lowest score (1) records that the majority of other people can be trusted and that there is an overall positive climate of trust in the country. The highest score (5) indicates that people are extremely cautious in dealing with others." Vision of Humanity, "Serbia: Global Peace Index, 2007," www.visionofhumanity.org/gpi/results/serbia/2007/ (accessed Sept. 1, 2009).

113. Fund for Peace, "Failed States Index," www.fundforpeace.org/web/index.php?option=com_content&task=view&id=99&Itemid=140 (accessed Sept. 1, 2009).

114. RiskMap 2008 assesses the level of political and security risks for businesses looking to operate in foreign countries. The political risk rating gauges "the likelihood of state or non-state political actors

- The Economist Intelligence Unit reports from 2000 to 2008 show high political tensions over the status of Kosovo. With the exception of the riots in 2004 and increasing levels of violence and insecurity in 2003, the insecurity is framed largely in the political context and the potential for the explosion of violence rather than in ongoing hostilities.[115]

These analyses indicate that while violence has been kept at relatively low to medium levels in Kosovo, insecurity and ethnic tensions remain a serious obstacle to long-term peace. In particular, the ongoing uncertainty over the status of independence had perpetuated the everyday tension and the security issues, particularly those facing ethnic minorities. Protests are common in Kosovo, both in the five years immediately after the conflict and today. Though most of these protests remain peaceful, the 2004 riots demonstrate just how quickly tensions in Kosovo can boil over to a potential reincitation of the conflict. While many youth-led organizations are actively contributing to peacebuilding and tolerance efforts, youth have also played a significant role in the ongoing instability, specifically in organizing and participating both in peaceful protests and in violent riots.

Kosovo's declaration of independence on February 17, 2008, further complicates security and stability issues there. The declaration incited a number of peaceful protests as well as violent riots among the Serb population. While 150,000 people gathered in a nonviolent protest in Belgrade, crowds later looted and set fire to the U.S. and other Western government embassies, killing one person, and Serb protestors in Bosnia attacked the U.S. consulate in Banja Luka. While the initial violence was perhaps inevitable and protests still occur regularly, the violence has not been sustained. Serbian Prime Minister Vojislav Koštunica said of the peaceful protests following the declaration of independence, "Above all, the youth of Serbia have sent out a message that they want law, justice and freedom, and that they reject the western policy of force."[116] The peaceful rallies on both sides are significant indicators of restraint and the potential for a nonviolent resolution in Kosovo; however, Kosovar Albanian-Serb relations have remained strained throughout Kosovo's first year of independence, and the fate of the independent state of Kosovo remains to be seen.[117]

---

negatively affecting business operations in a country," whereas the security risk rating gauges the likelihood of "state or non-state actors engaging in actions that harm the financial, physical and human assets of a company." Control Risks Group, *RiskMap 2008*.

115. Economist Intelligence Unit, "Country Report: Serbia," 2000–2008, www.eiu.com (subscription only, accessed Sept. 1, 2009).

116. B92 News, www.b92.net/eng/news/politics-article.php?yyyy=2008&mm=02&dd=22&nav_id=47900 (accessed Sept. 1, 2009).

117. Much of the violence immediately following the independence announcement was in areas surrounding Kosovo or in Kosovar Serbian enclaves in Kosovo, but not necessarily throughout Kosovo proper. However, the violence in Serbia and other surrounding areas is significant for Kosovo's stability, and as of this writing, many protests and violent clashes between Kosovar Serbs and Kosovar Albanians have also taken place in the newly established country.

Coding

Kosovo is rated has having a medium level of instability. This rating reflects the incidences of politically motivated violence, along with the ongoing tensions that continue to threaten the success of the reconstruction and transition process. However, since significant progress toward peace has been made and widespread violence has not emerged, the situation does not reflect a high or extreme level of instability.

Summary of Variables' Impact

Tables 4.1 through 4.7 summarize the information in this chapter, synthesizing the details in each variable and showing its impact on the youth demographic and the general level of stability in Kosovo. Tables 4.1 through 4.5 address independent variables, and tables 4.6 and 4.7 address dependent variables.

Conclusion

The extraordinarily high proportion of youth in Kosovo's population, combined with high unemployment, poor quality of the education system, and continued political uncertainty, could have been disastrous for the reconstruction process. But as table 4.5 shows, while tensions remain high, widespread violence and instability have been kept at bay. Three main factors help explain this precarious balance.

- International organizations' success in providing aid quelled the potentially explosive potential of the youth demographic while also tapping young people's potential to rebuild their society in the immediate aftermath of war.
- However, the short-term nature of the aid programs limited the impact of youth programming and caused a number of unintended negative consequences for young people, particularly in the delay of education reforms and the atrophy of the culture of volunteerism.
- Cultural and environmental factors, including the ongoing uncertainty over independence, prolonged unemployment, and the opportunity to leave Kosovo to seek a better life, complicate youth attitudes and behaviors.

The initial successes of the international community were largely responsible for curbing the potential danger of the disproportionate youth demographic (see tables 4.1 and 4.2). International organizations, regional security groups, and NGOs, using specific programs dedicated to youth empowerment, worked together to meet young people's needs during the initial humanitarian crisis, to empower youth to become constructive actors in their communities, and to provide forums for young voices to contribute to reconstruction dialogue. In fact, in the immediate aftermath of the conflict, young people were a significant part of the reconstruction process, providing aid to refugees and war-torn communities.

Table 4.1. Kosovo: International Involvement

Variables	Program Specifics	Impact
Foreign Governments	• Humanitarian aid and development initiatives, many with programs specifically for youth • Regional security groups highly involved in broad range of youth-oriented activities, ranging from meeting critical needs to empowerment programming	High positive impact
United Nations	• Humanitarian and refugee reintegration • Youth empowerment programming—political and social • Education reform • Involvement in sexual abuse, trafficking	High positive impact with programs despite negative impact of sexual abuse
Time Frame	• Short to medium term • Highly effective during this time • Potential for international community to remain in charge of Kosovo as a protectorate and uncertainty of future status contributes to increasing tension between Kosovar-Albanian and Kosovar-Serb communities	Medium positive impact
Overall Effectiveness		**High positive impact**

Table 4.2. Kosovo: NGO Involvement

Variables	Program Specifics	Impact
Coordination	• Inter-NGO competition drives programming, erodes local structures, and overpowers some coordination efforts	Medium negative impact
Types of Programming	• Psychosocial support • Reunification • Reintegration • Youth empowerment—political and social • Humanitarian	High positive impact, especially in short term
Level of Efforts (number of NGOs and international personnel)	• High, but the overwhelming presence of international organizations indirectly damages existing community service structures	Medium positive impact
Time Frame	• Short term, driven by emergency humanitarian funding • Drop-off in funding after first three years is a serious obstacle to continued progress on education reform and youth empowerment	Medium negative impact
Overall Effectiveness		**Low positive impact**

Table 4.3. Kosovo: Domestic Policy

Variables	Program Specifics	Impact
Focus on Youth	• Acute awareness of importance of addressing youth issues	Medium positive impact
Types of Programming	• Education reform • Unemployment recovery plans	Low positive impact
Overall Effectiveness		**Low positive impact**

Table 4.4. Kosovo: Cultural and Environmental Factors

Variables	Role	Impact
Exit Option	• Option to emigrate alters youth's decision-making logic	Unclear, both for positive impact of dampening youth aggression and for negative impact of promoting apathy
Overall Effectiveness		**Low positive impact**

Table 4.5. Kosovo: Demographic and Objective Standards

Population age 10–24	• 60% of population under age 25 • 21% of population between age 15–25 • 65% of population under age 30 • Total population (2001): 2.4 million
	Baseline • Average for eastern Europe: 34.5% under age 25; 15.9% age 15–25 (2000)
Level of Youth Participation	• 10–20% of KLA forces were under age 18 (1999)
Unemployment	• Youth unemployment rate (2004): 63%
	Baseline • Average for eastern Europe: 15.3% (2002)
GNI per Capita	• For Serbia: US$3,490.0* (2005) * Kosovo is one of the least developed areas of Serbia; therefore, GNI is lower than in Serbia overall
	Baseline • Average for Europe and Central Asia: US$3,968.10 (2005)
Overall Coding	• **Extremely high proportion of youth in the population**

Kosovo population statistics taken from UNMIK, "Kosovo State of the Environment Report," 2002, http://enrin.grida.no/htmls/kosovo/SoE/index.htm (accessed Sept. 1, 2009); baseline population statistics taken from U.S. Census Bureau, "International Data Base"; baseline of youth unemployment taken from United Nations, "The Millennium Development Goals Report 2007"; baseline for GNI per capita taken from World Bank, "Key Development Data and Statistics."

Figure 4.6. Kosovo: Level of Instability

Overall Description of Stability	• Significant drop in violence after conflict, but tensions remain high due to uncertainty over independence • Isolated violent rioting • Sex trafficking • Low levels of violence and crime
Youth Involvement	• Youth participation both in peaceful activities and in violent riots/protests
Youth's Effects on Overall Level of Instability	Medium level of instability, with youth contributing to both peaceful and violent protests, ongoing latent tensions and grievances among youth, who constitute an extremely high proportion of population

Table 4.7 Kosovo: Supporting Indicators of Level of Instability

Global Peace Index * For Serbia	• 2.181 on a scale of 1–5 (1 = most peaceful)
Failed States Index * For Serbia	• "Warning" level • 55th most vulnerable to collapse or conflict in 2006, out of 146 countries
RiskMap 2008	• High political risk • Medium security risk

And although activism has declined over time, dedicated youth remain active players in Kosovo's civil society.

The high level of international involvement was initially positive, helping many youth contribute to community development. But the short-term donor-driven programming has been a serious impediment to continued progress in education and youth programming and has had the indirect effect of damaging the existing community structures. Before the 1999 conflict, Kosovo citizens, particularly Kosovar Albanians, held strong traditions of rallying as a community in peaceful resistance against decades of discriminatory rule. But during reconstruction, the dominance of international actors at the expense of local participation alienated many citizens, and the same sentiment has not developed as much within the current youth population. The absence of Serbian control removes some of the motive for resistance and undoubtedly affects this altered sentiment. And yet, the fact that a majority of youth feel they cannot make a difference in their communities—and, moreover, would leave Kosovo if they could—speaks to the depth of the change.

Cultural and environmental factors further complicate the situation. (See table 4.3.) Although young people's future potential for success in Kosovo is hampered by the stagnant economy, and the uncertainty over independence has been a serious source of frustration, the possibility to leave Kosovo fundamentally alters their self-understanding as Kosovar citizens, as well as their decision-making logic on how (or whether) to participate in their communities.

Kosovo's declaration of independence in 2008 marks a turning point in the reconstruction process. Although there were a few isolated instances of rioting and low-level criminality, Kosovo has emerged rather well from the transition process. While the reconstruction actors were faced with an extremely large youth population, the high level of efforts designed specifically for that demographic across a wide range of key functions tapped into the youth potential to serve as active peacebuilders. But because of their short-term nature, these programs may not have the lasting impact that youth empowerment programming is intended to create. In 2009, a year after declaring its independence, Kosovo seems to have secured its status as an interdependent country. However, relations with Serbia and other regional actors remain tense, and, as evidenced by the peaceful protests and the violent riots that followed the declaration, the potential is there for either peaceful resolution or reincitation of the conflict.

Although the youth demographic's potential to derail the reconstruction process was largely avoided, unemployment and poor access to education remain largely unresolved issues. Thus, we see the same recipe today that spelled disaster in 1999: a large youth population facing increasing unemployment and frustration. And without a sustained effort by the international community to help the newly established Kosovar government handle these issues, instability may again flare into something much worse.

5

Cross-Case Analysis and Implications for Future Research

"We agree that we have destroyed this country. And it is us—the young people—that should be empowered to rebuild our communities. . . . We need basic training to make this country good again. It can't be the NGOs that do all the work for us. It has to be us." (Young man, 18, Liberia)[1]

"Although sometimes it seems as if things haven't changed much, I know they really have because I myself have changed. With my friends, we have made a big difference in Kosova. I used to see young people as only a simple part of the population, a part of everyday life. Today I see that young people have one of the most important political, educational and cultural roles in the community of a nation." (Dafina, 16, Kosovo)[2]

As these two young voices attest, many youth in post-conflict societies actively seek ways to become constructive members of their communities and help rebuild their nations. While most scholars and policymakers focus solely on young people's potential for violence, youth are, in fact, dynamic agents of change, pushing their societies in both directions: toward violence and toward peace. The following comparative case analysis reveals new insights into these youth roles during and after conflict. In each of these cases, the evidence suggests that the youth demographic's role is largely contextual, based on the efficiency of reconstruction programs in meeting youth needs, on how and in what sequence these programs are implemented, and on how well reconstruction actors understand the situation on the ground.

While this evidence strongly suggests a more complicated model of a large youth population's impact than currently exists, the observations drawn from the cross-case comparison are not conclusive. Rather, these hypotheses point to gaps in our understanding of the youth demographic's real impact during war-to-peace transitions. Further research in these areas will result in more concrete findings and establish "best practices" for addressing youth needs during reconstruction processes.

---

1. Vidar Ekehaug and Chernor Bah, "'Will You Listen?' Young Voices from Conflict Zones," report, www.unicef.org/publications/index_41267.html (accessed Sept. 1, 2009).
2. Women's Commission for Refugee Women and Children, "Youth Speak Out."

The three case studies of Mozambique, the Democratic Republic of the Congo, and Kosovo all show how important young people are in a reconstruction process. Although the dominant literature predicts that youth will have a negative or disruptive impact, these cases suggest that the youth role is not predetermined. In each case, the impact of the youth demographic, whether positive or negative, depended on the success of various policies and programs in addressing certain key issues, including protection, reintegration, education, and empowerment. Young people in Kosovo's refugee camps, child soldiers in the DRC, and street children in Mozambique had dramatically different experiences. Moreover, in each case, reconstruction actors used a variety of different approaches, ranging from child's rights advocacy to empowering youth in civil society, to help youth recover from war. And yet, certain critical youth needs, including the reintegration of young soldiers and refugees, access to education, and employment opportunities, were vital across the board. The question then becomes, why were reconstruction actors in one case more effective than those in another in responding to the needs and channeling the potential of the youth demographic? The observations presented in this chapter indicate that the answer hinges on the types of programs, the sequence in which the programs were implemented, and the cultural and environmental context in which the programs must operate.

This chapter begins with a cross-case analysis comparing the variables from each case, the relationship between effective programming and youth roles in post-conflict reconstruction, and the sequence in which these programs were implemented. It then examines the potential limits of the comparison. The second half of the chapter explores hypotheses drawn both from the individual cases and from the cross-case analysis to show where further research may lead to a holistic model of youth roles in post-conflict reconstruction.

Cross-Case Analysis

In all the cases, each type of actor, from the international community and domestic policymakers to NGOs and the local environment, was engaged in youth-related programs and influenced the reconstruction process. Perhaps ironically, the study suggests that the success of youth programming does not depend on the efforts of one actor over another (e.g., United Nations versus NGOs) or on the presence of specific "youth" or "children's" policy. What matters more in determining whether youth become a positive force for stability is how effectively certain critical transition functions are fulfilled—regardless of who implements them or whether they target youth specifically or communities as a whole. These critical functions include psychological and social support, DDR and reintegration programming to ease the transition into civilian life, and educational opportunities to provide youth with the tools to succeed in the future. As figure 5.1 illustrates, the

Figure 5.1. Comparative Impact of Variables on Youth and Stability

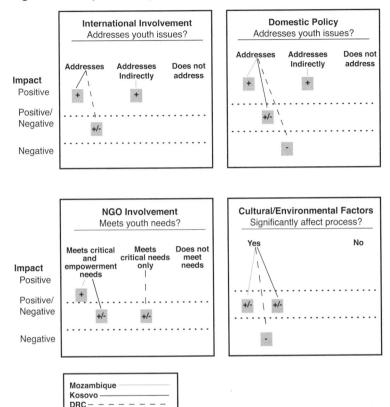

reconstruction actors' success in meeting these needs tends to reflect the relative success of the overarching reconstruction process.

The four boxes in figure 5.1 represent the four types of variables studied in each case: international involvement, domestic policy, NGO involvement, and cultural and environmental factors. The first three boxes sort the data to reflect whether intervening actors addressed youth issues during the reconstruction process, and then show whether their policies had a positive or negative impact on youth and stability. For example, NGOs in Mozambique had specific programs addressing both critical youth needs and empowerment issues. These programs had a positive impact on the youth they served and on the level of stability. The final box shows whether exogenous cultural and environmental factors had a significant impact on the reconstruction process and, if so, whether it was positive or negative.

The graph is meant to capture the impact of the policies, programs, and exogenous factors that affected youth during reconstruction. However, if the ratings for all four variables are examined together for each case, they also tend to describe the relative success of the reconstruction process as a whole. For example, the DRC saw two variables having a "negative" impact and two having a "positive/negative" impact, reflecting the failing reconstruction process and return to violence in the DRC. In Mozambique, three variables have a "positive" impact and one has "positive/negative," reflecting the relatively successful reconstruction program there. Figure 5.1 shows that the combined ability of reconstruction actors to meet youth needs, taking into account environmental and cultural factors, parallels the overall level of success of the reconstruction program; however, the data from the individual case studies suggest that actors' relative success in meting youth needs can also directly influence stability.

In the three cases studied, success in meeting youth needs did not depend on whether actors had policies that specifically addressed youth needs, or whether those implementing the programs were NGOs, international organizations, or domestic actors. In the DRC, the United Nations, NGOs, and domestic actors all had their own policies for children and youth, yet they were the least successful in meeting youth needs. Nor was it the presence of a specific type of actor (e.g., NGOs, the United Nations, or international organizations) that predicted success. In Kosovo, the overwhelming presence of NGOs inadvertently undermined the local civil society, and the UN mission in the DRC, despite its size, has struggled to provide even basic youth protection. Instead, the most successful case was where the range of actors' policies or programs, directly or indirectly, addressed the issues of youth protection, reintegration, education, and empowerment, and where cultural and environmental factors were an asset to those policies' and programs' implementation.

This conclusion adds a new dimension to previous understandings of youth roles in conflict and post-conflict reconstruction. As discussed in chapter 1, most theories have either focused on youth's destabilizing potential, the structures that sway youth decision making toward conflict-causing activities, or the dual roles of youth as potential troublemakers or peacemakers.[3] More recent studies have made the case for a more dynamic understanding of youth roles in conflict, where youth roles depend on other structures, such as NGO intervention or economic and cultural environments. This project not only supports this dynamic view but goes further, using in-depth case studies analyzed across shared variables to systematically draw the connection that effective programming in these critical areas can shape youth roles during the post-conflict period. The evidence in the three cases shows that reconstruction programs can alter, for good or ill, the same decision-making structures that lead youth to destabilizing behavior, so that youth are more or less likely to participate in peacebuilding. If this is the case, it is important to understand what constitutes *efficiency* in a reconstruction context. The cases suggest that rather than considering money, manpower,

---

3.   Urdal, "A Clash of Generations?" 612–13; Collier and Hoeffler, "Greed and Grievance in Civil War," 569; Zakaria, "The Politics of Rage."

or specific youth policy, efficiency looks at how well these reconstruction actors are able to address youth needs given the institutional, environmental, and cultural constraints. For example, competition among NGOs is an institutional constraint that NGOs must overcome if they are to have the optimal impact, and a harsh environment can hinder the ability of all reconstruction actors to implement programs at their full capacity.

Comparative Analysis of Independent Variables: Function over Form

Impact of International Involvement

A comparative analysis of the variable categories (international involvement, domestic policy, NGO involvement, and cultural/environmental factors) across the cases provides further support for the emphasis on function over form. Further, it highlights what types of programs succeeded in all three cases and what factors undermined the process. For example, in examining international involvement, we see that in each of the three countries, the UN mission played a large role in facilitating the transition and building the country's new institutions. But in each case, the United Nations took on distinctly different responsibilities, with varying success. In Mozambique, the United Nations managed the DDR process and reintegration of refugees. While this program did not include a youth-specific policy, the demobilization and reintegration process was relatively successful, and it fulfilled the critical function of reintegration because young people were included in the population of soldiers and refugees who benefited from the programs.

In the DRC, the UN mission took on a strong advocacy and protection role, with an acute focus on children's rights, while serving only as an implementing agent for the DDR/DDRRR process. In this case, while the efforts of the international community, including the United Nations, have had a small positive impact in treating the symptoms of the humanitarian crisis and demobilizing soldiers, the program has fallen short in fulfilling its mandate to protect children and youth. The inability to fulfill this goal in the DRC, while due in large part to domestic actors' mismanagement of the DDR program, had a significant impact on the overall process—not because of the failure of the international community but because of the unfulfilled requirement of a complete DDR process.

The differences between the two DDR programs also highlight that having a separate, youth-specific policy is not essential to successful programming. In the DRC, nearly every agency involved, from the United Nations to CONADER, was aware of the importance of children's issues and developed separate strategies to deal with children and adults. This distinction between children and adults was exemplified in the Operational Framework outlining the precise mechanisms for children's DDR. And yet, the child-oriented programming in the DRC was *least* effective in meeting the youth needs, and in fact, the incomplete children's DDR/DDRRR contributed to the ongoing instability. By contrast, Mozambique, where youth were acknowledged as a vulnerable group but where youth issues were not treated as a separate policy objective, had much greater success in reintegrating youth soldiers.

In Kosovo, the international community, including the United Nations and regional security groups, took on a distinctly different function. In this case, they tried to meet immediate humanitarian needs and also work with youth to channel their energy into constructive activities. The international community was extremely successful, at least in the short term, in fulfilling these objectives and was able to channel young people's energy toward community building activities and also to help them develop as a cohesive voice in the reconstruction process. For example, the international community not only helped young people in the refugee camps organize to pick up trash or plan events in the camps, they helped these youth groups develop into a youth civil society that could continue to work after the humanitarian crisis was over. Often the NGO community rather than international or regional organizations provides this type of programming. In Kosovo, however, regional actors were just as effective, if not more so, in fulfilling this function. And considering the high population of youth with little to do in the refugee camps, this proved integral to the short-term success of the reconstruction process.

Impact of Domestic Policy

In each case, domestic actors took on some degree of responsibility for educational reform—again, with varying success. Across the board, reconstruction actors recognized that education was an important factor in the transition process. However, as Kosovo demonstrates, it does not have to be domestic actors who lead the charge for education reform. While the exclusive manner in which international actors in Kosovo carried out education and curriculum reform had some indirect negative consequences, those actors' efforts have made some significant headway in improving the educational environment, which may not otherwise have been possible considering the competing interests of the domestic parties. Excluding domestic actors from the process, though certainly not ideal, is sometimes appropriate, especially in cases where policymakers use control over curriculum to perpetuate ethnonationalist sentiments.

The positive domestic policy in Mozambique differs from the negative impact in the DRC not just in the quality of education reform but in the idiosyncratic policies unique to the domestic actors in these situations. Whereas, in many conflicts, the justice process is led on top levels by international agents such as the United Nations or the ICC, Mozambique implemented its own amnesty policy, which helped create a culture of reconciliation and indirectly facilitated the reintegration of former youth combatants. In the DRC, the national government took on most of the responsibility for DDR/DDRRR, a function that usually falls to the United Nations. But the domestic government's poor management of the DDR program's funds prevented the implementing agents, including the United Nations and NGOs, from completing the DDR program.

In both countries, the consequences of the domestic programs for youth did not depend on whether domestic actors were responsible for a specific type of program, such as education reform or reintegration, but on *how effectively* domestic programs, whatever they were, met specific vital youth needs. Because the DRC's domestic actors failed in implementing the DDR process—especially in reintegration—they had a serious negative influence on the youth reconstruction process as a whole. In Mozambique, amnesty for crimes committed by the average soldier indirectly helped meet the need of youth reintegration. These examples underscore the critical importance of successful DDR and reintegration programs, and not necessarily of domestic as opposed to international policy.

Impact of NGOs

Of the three types of actors—international, domestic, and NGO—NGOs are often the actors most visibly focused on key youth needs. While NGOs can be successful in meeting these needs, evidence from the three cases suggests that a high level of NGO involvement is no predictor of success. Both the DRC and Kosovo were inundated with NGOs, many of them focused on youth and children's issues. And yet, it was in Mozambique that NGOs were most effective in meeting youth needs.

It seems that the crucial element for NGOs' successful youth programming lies not in the number of organizations or personnel involved but in their efficacy in fulfilling certain key functions or needs. For instance, in Mozambique a small number of NGOs were able to dedicate their resources to a few issues that had fallen through the gaps of the UN mission and the domestic policy program. By contrast, in both the DRC and Kosovo, NGO programming was severely limited by poor coordination, competition, and dependence on international donors focused on immediate results rather than long-term development. This frenzy of NGOs competing for grants limited the individual organizations' ability to accurately assess and meet needs based on the specific circumstances on the ground, which has contributed to a culture of distrust of the international community.

In all three cases, NGOs often relied on emergency or transition funds to pay for their programs. The donors' stipulations that these funds' impact must be measured in a relatively short time create a tunnel vision for immediate results and, therefore, favor programs that apply superficial solutions to problems but do little to cure the root cause.[4] For instance, the NGO community in Kosovo created various institutions and youth centers to give young people the opportunity to

---

4. This trend was also observed in Northern Uganda. See Annan, Blattman, and Horton, "The State of Youth and Youth Protection in Northern Uganda."

take classes, participate in workshops, and contribute to their communities. But the creation of youth centers did not address the broader need for better-quality vocational and technical training to prepare youth to be constructive members of the workforce. Without long-term funding, most of these centers have shut down or become dysfunctional. This issue of meeting immediate needs without resolving the underlying issues is a problem for nearly all the actors involved in the reconstruction process. However, it is especially apparent in the NGO community, because the dependency on donor funding demands that these organizations balance their responsibility to the donor and to the receiving community. Under these circumstances, it is easier to institute programs that satisfy immediate needs, helping the community and satisfying donor requirements, than to defend the financing for a long-term endeavor that attempts to resolve more complicated, less obvious issues.

Also, the needs that NGOs often fulfill do not necessarily depend on the NGO structure as the mechanism for resolution. For instance, in Kosovo, regional security groups were just as effective as NGOs in instituting youth empowerment programs and have stayed funded longer than many NGOs. In Mozambique, many NGOs opted not to involve themselves in the reintegration efforts, because their involvement could have hindered the local processes. In these cases, it was not necessarily important who implemented the programs, but rather that these specific needs be met effectively.

Impact of Cultural and Environmental Factors

Despite the best efforts of international, domestic, and non-governmental actors to fulfill key requirements, cultural and environmental factors can exert a significant and sometimes uncontrollable exogenous influence on reconstruction. These factors may affect specific actors or the entire structure of the reconstruction process. In Kosovo, for example, the option for emigration has an impact on the decision-making logic of the youth demographic, changing how youth choose to express their frustrations. In the DRC, the combined effects of the harsh terrain and a culture of impunity affected every aspect of the reconstruction process, hindering the ability of all the actors involved to effectively carry out their programs.

The influence of cultural and environmental factors is therefore important not only in explaining the youth response to the policies implemented, but it may also affect how well actors are able to fulfill their designated responsibilities. Even where the level of efforts may not be especially high, as in Mozambique, a positive influence from cultural factors can help ease the process and tip the scales in favor of successful reconstruction and the emergence of a constructive youth population. Conversely, where the level of efforts is extremely high, as in the DRC, negative environmental and cultural factors can offset reconstruction actors' ability to meet the demands of the peacebuilding process.

By comparing the influence of the various actors in each of the three cases, it becomes apparent that it is not the efforts of any one group, such as NGOs, to cater to the youth demographic that make for a successful youth policy. NGOs in Mozambique did not single-handedly meet youth needs, and the government's mismanagement of the DDR process was not the only problem plaguing reconstruction in the DRC. Rather, each actor can try to fulfill certain functions (or share the responsibility with other actors), taking into account the cultural and environmental context. For example, international actors in Kosovo can choose to manage education reform in light of a competing domestic agenda. Their success or failure in fulfilling that function has a positive or negative affect on youth, the reconstruction process, and the overall stability of the country. The combined results, shown in figure 5.1, are a good indicator of the general direction of the reconstruction process.

Shaping Youth Roles in Post-conflict Reconstruction

The Youth Demographic as a Dependent Variable

The finding that the type of role the youth demographic plays during post-conflict reconstruction depends on effective implementation of certain reconstruction activities is a significant departure from the established scholarship on youth in conflict. As chapter 1 explains, the dominant theories concerning the role of the youth demographic in conflict claim that a large proportion of young men in the population is a uniformly destabilizing factor. In these models, the population of youth age 10 to 24 then represents an *independent variable* that can exert only a negative influence: a large proportion of youth either increases the potential for internal conflict or is a potential spoiler in the peacebuilding process. From this perspective, very little can be done to manage youth's potential for creating instability.

In direct contrast with the dominant view, the evidence from the cases of Mozambique, the DRC, and Kosovo supports an argument, similar to Siobhán McEvoy-Levy's, that the role of the youth demographic is more accurately a *dependent variable:* youth's impact, whether positive or negative, is not predetermined but is guided by how well youth needs are met. As McEvoy-Levy argues, youth do not have to be a destabilizing force; they also have the potential to contribute to the process of community development and conflict resolution. The spontaneous emergence of youth peacebuilding in Kosovo is case-in-point evidence of how young people can contribute to community development with the help of capacity-building reconstruction programs. The analysis from this study suggests that this transformation from "troublemaker" to "peacemaker" during post-conflict reconstruction depends on how well policymakers can implement youth programming and resolve issues key to the young people's successful transition from war to peace and from child to adult. For instance, effective programming in Mozambique allowed many young ex-combatants both to reintegrate into civilian life and to become agents for conflict resolution, but in the DRC, ineffective programming created a situation in which young people were particularly vulnerable to (re)recruitment into armed forces, thus contributing to the ongoing instability.

Approaches to Youth Programming

While the types of programs or functions that needed to be implemented were similar across all three cases (demobilization, reintegration, education reform, and so on), the varying success of the different methods used to fulfill them points to "best practices" in youth programming and also shows how some approaches can limit or even negate a program's positive impact. In the immediate aftermath of war, organizations tend to focus on humanitarian and psychosocial needs while paying less attention to educational, economic, and empowerment needs.[5] However, as Yvonne Kemper demonstrates with her evaluation of rights-based, economic, and sociopolitical approaches to youth policy, the theoretical framework behind a certain program defines the extent to which that program can foster youth development. For instance, a successful children's-advocacy program in the DRC can protect children, but it cannot empower them to work for community development. Therefore, while advocacy is necessary, the most effective protection programs, such as Search for Common Ground's *Sisi Watoto* radio program, also include youth participation. This program reached out to communities to protect children and help them find demobilization centers, while also giving the youth who ran the program an opportunity to contribute to the peacemaking process. While the type of programming—rights-based, economic, or sociopolitical—may determine the potential impact of youth roles, the case study analysis suggests that the successful implementation of youth policy also depends on the institutional and environmental context, including the level of competition among implementing organizations and the influence of cultural-environmental factors.

Critical Transition Functions

Reintegration

The relative success of reintegration programs across the three cases shows how a program's theoretical framework determines its potential impact. Beyond the immediate necessities of food and shelter, one of the most important functions emphasized in each case study is an effective reintegration program. Whether for child soldiers or youth refugees, reintegration is a critical need that, left unmet, can become a serious liability for the overall reconstruction process. However,

---

5. Ibid., 72.

reintegration for youth and children is most commonly placed within a rights-based, or advocacy, framework that focuses on family reunification. For instance, many children in the DRC were reunited with their families but, without effective reintegration, were still vulnerable to rerecruitment, with negative results for stability.

Rather, the most effective type of reintegration programming goes beyond family reunification. These programs work with communities to facilitate children's and youth's transition back into their communities and provide young people with opportunities to continue to succeed. It is not necessarily the physical reunification with family members that matters, but rather the acceptance back into their *community* and the reestablishment of youth roles within that community. In some cases, this is accomplished through vocational training that teaches participants the skills necessary to generate an income. In other cases, such as Mozambique, reintegration programming can involve traditional religious practices to absolve young people of their previous crimes. Conflict resolution workshops and youth volunteer corps are also especially successful in helping youth reconcile issues remaining from the war and in giving young people a strong sense of community involvement and an outlet for their frustrations.

Given the influence that cultural and environmental factors have on the process, a "one-size fits all" approach to reintegration will not prove effective. Reintegration may be easier in some cultures than in others—for example, the stigma of sorcery associated with young women in the DRC made reintegration much harder there than in Mozambique. While the success of reintegration programming depends in part on the policy framework itself, the cultural environment and the ability of domestic and international actors to effectively carry out their programming within that context also has a significant effect. Therefore, any programming, to be effective in fulfilling reintegration, must take into account these contextual factors.

Education

Providing high-quality educational programming is another important function for the reconstruction process, especially in areas with a younger population. Without regular schooling (as was the case in the DRC), children not only miss out on critical learning opportunities but are also deprived of a daily routine, leaving them with free time to engage in less productive pursuits. For the older adolescents and young adults who must navigate a dual transition from child to adult and from war to peace, educational opportunities, including regular schooling and specialized support such as classes in health, technology, and vocational skills, are essential tools to their becoming productive members of society. Because the experience of war interrupted the normal processes of childhood development within society, it is especially important during the reconstruction processes to develop in the younger generation the human capital necessary for future progress. The youth surveyed for Kosovo's 2006 Human Development Report, for example, made it clear that they were not satisfied with the educational opportunities in Kosovo. Indeed, many thought that a chance for a better future meant leaving Kosovo. By failing to invest in this generation, Kosovo may have both the immediate problem of a large proportion of its population frustrated with nothing to do and the long-term problem of no skilled labor force to contribute to economic progress. But just as with reintegration, the institutional and cultural/environmental context will also affect the extent to which educational programming satisfies youth needs. For example, the quality of the prewar education system in the DRC, the use of the education system as a nationalist symbol in Kosovo, and the competition between implementing agencies during the reconstruction process all served as obstacles to educational development.

Both reintegration and education, in their various forms, are critical functions that must be fulfilled during the reconstruction process. However, both types of programming serve mainly to mitigate the potentially negative effects of a large youth demographic. Once immediate needs have been met, reintegration and education restore a sense of normality and provide a mechanism to address youth frustrations immediately following the conflict. As soldiers, these young people held positions of relative power and were able to secure for themselves daily necessities such as food and shelter. Participation in reintegration programs allows ex-combatants to return to a civilian life armed with new tools to make money and take care of themselves and their families. These programs, however, generally serve the individual and do not take the next step: empowering youth to play a positive role in rebuilding their country.

Empowerment Programming

While successful reintegration and education programs can mitigate the potentially negative role of the youth demographic, successful economic, social, and political empowerment programming can enhance the youth demographic's potential as a force for peace. The evidence from Kosovo and Mozambique demonstrates that where empowerment programs are instituted, they can be effective in tapping into the energy and vital potential of youth and providing them with the types of skills needed to play a constructive role in their communities. Whereas a vocational education program in carpentry may last for a few months, programs like ProPaz and the Kosovo Youth Congress continue to serve not just the youth who participate in them but also the local communities. By building youth capacity through participatory mechanisms, these programs provide the next generation of leaders with essential skills and experience to continue the process of reconstruction and reconciliation into the future.

Sequencing in Youth Programs

While the success of empowerment programs is a powerful testament to young people's potential as a positive force in reconstruction, these programs could not have taken place until critical needs, from food, protection, and medical care to reunification and reintegration, were met. That is, the sequencing of programs is crucial to successful implementation. "Sequencing" means determining *when* to implement different reconstruction and nation-building programs, from security sector reform to building democratic institutions. The evidence from the cases suggests that sequencing is also crucial to successful youth programming during reconstruction. For example, in Kosovo, humanitarian issues were solved relatively quickly. Since NATO and UNHCR were handling security issues and the refugee crisis, other agencies did not need to provide basic care. Instead, they could provide development programming and focus on helping the emerging youth activist groups develop into a successful network of organizations. In Mozambique, with the DDR program completed, groups like ProPaz and the Rebuilding Hope Foundation were able to use their resources to fill in any gaps in the UN reconstruction program and give former youth soldiers an outlet to become an active force for reconciliation and rebuilding. In these cases, it did not matter *who* was sponsoring the program, only that each phase was successfully completed and that actors could concentrate their resources on their own initiatives rather than try to remedy broken programs.

The importance of sequencing for youth programs during reconstruction parallels some aspects of the research on the importance of sequencing to establish rule of law in democratic transitions.[6] The transition to democracy can be a tumultuous process, and some scholars argue that pushing the process before the necessary institutions are in place can hamper the prospects for successful democratization. For instance, the CSIS definition of post-conflict reconstruction examined in chapter 1 describes four pillars, each essential to the reconstruction process: security and public safety, justice and reconciliation, governance and participation, and economic and social progress.[7] Alternatively, the United Nations Post-conflict Stabilization, Peacebuilding, and Recovery Framework's module for DDR and post-conflict reconstruction outlines a progression of events (including these four pillars) to facilitate the transition from conflict to peace. According to this module, the process of reconstruction will cover four stages along a continuum from conflict and humanitarian relief to post-conflict stabilization, transition and transformation, and peace and development.[8] In practice, these four stages may overlap or take place simultaneously, yet each stage represents

---

6.   See Francis Fukuyama et al., "The Debate on 'Sequencing,'" *Journal of Democracy* 18, no. 3 (2007).

7.   CSIS, "The Post-conflict Reconstruction Project."

8.   United Nations, "United Nations Integrated DDR Standards," www.unddr.org/iddrs/framework.php (accessed Aug. 1, 2009).

a critical progression in the reconstruction process toward achieving a peaceful and stable environment. (See table 5.2.)

According to the UN module, during the conflict phase the United Nations can provide humanitarian relief and help facilitate a cease-fire and peace treaty. During the post-conflict stabilization phase, usually the first few months after a peace treaty, the United Nations and other coordinating parties begin implementing the agreements and assessing the situation to stabilize the level of violence. The transition-and-transformation phase should include the bulk of DDR programming, along with the establishment of a transitional authority and the implementation of other transition programming, such as development of democratic procedures and institutions. Finally, during the peace-and-development phase, the DDR program should be largely complete, and the United Nations and other international actors can focus on strategies for poverty reduction or development.

Although, in reality, the phases will overlap, the evidence from the cases suggests that strong sequencing is important, both for reconstruction efforts and for youth programming. In the same way that general reconstruction programs build on each other, the different types of youth programs also follow a sequence, in which the success of youth empowerment programming depends on first establishing an environment conducive to the process. Failing to satisfy one aspect of youth programming on the reconstruction continuum (e.g., reintegration) before moving on to another (e.g., empowerment), or providing inappropriate programming to fulfill the requirements of a particular phase, may hamper the overall progression of reconstruction efforts. For instance, unlike the successful youth empowerment programming in Kosovo, youth empowerment for peacebuilding in the DRC was unlikely to occur until a more successful reintegration program was in place. Even though thousands of soldiers in the DRC were demobilized, the process was still incomplete, and most actors, including the UN mission and NGOs, were focused on dealing with immediate humanitarian issues.

Figure 5.2 illustrates these parallels by aligning the UN post-conflict sequence with a similar sequence for youth programming. For instance, in the second phase, "post-conflict stabilization," the youth programming needed is advocacy and post-conflict relief. In the third phase of the sequence, youth DDR matches up with the overarching goals of "transition and recovery," and so on.

The parallels between the sequencing for conflict transformation and democratization and the sequencing for youth programming point to a direct relationship between the youth demographic and rule of law. Just as the UN post-conflict reconstruction continuum highlights the need to establish safety and security before implementing transition or development programs, the initial programming for children and youth is linked to establishing rule of law, or quelling the negative potential of the youth demographic. Continuing in sequence, once basic rule-of-law institutions are established, the country can continue working toward

Figure 5.2. Sequencing in Post-conflict Reconstruction and Youth Programming

UN Post-Conflict Continuum

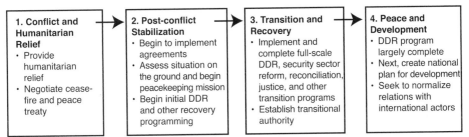

UN Post-Conflict Continuum adapted from United Nations, "United Nations Integrated DDR Standards."

Youth Programming Sequence

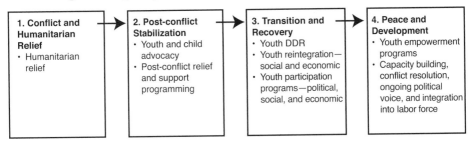

democratic transformation. In the same way, the next types of youth programs in the sequence can then focus on more long-term and development-oriented goals such as youth capacity building and empowerment.

This progression is especially apparent in Mozambique. (For a summary of the sequencing in all three cases, see figure 5.3.) Just as the reconstruction program in Mozambique sought to establish rule of law and complete the DDR program before holding national elections, the programs affecting youth first sought to satisfy immediate needs, then to achieve social reintegration, and finally to develop youth empowerment and conflict resolution programs allowing young adults to serve as leaders in the peacebuilding process. In Kosovo, the same sequence occurred, although in a much shorter time frame. Immediate needs were satisfied relatively quickly, and reconstruction actors began implementing youth reintegration and empowerment programming right away. However, Kosovo's overall progress has not kept pace with youth development, as the slow development of the economic and education systems remains a significant obstacle to future youth development.

Whereas Mozambique and Kosovo each had a degree of sequencing, the reconstruction process in the DRC tried to do most tasks simultaneously. Elections were held before the DDR process was completed, and the country is still struggling with implementing reintegration programming. With youth policy, instead of making a progression from protection to sociopolitical and economic reintegration, the majority of youth programs in the DRC are stuck in an advocacy and children's-protection framework, and most young people have yet to benefit from reintegration programming that could help them in the transition to civilian life.

This evidence demonstrates that effectively fulfilling the critical transition functions also depends on the sequence in which programs are implemented. Similar to the sequencing of the overarching program, the progression from youth humanitarian and protection programming to reintegration and empowerment allows for each program to build on the successes of the last.

Potential Limits in Cross-Case Comparison

Although each country studied went through a number of processes that can be compared from case to case, there are also certain differences that could potentially limit comparability. Specifically, the differences in region, conflict causation, and classification as "post-conflict" could all affect the validity of the observations drawn from comparison. But these differences may, in many ways, prove immaterial and may actually contribute to a more comprehensive study of youth in different types of post-conflict situations.

Regional Differences and Level of International Involvement

Because both Mozambique and the DRC are in sub-Saharan Africa, their geographic similarities coincide with similar histories of colonialism, allowing for a relatively smooth comparison. Kosovo, however, stands out as the only European example in the study, and its European location did influence the reconstruction efforts. As a result, its experience during post-conflict reconstruction was quite different from the process in either the DRC or Mozambique in a few key areas.

First, compared to Mozambique or the DRC, Kosovo's level of development before the conflict was significantly higher. Indeed, although Kosovo was the one of the poorest places in FRY/Serbia, its infrastructure was more developed than Mozambique's or the DRC's, and it also had many more experienced civic administrators than either African nation. However, the conflict in Kosovo and the NATO air campaign destroyed most of the physical infrastructure, and the interim international administration forced Kosovo to overhaul its political institutions, creating a situation more similar to that in Mozambique or the DRC. While Kosovo's more advanced development may have made the process of reconstruction easier, this did not predetermine the level of success, since Kosovo does not represent the most stable case of the three cases.

Figure 5.3. Sequencing of Reconstruction and Youth Programming in the Case Studies

Mozambique

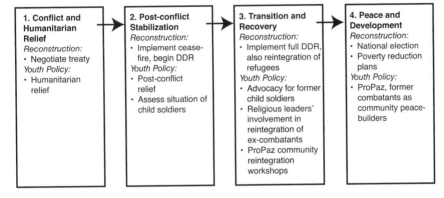

Kosovo

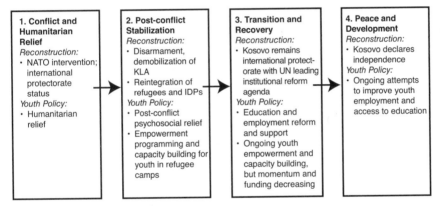

Democratic Republic of the Congo

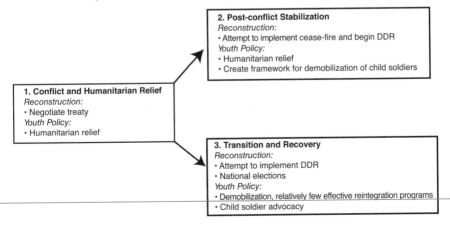

Second, Kosovo's position in Eastern Europe is largely responsible for its attracting so much attention from the international community, and as a result, its reconstruction process saw a higher level of involvement from foreign governments and regional security groups than did the sub-Saharan African countries. However, while Kosovo did benefit from the international attention in ways that could have aided the processes in the DRC and Mozambique, the international involvement was a mixed blessing. In fact, the overwhelming international presence indirectly damaged some of the existing community structures, whereas a lower level of involvement might have allowed for more local participation, as happened in Mozambique. The research design is intended to allow for a comparison between the high level of international involvement in Kosovo and the lower level of involvement in both the DRC and Mozambique. Therefore, while Kosovo's location caused the high level of international involvement, it is not the presence of the international community that the study is evaluating, but the effectiveness of its programs in one country relative to another.

In line with the hypothesis-generating methodology outlined by Stephen van Evera, Kosovo's inclusion in the study broadens the scope of comparison and adds an important level of variation across the cases.[9] Instead of limiting the study to issues prevalent in the sub-Saharan African context, the cross-regional comparison broadens the scope of inquiry, particularly in terms of the types of youth involvement. Whereas in Mozambique and the DRC, youth were mainly involved in the conflict as soldiers, the evidence of youth involvement in Kosovo is integral to including the full range of youth roles. The similarities and differences between youth empowerment programming in Europe and sub-Saharan Africa highlight the types of needs that are important independent of culture or regional development.

The cross-regional comparison also provides variability in the international involvement and NGO variables. Analyzing the impact of the high-level yet short-term NGO involvement in Kosovo along with the NGO involvement in the DRC and Mozambique underscores both the limits of the NGO role and the benefits of local participation in international programming. In addition, although Kosovo overcame the humanitarian crisis more easily than either the DRC or Mozambique, by comparing the success of youth empowerment programming in Kosovo and Mozambique, we can avoid restricting the conclusions to a purely European or "developed" context. Also, the relative ease with which the programs were implemented in Kosovo compared with the DRC elicits inferences about the differences in humanitarian as opposed to development programming in general.

---

9.   See the methodology discussion in chapter 1. Stephen van Evera, *Guide to Methods for Students of Political Science* (Ithaca, N.Y.: Cornell University Press, 1997).

Conflict Causation

No two cases of intrastate conflict are exactly alike, and the same is true of the cases presented in this study. The conflicts in Mozambique and the DRC stem from movements for independence from colonial regimes, whereas the conflict in Kosovo is linked to nationalist movements associated with certain ethnic groups. In Mozambique, the parties competing for control were generally divided by political ideology, whereas the divisions in the DRC and Kosovo fell along ethnic and geographic lines.

While these issues constitute significant differences across the cases, the struggles for power and territorial control ring true across the cases, and the positions that the countries found themselves in following the conflicts are sufficiently similar to enable comparison. While Kosovo's civil conflict does not trace back to colonial roots, its experiences under the control of both the Federation of Yugoslavia and Serbia have some similarities to colonization, for example, in the arbitrary establishment of borders without regard for existing cultural, linguistic, or ethnic boundaries. Although the conflict in Mozambique was not ethnically divided, the strong convictions on both sides spurred a long-drawn-out civil war that was just as divisive as Kosovo's, with similar trends of violence, terrorism, and youth involvement. Therefore, whereas the lack of ethnic divisions may have made the reconciliation process easier, Mozambique had to overcome similar issues related to the reintegration of children and youth who had been active participants in a nationally divisive and deadly war.

Classification as "Post-conflict"

Finally, the ongoing violence in the DRC raises the question of whether it can even be classified as being in a post-conflict phase at all. All three cases represent relatively recent conflicts, and because reconstruction processes generally take decades to evolve, the first five to ten years after the signing of a cease-fire or peace treaty may represent only a blip in the history of the conflict. However, these first years are also extremely critical and formative for the future development of the country.

During these first years after signing the peace accord in late 2002, parties in the DRC have volunteered for disarmament and begun the transition toward establishing a new government, and the international community has implemented a number of reconstruction programs. Therefore, the DRC is best categorized as a case of post-conflict reconstruction. These efforts fit into former UN secretary-general Boutros Boutros-Gahli's description of the reconstruction process (discussed in chapter 1) as "foster[ing] economic and social cooperation with the purpose of building confidence among previously warring parties, developing the social, political and economic infrastructure to prevent future violence, and laying the foundations for a durable peace."[10] This means that the international community recognizes the process of post-conflict reconstruction as encompassing the postaccord peacebuilding process, from implementing a UN mission to supporting the establishment of new national institutions and fostering continued economic and political development.[11] For the purposes of this study, miscategorizing the DRC as an "ongoing conflict" would also ignore the fact that the ongoing instability is partially a result of the ineffective reconstruction program. Therefore, while the future of the conflict may be uncertain, the efforts in the period following the Lusaka Accord and the Global and All-Inclusive Agreement can be best understood as post-conflict reconstruction.

The inclusion of cases with different degrees of success in establishing peace and stability during the reconstruction phase is also critical for variations within the research design. As noted in chapter 1, the case studies were selected to provide extreme variations across the dependent variable of stability. These variations are necessary for drawing hypotheses about the relationships between the youth demographic, reconstruction programming, and the success of peacebuilding processes. Because this study is limited in the number of cases it can include, only the DRC was chosen as the example of extreme instability. A research design that uses a greater number of cases to represent stable, medium, and unstable outcomes would undoubtedly provide greater insight; however, this was not possible within the confines of this study.

Because the conflicts in the DRC and Kosovo are so recent—and, in the case of the DRC, perhaps ongoing—discussions of the overall success or failure of the entire reconstruction process may not be entirely conclusive. Dynamics on the ground in both places have the potential to change abruptly. However, observations and comparisons about the effectiveness of peacebuilding and reconstruction policies during the first five years after each conflict offer important insights and can help predict long-term outcomes.

Implications for Further Research

This study contributes to our knowledge about youth in post-conflict reconstruction in two ways. First, whereas previous studies had not drawn extensive comparisons across cases, the study contributes to the developing field of research on youth roles in conflict by providing a cross-case analysis of post-conflict situations. The common threads traced through the reconstruction periods in Mozambique, the DRC, and Kosovo show that meeting certain critical needs, from physical and mental health to reintegration, education, and empowerment, is essential to a successful youth policy and that a "youth bulge" need not be a

---

10. Doyle and Sambanis, *Making War and Building Peace*, 11.

11. United Nations, "United Nations Integrated DDR Standards."

destabilizing force. The youth role is malleable and depends on how other actors address these critical issues. In fact, if reconstruction actors successfully address these critical youth needs, a large youth population can be an asset for conflict transformation.

Second and perhaps more important, the heuristic method provides the framework for exploring linkages within and across cases, generating hypotheses, and developing questions that will direct future research in the field. From this perspective, the study adds to the field not only through the observations drawn from the comparative analysis but also by pointing to questions that remain unanswered. Future research on these questions can lead to more definitive conclusions about the role of youth in post-conflict reconstruction. In this vein, the following section uses the cross-case comparison to draw connections to other areas of conflict research and to pose questions critical to improving our understanding of effective peacebuilding mechanisms and the dynamic role of youth in conflict.

Designing Efficient Post-conflict Reconstruction Programs

If reintegration, education, income-generating activities, and empowerment are the progression of critical tasks that need to be fulfilled for the youth demographic during post-conflict reconstruction, then a number of new questions arise about how best and most effectively to implement these activities. Since knowing what functions need to be fulfilled is the first step in successful reconstruction, actors can then evaluate the situation on the ground to design the best way to execute programs. As long as these programs meet certain requirements—successful disarmament, reintegration, education reform, and so on—then it is not necessary that one type of actor implement these programs. Instead, leaders must evaluate which actor can best fulfill each need and choose the implementation mechanism that best fits the circumstances. The delegation of tasks can then depend on the capacities of international, non-governmental, and domestic organizations to operate in the host country, along with the cultural and environmental factors that may affect the process.

This seems like common sense, and practitioners and scholars agree that assessing specific circumstances is integral to designing a successful post-conflict reconstruction program. But in practice, there is not always a complete assessment of the situation, or coordination among domestic, international, and regional actors, before reconstruction begins. Instead, while the UN mission is just getting off the ground, NGOs tend to flood the reconstruction scene, each trying to stake out its own turf in the process.

Other scholars have argued that the success of a peacekeeping mission rests solely on its funding and manpower.[12] But this study's findings on the importance

---

12. See Dobbins, *The UN's Role in Nation-Building.*

of specific functions, rather than form or force, refute such arguments. The UN mission in the DRC is the largest UN peacekeeping force to date. It has also been one of the least successful. Although, as in Kosovo, having NATO, the United Nations, and other regional and non-governmental organizations flock to the scene and implement a wide range of programming can be successful, it may not be necessary. In fact, the overwhelming presence of the international community can actually hinder reconstruction. Instead, it may be that the success of peacekeeping and reconstruction missions depends on the *efficient use* of resources appropriate to the demands of the situation.

These findings on the efficiency of reconstruction processes suggest several additional avenues of research:

How important is effort relative to efficiency? What is the best measure of "effort" during reconstruction? Is effort the per-capita spending? Per-capita spending for targeted demographics? The ratio of peacekeepers to local citizens? Is the level of effort a political investment that depends on whether the country is strategically important to other actors?

The cases: The level of effort varied widely across the cases, with the most money dedicated to the DRC and the most political investment in Kosovo. Yet Mozambique realized the greatest stability.

How long must the level of effort remain high to have the most successful reconstruction program?

The cases: The issue of short-term versus long-term funding arose in each of the cases, with varying levels of impact on the reconstruction program. Particularly in Kosovo, the time frame of international involvement affected the degree of success and potential long-term impact of youth-related programming.

Which actors are best or least suited for efficiently carrying out which tasks?

The cases: In the DRC, domestic actors were responsible for the DDR program, whereas in Mozambique, the United Nations took on most of the responsibility. While it is clear that the DDR program is the essential aspect, are there circumstances in which certain actors (for example, an unstable government) are simply unable or unmotivated to carry out DDR? Should the international community implement DDR or other reconstruction programs if other key actors are unwilling or unable?

What features of the reconstruction process contribute to efficiency?

The cases: The evidence suggests that sequencing, cooperation, coordination, and environmental factors affect efficiency. However, the number of cases in this study limits the potential findings. Other case studies may provide additional insight into whether other factors, such as per-capita manpower or the type of UN mandate, contribute to efficiency.

Is a reconstruction mission more effective when guided by a lead organizing body, or does an overarching organization mechanism burden the process with bureaucratic delays?

The cases: The process in Mozambique was led predominantly by the United Nations, whereas in Kosovo, the United Nations, NATO, and a number of other regional organizations shared the responsibility. However, in both cases, local actors expressed disdain for how slowly the process took to implement and for the lead agencies' disregard of local actors.

What makes youth-oriented programming most efficient? Are community-based programs more efficient than demographic-specific programs in creating results for young people?

The cases: In Mozambique, the community-driven programs that did not target specific populations were especially effective, and in the DRC, the child-specific programs were the *least* effective. In Kosovo, the youth-oriented initiatives had a positive impact on the greater community, especially in the refugee camps, rather than on just the youth population.

Domestic Capacity

The ability of domestic actors to fulfill certain responsibilities during the reconstruction process is a crucial factor to assess early on. Whereas the national government in the DRC took on a function that it did not have the capacity to manage effectively, in Kosovo the international community shut out capable local actors from involvement in the reconstruction process. In both cases, the inept assessment of domestic capabilities had a detrimental effect on the overall process. The evidence suggests that wherever possible, the participation of domestic actors in the reconstruction process is especially beneficial, because local actors become invested in the peace process rather than having the reforms imposed by foreign actors. Again, this finding is not new to the field, but it is not always applied in practice. Accurate assessment of the domestic actors' capabilities is essential. In Mozambique, some local actors were capable of taking on the responsibility for overcoming barriers to reintegration, but they were not necessarily capable of managing the entire DDR process. The selection process for which mechanism to use in implementing the various reconstruction functions should include a preference for domestic actors wherever possible but should not rely on a fragile government to shoulder an overwhelming share of the responsibility.

These observations about domestic policy suggest the following potential research questions:

What factors are indicative of domestic capacity? Are they institutional? Cultural? Dependent on the nature of the conflict itself?

The cases: In the DRC, domestic capacity was related to corruption in managing the DDR program. In Kosovo, on the other hand, domestic actors were ignored (in education reforms, for example) as international actors felt that ethnic tensions could preclude effective policy. In Mozambique, capacity was related to traditional culture.

What are the most efficient ways to measure domestic capacity, and when should this assessment be made?

The cases: Had international actors better assessed domestic capacity in the DRC, the government may not have been given such control over the DDR process. However, how and when this assessment can be made in practice is unclear. There is often a short time frame to consider, as well as stipulations (such as permission from the host country) for the United Nations to enter a country and take the lead in reconstruction efforts.

How do local understandings of youth affect the ability of domestic actors to contribute to successful youth policy and programming?

The cases: In Mozambique, cultural mores made it easier for local actors to facilitate the reintegration of former youth soldiers. In the DRC, local attitudes toward human rights, or the so-called culture of impunity, along with fears and accusations of sorcery, had the opposite effect, hindering international and NGO operations. Yet to what extent do these cultural factors govern the process?

Impact of Exogenous Factors

Cultural and environmental factors must also figure in the design of reconstruction programs, since they also influence who might be best suited to take on various responsibilities. For instance, difficult terrain and lack of transportation infrastructure may make operations much more difficult for NGOs than for UN peacekeepers or military personnel.

Moreover, although foreign actors can intervene and construct a negative peace by using force to prevent further outbreaks of violence, a positive peace, in which the citizens work together to reconcile a country after conflict, depends on whether domestic actors and citizens are invested in the reconstruction process. If, as in Mozambique, the domestic culture lends itself to facilitating reintegration projects, then excluding these actors could be significantly detrimental to the legitimacy and long-term impact of the reconstruction process.

These understandings of cultural and environmental factors suggest these potential research questions:

To what extent can cultural or logistical factors improve or undermine the effectiveness of reconstruction efforts? What is the best way to measure or categorize these factors?

The cases: Although cultural factors helped the process in Mozambique, in the DRC they were a significant burden. Yet actors may not have been able to predict the impact of these factors without experience on the ground or an accurate situational assessment.

Which actors are better able to operate in different cultural, environmental, or logistical situations?

The cases: Although local actors played a large role in reintegration in Mozambique, in Kosovo international actors took on the bulk of education reform. Yet, because the education system is so intrinsically tied to national identities, the exclusion of the domestic community frustrated the local population. In these cases, the different cultural environments influenced which type of actor may have been a better fit to facilitate certain programs.

NGO Efficiency

The effectiveness of the international community, from UN personnel to regional security forces and NGOs, is not a unidirectional continuum, where increased money and manpower necessarily produce a more effective mission. Rather, international actors, including NGOs, must meet the demand for aid in an effective manner. In certain cases, as in the DRC, the need for aid may be unusually high and therefore require a high level of international involvement. However, particularly in the NGO community, the presence of either too few or too many actors is detrimental to the process. And yet, it is not clear exactly how to calculate what level of NGO support is enough and what factors, such as cooperation and coordination, contribute to an effective NGO program.

Future research on NGO activity may point to a need to reform the current methods of coordination. It is clear from the case studies that grant-seeking competition and the desire to stake a claim on a piece of the humanitarian market undermines the efficacy of the reconstruction process. As discussed in chapter 1, although the NGO and humanitarian community operates with the goal of helping others rather than seeking profit, funding structures constrain them in many ways to behave like profit seekers in an economic market, and this behavior can be counterproductive.[13] However, there is no obvious solution for NGO competition.

One way to frame the issue of NGO competition is to apply a simple economic model of diminishing marginal returns. In the theory of diminishing marginal returns, each unit of increase in production inputs produces a corresponding but diminishing increase in output returns, up to a point where each increase in input may actually serve to *decrease* overall productivity. This is easily understood

---

if the production inputs are chefs in a kitchen. Each added chef can make more bread, but as the kitchen becomes cramped, productivity actually decreases. Similarly, because of competition among organizations and the increasing demands for cooperation, there comes a point where fewer NGOs operating in the same area will be more effective in supporting the community, and a greater number of NGOs may actually become detrimental to the overall process. This is especially clear in the case of Kosovo, where organizations such as regional security groups, which were not as encumbered by competition, were just as able, if not more so, to implement the types of youth-oriented programs often reserved for non-governmental actors.

The findings on NGO activity bring up further questions:

What is the best measure of the level of NGO effort in comparison to the demands of the situation?

The cases: As with international effort, it is unclear from the cases whether NGO effort is best measured by per-capita financing, personnel, or some other measurement.

What are the determinants for effective coordination? In what cases has the working relationship between NGOs and other actors (international, domestic, and other NGOs) been most or least effective, and why?

The cases: Effective coordination among NGOs was important across all three cases. In Mozambique, a small number of NGOs were able to cooperate relatively efficiently, whereas in the DRC, coordination was extremely difficult. However, it remains unclear which factors, from the effect of the international managing body to environmental aspects, lead to the best coordination results.

How can the NGO environment be reformed to avoid behaviors, such as competition, that undermine the efficacy of the reconstruction process?

The cases: Competition for grants, particularly in Kosovo, was a significant impediment to the reconstruction process, whereas in Mozambique, competition was less an obstacle to NGO performance. However, it is unclear what remedy might be used to avoid the detrimental effects of competition.

Humanitarian versus Development Programs

In all three case studies, the distinctions between humanitarian and development programming and short-term, or transition, versus long-term funding affected the success of the reconstruction process, particularly for youth programs. The first few years immediately following the conflict in each of these cases were marked by emergency or transition efforts to resolve the immediate crisis situations, for example, facilitating the mass return of refugees and internally displaced persons; providing food, shelter, and medicine to those in need; and demobilizing the various armed factions. Indeed, these issues require immediate attention, and the reconstruction process cannot progress without successfully addressing them. However, emergency and transition programming is, by definition, temporary. Whereas humanitarian programs attempt to alleviate crisis conditions—for example, by protecting youth affected by conflict—development programs, such as those focused on youth empowerment and education, try to create long-term solutions. The success of these programs is measured over longer periods of time, and the end goal—for example, fostering leadership and civil society for the next generation—reaches much further into the future than in emergency or transition efforts. The progression from a humanitarian to a development focus is particularly important in post-conflict reconstruction, since the requirements of successful reconstruction cover the spectrum from providing emergency relief to developing transition institutions and facilitating long-term development. The evidence from the three cases also demonstrates how the concentration on short-term or emergency relief programs dictates the limits of the reconstruction process as a whole. For example, because violence in the DRC was ongoing and the DDR/DDRRR program, particularly for children, was forced to operate on an ad-hoc or emergency footing, the reconstruction actors were constantly faced with providing short-term remedies for the humanitarian crisis and were therefore unable to adequately address larger issues essential for longer-term development. In Mozambique, while the humanitarian efforts and transition initiatives were largely successful, the post-conflict reconstruction process stopped short of any kind of long-term development programming.

Because there is more international aid available for emergency relief than for long-term development, a tension arises in the reconstruction process when a reliance on short-term financing dictates the mechanisms used to achieve long-term goals. For instance, although the quick resolution of humanitarian issues in Kosovo allowed funding to be directed to other initiatives, the demand for immediate results and the drop in funding after the first few years stifled the potential for long-term results. This trend was particularly evident with both the proliferation of youth centers in Kosovo and the attempts at education and curriculum reform, which were funded by transition initiatives and emergency donations. By 2004, neither of these programs was receiving sufficient funding, and therefore the same level of efforts could not be sustained. As a result, many of the youth centers no longer operate, and the continued progress of education reform remains in jeopardy.

These observations about humanitarian and development programs suggest the following avenues for further research:

To what extent can short-term humanitarian aid hinder the process of achieving long-term goals?

The cases: In the DRC, humanitarian aid has been cited as one potential factor in causing the conflict. In Kosovo, the short-term nature of funding has stifled the potential impact of the reconstruction program. However, the extent to which funding determines impact remains unclear.

How is the transition from emergency relief operations (and short-term funding) to development-oriented operations (and long-term funding) best facilitated?

The cases: Since the reconstruction process encompasses both humanitarian and development programming, the transition to long-term development is related to the sequencing of general reconstruction and youth-related programs. The question of sustaining funding, however, remains a significant obstacle.

Does there need to be more donors willing to offer grants for long-term projects, or can the United Nations better facilitate the transition with its own programs for emergency relief, humanitarian efforts (Office for the Coordination of Humanitarian Affairs), and development (UNDP)?

The cases: In Mozambique, the post-conflict reconstruction program delegated development issues at the end of the ONUMOZ mission to UNDP. In Kosovo, however, regional security groups are responsible for a significant part of the financing for ongoing development programs.

Bridging Advocacy and Empowerment

Just as the balance between humanitarian and development programming defines the overall limits of post-conflict reconstruction efforts, the balance between youth advocacy campaigns and sociopolitical empowerment programs also determines the extent to which youth programming can influence the youth demographic's role. Like other humanitarian programming, rights-based initiatives are necessary and are complimentary to other sociopolitical and economic empowerment programs. And yet, on their own, they are limited by their own structure. While the Convention on the Rights of the Child is intended as a means to help children develop to their full potential,[14] programs that use a child's rights–based structure tend to respond to the need for emergency protection and support but do not go further to address long-term reintegration or empowerment needs. In addition, the international definitions of "child" and "adult" limit who can receive such support and shape the mechanisms through which advocacy programs are carried out. For example, the goal of children's rights protection tends to favor an adult-dominated process rather than youth participation. As a result, rights-based and advocacy programming does not

---

14. UNICEF, "Understanding the Convention on the Rights of the Child," www.unicef.org/crc/http://www.unicef.org/crc/index_understanding.html (accessed Sept. 1, 2009).

address the full spectrum of youth needs and move beyond the potentially de-stabilizing effects of a large youth demographic by developing the potential for a positive youth role in the reconstruction process.

Where advocacy falls short, particularly in reaching adolescents and older youth, the successful programs seen in all three cases demonstrate that youth empowerment programming can be more effective than rights-based and advocacy programming alone. Empowerment or sociopolitical programming not only pro-vides youth with a constructive way to occupy their time but also gives them skills they can use well into the future. Many of the youth empowerment programs examined in this study also involved some type of community participation and, therefore, allowed the programs not only to benefit the youth participants but also to contribute to community development. Youth empowerment programming in Kosovo, for example, was particularly successful in preventing the emergence of the youth demographic as a destabilizing force, by channeling youth frustrations into productive projects that provided concrete community benefits, especially in the refugee camps.

Despite the successes of youth empowerment programming in both Kosovo and Mozambique, the situations have cycled back to a "greed-grievance" or "youth bulge" scenario, where youth have the potential to become a destabiliz-ing factor. It appears that although the initial youth programming effectively countered the potential for disruption, the structural issues affecting youth have yet to be resolved: in Kosovo, the youth unemployment rate has yet to fall, access to higher education is still quite limited, and ethnic tensions remain high. Un-til these issues are handled, there remains great potential for youth frustrations to resurface in destructive ways. In Mozambique, empowerment programming was successful in promoting community reconciliation, but extreme poverty also opens the door for the youth demographic to reemerge as a destabilizing factor.

While both these cases provide evidence of the positive benefits of youth empowerment programming, their return to a potentially dangerous youth bulge scenario demonstrates that efforts to address youth issues do not take place in isolation. Rather, they are a small (yet significant) factor in the greater reconstruc-tion context. Although successful youth programming can prevent youth from turning to violence and can harness youth energies for community development, the impact of these programs still depends on the general trajectory of the post-conflict environment and on the issues left unresolved since the conflict.

The endeavor to address the youth demographic's potential dual role in per-petuating violence and building peace also parallels the tension between creat-ing a positive and a negative peace. Whereas negative peacebuilding establishes the absence of violence, a positive peace is much harder to achieve and requires that parties resolve the underlying issues that fueled the conflict. Similarly, while the steps taken to prevent young people's emergence as a destabilizing factor can help avert potential disruption of the reconstruction process, such policies do not provide solutions to the *root causes* of the youth demographic's destabilizing behavior, as the case thus far in Kosovo demonstrates. With the majority of young people wanting to emigrate, the ongoing protests, and low-level youth violence, it is clear that achieving the "negative peace" with the youth demographic in the short term, without finding solutions to the causal issues, such as youth unemployment and poor access to quality education, is not enough.

The observations about the balance between advocacy and empowerment suggest a number of important questions for future research:

How can the legal gaps that limit the advocacy structure be bridged to include the young adult and adolescent demographic?

The cases: Particularly in the DRC and Mozambique, where there were extensive efforts to demobilize child soldiers, the international legal definitions created divisions that did not necessarily enhance, and in some ways actually impeded, the reconstruction efforts.

How can children's advocacy programs incorporate lessons from empowerment program design to become more effective?

The cases: The culture of impunity in the DRC has compelled NGOs and other aid organizations to focus primarily on human rights awareness campaigns. However, only a few of these programs incorporate children and youth participation as a way both to promote human rights awareness and to provide young people with a constructive connection to their communities.

What are the limits of youth empowerment programming, and how can reconstruction actors reshape policies and programs to prevent a recycling to the "greed-grievance" or "youth bulge" structure?

The cases: The long-term implications of empowerment programming in Kosovo remain to be seen. In Mozambique, however, it seems evident that youth peacebuilding and community service cannot have an extensive impact when they take place in an environment that continues to be plagued by extreme poverty and humanitarian crises.

If the goals of empowerment programming mirror the goals of creating a "positive peace," can these types of programs be sustained through the reconstruction process?

The cases: While programs in Kosovo and Mozambique fostered short-term leadership development, the commitment to empowering youth and reforming education has not been sustained beyond the initial reconstruction process. Are outside actors capable of continuing these programs? If not, what is the best method to internalize these programs into the domestic sphere?

Youth Agency versus Manipulation

Thus far, this chapter has explored how youth programming fits into the broader reconstruction context. But there is still the question of how young people's role in the post-conflict environment, whether as active social and political agents or as a resource for elite actors to manipulate, affects the reconstruction process. The line between agency and manipulation is gray. Because conflict tends to be a consequence of elites struggling for power, the role that youth play will necessarily depend on what the fighting is about and who the main stakeholders are. In the cases examined in this study, there is more evidence of elites manipulating youth to perpetuate conflict than of youth causing conflict through their own agency. For example, the youth involvement in destabilizing the DRC shows the dangerous potential of the youth demographic but does not necessarily fit the definition of youth "spoiling" the peace. A spoiler actively seeks to prevent a peaceful resolution. In the DRC, child and youth soldiers were manipulated by elites using brutal tactics to spoil an existing peace, but they were not spoilers themselves. Although youth participated in the violence, the violence was not youth driven.

Part of the reason for this finding may lie in the selection of cases, since the forced recruitment of child soldiers was prevalent in two of the three cases. Specifically, in the DRC, the absence of an independent and youth-driven role in perpetuating the instability may be a result of the comparatively young youth population. Not only does the DRC have a high proportion of youth, but in 2003 nearly half of the population (47 percent) was under age 15.[15] Although children were frequent participants in armed groups, they were so young that they could not likely have organized on their own to have an independent effect on the reconstruction process. In these cases, children and youth represented a threat to the stability of the process because they were particularly vulnerable to recruitment. Thus, their destabilizing potential lay in their capacity to be manipulated by elite actors.

The evidence from the cases, however, is not limited to instances of youth manipulated into contributing to conflict. In the DRC there are a number of instances of youth agency perpetuating violence—for example, the youth recruitment gangs loyal to Gen. Laurent Nkunda and the OPEC Boys, who dominated the black market for oil between the DRC and Uganda. In Kosovo, youth were agents of both peace and violence, through student protests and riots, youth networking, and political involvement. Although the data from the three cases do not present conclusive evidence that youth behavior during post-conflict reconstruction parallels the type of role that an elite or adult "spoiler" plays, the evidence does suggest that this potential may exist in other cases and that a large youth population can be an independent force, whether for destabilization or for peace. Further research on youth participation in conflict and post-conflict

15. U.S. Census Bureau, "International Data Base Population Pyramids."

reconstruction may be able to clarify this distinction between youth agency and youth manipulation in conflict causation and post-conflict reconstruction.

Additional analysis of this relationship may reveal, as the evidence from the three cases suggests, that when youth emerge as a destabilizing factor, they are usually manipulated by the proponents of the conflict or are acting within existing structures for violence. For example, children may be forced or co-opted into serving in militias, but they did not ignite the violence, nor do they form the militias. Because participation in the ongoing violence does not always require youth to take much initiative, it may be more likely that young people are susceptible to becoming a source of instability, as suggested by Collier and Hoeffler and by Zakaria.[16] On the other hand, playing a positive role in peacebuilding processes requires youth to take initiative, organize, and rally their peers independently of other actors. In Kosovo, for example, the youth-led movements in the refugee camps and the student movements for independence began on their own, requiring youth to take the initiative (though they were later supported by other actors). But because exerting a positive influence requires greater agency, it is also more difficult to achieve.

This distinction between agency in peacebuilding and manipulation into violence helps explain why current scholars have dismissed the youth demographic as an exclusively destabilizing factor. It also may be one of the reasons why empowerment programming is not usually the focus of international donors. If it is easier for youth to be manipulated or to resort to violence, then donors understand that it is especially important to design programs that prevent recruitment and protect children. However, donors are less likely to tackle the issue of youth empowerment, since helping young people become independent agents of peace in their communities requires a lot more effort than merely keeping them out of armed groups.

Also, it is more difficult to evaluate the success of a youth empowerment program than, say, a demobilization program, because these more development-oriented programs do not necessarily produce direct results, and the skills that participants develop through them are relevant for their participation in society throughout their lifetime, not just in their adolescent and young adult years. In fact, the long-term goal of many youth empowerment, leadership, and development programs is to facilitate the transition from youth to adulthood, so that children and youth affected by conflict can become productive members of their society. Tracking the success of these programs—similar to tracking the success of education—requires follow-up with participants in the years after the program has concluded. Not only is this problematic for evaluating the program's impact, but it also represents a significant obstacle to attracting donors, who often require that organizations clearly demonstrate mechanisms to assess their impact.

---

16. Collier and Hoeffler, "Greed and Grievance in Civil War"; Zakaria, "The Politics of Rage."

The findings on the differences between manipulation and agency suggest other possible avenues for research:

To what degree do geography and culture affect the nature—as manipulated agent or active agent—of the youth role? Do differences depend on relative economic development? On cultural understandings of youth? On methods of warfare?

The cases: Of the three cases, youth in Kosovo initially took the greatest initiative in participating in peacebuilding processes. Youth in Mozambique also took an active, though lesser, role in peacebuilding. It is not clear whether reconstruction policy contributed to this difference, or whether the difference was rooted in the cultural or economic environment.

To what extent do youth exhibit agency before, as distinct from after, a conflict?

The cases: Most literature on youth in conflict areas focuses on youth and conflict causation. Since there appears to be a significant difference between youth manipulation and agency in a post-conflict context, there may be a similar distinction during conflict causation.

What is the best way to evaluate the long-term impact of empowerment programming? By tracking individual participants? By examining generational trends?

The cases: The conflicts in Kosovo and Mozambique were relatively recent, and the long-term impact of empowerment programming may not be known for some time. However, it will be particularly difficult to capture the cross-generational impact of this type of programming. Northern Ireland may be a case in which both the conflict and post-conflict periods have been of sufficient duration that a cross-generational study could reveal important insights regarding the impact of youth programming.

Gender

Finally, one factor that has been present across all three cases, but not discussed at length, is the role of gender and of sexual violence and its effects on the youth population in the reconstruction process.[17] Particularly in the DRC and Kosovo, sexual violence has become extremely prevalent. In the DRC it is used as a weapon of war, as perpetrators terrorize villages and rape the women and girls who serve in armed groups. In Kosovo, sex trafficking has become a serious danger for young Kosovar women. It is not immediately clear how sexual violence, particularly rape and forced marriage, as a tool for waging war affects the behavior of the youth demographic in a post-conflict setting, but it must not be discounted

---

17. For an exploration of issues of gender and youth in post-conflict reconstruction, Annan et al.'s April 2008 SWAY report provides some important findings in the context of Northern Uganda. Annan et al., "The State of Female Youth in Northern Uganda."

as a significant characteristic of the conflict. The importance of women's participation in peacebuilding is gaining more and more acknowledgment in the field.[18] Because women are integral to the peace process, gender-motivated violence may serve as a significant obstacle to reconstruction by physically and psychologically depriving women of the ability to exert independent influence and by tearing apart the family and community structures necessary for a successful transition from war to peace.

For youth, sexual violence is especially traumatizing. Young women subjected to sexual violence at a young age are not only psychologically and physically traumatized, but in many areas, including the DRC and Kosovo, their communities shun them because of cultural stigmas. This not only makes young women more vulnerable but also disrupts the normal familial structures and methods of community learning that facilitate young women's transition to adulthood. While it is clear that girls and young women are distinctly affected by conflict, programs for children and youth often do not provide adequate gender-specific support. In fact, in both cases of demobilization of child soldiers, while girls and young women were estimated to represent up to 40 percent of child soldiers, they were largely left out of the reintegration process. The girls and young women who were included in the DDR programs may not have received the specific tools and support they need to make the transition back to civilian life. For example, the kits that former child soldiers receive upon demobilization are often not gender specific, leaving out sanitary items or other things that young women may need. While the implications of sexual violence and the unequal treatment of genders within the reconstruction process are not clear from the evidence provided in this study, further investigation of the connection between women as agents of peace and sexual violence as a deliberate tool for destabilization could reveal important findings for the field of youth development and post-conflict reconstruction. Here are some questions regarding gender that could guide future research on the relationship between gender and youth roles in conflict:

To what extent is gender-motivated violence and sexual terrorism an instrument, rather than a symptom, of modern civil war? What does the subordination and humiliation of women mean for the potential for peace?

The cases: Parties seeking to perpetuate the instability in the DRC deliberately use sexual violence. In Kosovo, sexual violence was also evident during the conflict, but the rising trend of sex trafficking appears to be mainly a symptom of

---

18. Chineze J. Onyejekwe, "Women, War, Peace-Building and Reconstruction," *International Social Science Journal* 57, no. 2 (2005); Elisabeth Rehn and Ellen Johnson Sirleaf, "Women, War and Peace: The Independent Experts' Assessment on the Impact of Armed Conflict on Women and Women's Role in Peace-Building" (United Nations Development Fund for Women, report, 2002, www.unifem.org/resources/item_detail. php?ProductID=17 (accessed Sept. 1, 2009); International Crisis Group, "Beyond Victimhood: Women's Peacebuilding in Sudan, Congo and Uganda," *Africa Report*, no. 112 (June 28, 2006), www.crisisgroup.org/home/index.cfm?id=4185&CFID=13912551&CFTOKEN=5093512 (accessed Sept. 1, 2009).

the current situation. In Mozambique, where reconstruction has been relatively successful, sexual violence played a much lesser role in the conflict.

How does sexual violence disrupt the normal familial or community structures, and to what extent does this affect the process of national reconstruction and peacebuilding? Are there any trends in how young women who have been victims of sexual violence behave and are treated during the reconstruction period compared with other young women and young men?

The cases: In the DRC, young girls are often kicked out of their communities, thus being made even more vulnerable by the sexual assault they have already endured. Some girls were then forced to join militias out of necessity, to meet basic needs such as food and shelter. Women are critical agents in the peacebuilding process, and sexual violence against them may alter their personal understandings of conflict, as well as their opportunity and desire to engage in destabilizing or peacebuilding efforts.

To what extent to do cultural norms regarding sexual assault determine the possibilities for successful reintegration? And what types of programs have been most effective in aiding victims of sexual assault: advocacy or empowerment?

The cases: In both Kosovo and the DRC, scholars have noted a cultural stigma toward young women who have been raped or sexually assaulted. In Mozambique, however, this discussion was largely absent from the analysis of youth roles in conflict.

Conclusion

The conventional wisdom on youth in conflict holds that a country with a disproportionately high youth population is more likely than a country with a smaller youth cohort to fall into conflict. From this perspective, the youth population is a one-dimensional force for destabilization. If so, then a large youth population would also have a destabilizing potential during a post-conflict reconstruction process. However, the evidence shows otherwise. This study provides a number of key findings on how youth affect the post-conflict reconstruction process.

The youth demographic is not simply a destabilizing force. Young people can be agents of peace as well as instability. Despite the menacing youth gangs, child soldiers, and teenage terrorists dominating news headlines, a deeper look at the situation on the ground in conflict zones shows that youth play a more dynamic role than was thought. Young people can be both positive and negative agents of change. The evidence from the case studies of Mozambique, the Democratic Republic of the Congo, and Kosovo reveals that young people in post-conflict situations have the potential to riot, commit violent crimes, join rebel movements, and perpetuate conflict, but also to contribute to peacebuilding as leaders in community reconciliation, entrepreneurs, and active members of civil society.

Whether the youth demographic emerges as a force for violence or for peace depends largely on the actions of other actors in the reconstruction process. Without successful DDR, access to education or jobs, and opportunities to have their voices heard in the reconstruction process, young people can easily become a resource for elites seeking to spoil reconstruction, or they can independently contribute to destabilization thorough riots, gang militancy, and terrorism. However, if reconstruction actors can provide youth with the needed opportunities, the cases show that youth are just as likely to contribute to conflict resolution and community development. Therefore, although the youth demographic is just one cog in the greater reconstruction machine, how well the international community and domestic leaders address youth issues has a significant impact on the level of stability during the reconstruction process and on the ultimate success of the peacebuilding mission.

In a post-conflict environment, youth roles do not depend on who is implementing youth programs or even on whether there is a specific youth policy. Rather, youth roles are shaped by how effectively reconstruction actors meet certain functions.

In all three cases, certain tasks—among them disarmament, demobilization, and reintegration; access to education; employment or skills training; and empowerment in civil society—proved critical to meeting youth needs during reconstruction. While certain actors may be more capable than others of taking on a particular task, what matters is that each task be implemented effectively.

Success in meeting these requirements depends on both the sequence in which programs are implemented and the type of program design. Each critical youth function, from protection to reintegration and empowerment, builds on the success of the preceding function: youth empowerment cannot be successful without first ensuring that young people's basic needs are met. While in reality the stages may overlap, each represents a critical progression: (1) providing humanitarian aid; (2) reintegration; and (3) facilitating youth empowerment in the nation's political, social, and economic structures.

Different types of programs are better suited for different functions. Whereas an advocacy framework is well suited to providing protection and quelling the negative potential of the youth demographic, sociopolitical and empowerment approaches provide platforms to support young people in becoming agents of peace.

Finally, the distinction between youth agency and manipulation is crucial to understanding how the youth demographic affects conflict environments. Youth play a variety of roles during the reconstruction processes: soldiers, protesters, peace advocates, entrepreneurs, and community leaders. In the cases studied, when youth played a destabilizing part, their actions were often orchestrated by elite actors. But when young people played positive roles, their movements, organizations, and activities were often youth driven and youth led.

The dynamic role of youth in post-conflict reconstruction suggests that long-term youth empowerment programming has the capacity both to reduce the youth demographic's destabilizing potential and also to train the next generation in methods of peace and conflict resolution. Just as the post-conflict reconstruction phase is a significant transition for a nation, the young adults living through this period constitute the transition generation. Thus, addressing youth needs such as reintegration and access to education during reconstruction is necessary, first, to help stabilize the nation during the transition period. Perhaps more importantly, effectively fulfilling these transition functions is also critical to future development: The ways that young people who lived through the horrors of war experience the peacemaking process, from undergoing a demobilization-and-reintegration program to participating in conflict resolution workshops, or even simply observing the process, will shape their understanding of peace, community, and their role as citizens. As these young men and women become the next generation of adults leading the country, their experiences during reconstruction will influence the nation's trajectory in the transition from war to peace.

Appendix

List of Acronyms

AFDL	Alliance des Forces Démocratiques pour la Libération du Congo (Alliance of Democratic Forces for the Liberation of the Congo)
ANC	African National Congress
CCPN	Community Child Protection Network
CNDP	Congrès National pour la Dèfense du Peuple (National Congress for the Defense of the People)
CO	Orientation Centers (for the DDR program in DRC)
CONADER	Commission Nationale de la Désarmement, Démobilization et Réinsertion (National Commission for Disarmament, Demobilization and Reintegration in the DRC)
CRC	Convention on the Rights of the Child
DDR	Disarmament, demobilization, and reintegration
DDRRR	Disarmament, demobilization, repatriation, resettlement, and reintegration
DRC	Democratic Republic of the Congo
ex-FAR	Former Forces Armées Rwandaises (Rwandan Armed Forces)
EYES	Effective Youth Empowerment Strategy (in Kosovo)
FARDC	Forces Armées de la République Démocratique du Congo (Armed Forces of the Democratic Republic of the Congo)
FDLR	Forces Démocratiques de Liberation du Rwanda
Frelimo	Frente de Libertação de Moçambique (Liberation Front of Mozambique)
GPA	General Peace Agreement (for Mozambique)
ICC	International Criminal Court
ICRC	International Committee of the Red Cross

IDP	Internally displaced person
ILO	International Labour Organization
IOM	International Migration Organization
IRC	International Rescue Committee
KFOR	Kosovo International Security Forces
KLA	Kosovo Liberation Army
KYC	Kosovo Youth Council
MDRP	Multi-country Demobilization and Reintegration Program
MLC	Mouvement pour la Libération du Congo (Movement for the Liberation of the Congo)
MONUC	United Nations Organization Mission in the Democratic Republic of the Congo
NATO	North Atlantic Treaty Organization
NGO	Non-governmental organization
OFDA	Office of U.S. Foreign Disaster Assistance
ONUMOZ	United Nations Operation in Mozambique
OSCE	Organization for Security and Co-operation in Europe
OSD	Occupational Skills Development Program (in Mozambique)
PN-DDR	National Plan for Disarmament, Demobilization, and Reintegration (in the DRC)
QIP	"Quick impact projects" (in Mozambique)
Renamo	Resistência Nacional Moçambicana (Mozambican National Resistance)
RCD	Rassemblement Congolais pour la Démocratie (Congolese Rally for Democracy)
RCD-Goma	Rassemblement Congolais pour la Démocratie–Goma
RSS	Reintegration Support Scheme (in Mozambique)
SE*CA	Synergie d'Education Communautaire et d'Appui à la Transition (Synergy of Community Education and Transitional Support)
UNDP	United Nations Development Program
UNESCO	United Nations Educational, Scientific, and Cultural Organization
UNHCR	United Nations High Commissioner for Refugees
UNICEF	United Nations Children's Fund
UNMIK	United Nations Interim Administration Mission in Kosovo

UNOHAC	United Nations Office for the Coordination of Humanitarian Assistance
USAID	United States Agency for International Development
YPCPP	Youth Post-conflict Participation Project (in Kosovo)

Bibliography

Action for the Rights of Children (ARC). "Critical Issues: Child Soldiers." UNHCR and International Save the Children Alliance, 2001. www.unhcr.org/3f83de714.html (accessed Aug. 1, 2009).

Aird, Sarah, Boia Efraime Jr., and Antoinette Errante. "Mozambique: The Battle Continues for Former Child Soldiers." Youth Advocate Program International Resource Paper, 2001, 1–11. www.nabuur.com/files/attach/2008/07/task/doc_44537b29343bb.pdf (accessed Aug. 25, 2009).

Alden, Chris. "The UN and the Resolution of Conflict in Mozambique." *Journal of Modern African Studies* 33, no. 1 (1995): 103–28.

———. *Mozambique and the Construction of the New African State: From Negotiations to Nation Building.* New York: Palgrave, 2001.

———. "Making Old Soldiers Fade Away: Lessons from the Reintegration of Demobilized Soldiers in Mozambique." *Security Dialogue* 33, no. 3 (2002): 341–56.

Ali, Taisier, Mohamed Ahmed, and Robert O. Matthews. *Civil Wars in Africa: Roots and Resolution.* Montreal: McGill-Queen's University Press, 1999.

Amnesty International. "Democratic Republic of Congo: Children at War, Creating Hope for the Future." Report, 2006, www.anmestyusa.org/document.php?id=ENGAFR6201720068lang=e(accessed Sept. 1, 2009).

Annan, Jeannie, Christopher Blattman, Khristopher Carlson, and Dyan Mazurana. "The State of Female Youth in Northern Uganda: Findings from the Survey of War Affected Youth (SWAY)." Report produced for UNICEF Uganda, 2008. http://wikis.uit.tufts.edu/confluence/display/FIC/The+State+of+Female+Youth+in+Northern+Uganda (accessed Sept. 1, 2009).

Annan, Jeannie, Christopher Blattman, and Roger Horton. "The State of Youth and Youth Protection in Northern Uganda: Findings from the Survey of War Affected Youth (SWAY)." Report produced for UNICEF Uganda, 2006. http://chrisblattman.com/documents/policy/sway/SWAY.Phase1.FinalReport.pdf (accessed Sept. 1, 2009).

B92 News. "Koštunica: Youth Show They Want Justice." *B92*, Feb. 22, 2008.

Bache, Ian, and Andrew Taylor. "The Politics of Policy Resistance: Reconstructing Higher Education in Kosovo." *Journal of Public Policy* 23, no. 3 (2003): 279–300.

Bashir, Sajitha. "Democratic Republic of Congo: Country Status Report on Education, Priorities and Options for Regenerating the Education Sector." World Bank Report No. 30860-ZR, Nov. 15, 2004. www-wds.worldbank.org/external/default/WDSContentServer/WDSP/IB/2004/12/28/000012009_20041228 095516/Rendered/PDF/308600ZR.pdf (accessed Sept. 23, 2009).

BBC. "Kosovo UN Troops 'Fuel Sex Trade.'" *BBC News*, May 6, 2004.

Bell, Martin. "Child Alert: Democratic Republic of Congo." Report produced for UNICEF, 2006. www.unicef.org/childalert/drc/ (accessed Sept. 1, 2009).

Boothby, Neil, Jennifer Crawford, and Jason Halperin. "Mozambique Child Soldier Life Outcome Study: Lessons Learned in Rehabilitation and Reintegration Efforts." *Global Public Health* 1, no. 1 (2006): 87–107.

Boothby, Neil G., and Christine M. Knudsen. "Children of the Gun." *Scientific American* 282, no. 6 (2000): 60–65.

Borer, Tristan Anne, John Darby, and Siobhán McEvoy-Levy. 2006. *Peacebuilding after Peace Accords: The Challenges of Violence, Truth, and Youth*. South Bend, Ind.: University of Notre Dame Press, 2006.

Boulden, Jane. *Dealing with Conflict in Africa: The United Nations and Regional Organizations*. New York: Palgrave Macmillan, 2003.

Boyden, Jo, and Joanna de Berry. *Children and Youth on the Front Line: Ethnography, Armed Conflict and Displacement*. Vol. 14 of *Studies in Forced Migration*. New York: Berghahn, 2004.

Boyden, Jo, and Gillian Mann. "Children's Risk, Resilience and Coping in Extreme Situations." In *Handbook for Working with Children and Youth: Pathways to Resilience Across Cultures and Contexts*. Edited by Michael Ungar. Thousand Oaks, CA: SAGE, 2005.

Brett, Rachel, and Irma Specht. *Young Soldiers: Why They Choose to Fight*. Boulder, Colo.: Lynne Rienner, 2004.

Busumtwi-Sam, James. "Sustainable Peace and Development in Africa." *Studies in Comparative International Development* 37, no. 3 (2002): 91–118.

Center for Strategic and International Studies (CSIS). "The Post-conflict Reconstruction Project." www.csis.org/isp/pcr/ (accessed Sept. 1, 2009).

Central Intelligence Agency (CIA). "The World Factbook: Mozambique." www.cia.gov/library/publications/the-world-factbook/geos/mz.html (accessed Sept. 1, 2009).

Chege, Michael. "Sierra Leone: The State That Came Back from the Dead." *Washington Quarterly* 25, no. 3 (2002): 147–60.

Coalition to Stop the Use of Child Soldiers. "Child Soldiers Global Report 2001—Federal Republic of Yugoslavia, 2001." www.unhcr.org/refworld/docid/498805fbc.html (accessed Sept. 1, 2009).

———. "Democratic Republic of the Congo: Priorities for Children Associated with Armed Forces and Groups." Report, 2007. www.reliefweb.int/rw/RWB. NSF/db900SID/TBRL-75QQQX?OpenDocument (accessed Sept. 1, 2009).

Cobban, Helena. *Amnesty after Atrocity?: Healing Nations after Genocide and War Crimes*. Boulder, Colo.: Paradigm, 2007.

Coelho, João Paulo Borges, and Alex Vines. "Pilot Study on Demobilization and Reintegration of Ex-Combatants in Mozambique." Report, Oxford Refugee Studies Programme, University of Oxford, 1994.

Collier, Paul, and Anke Hoeffler. "Greed and Grievance in Civil War." *Oxford Economic Papers* 56, no. 4 (2004): 563–95.

Conciliation Resources. General Peace Agreement for Mozambique. Aug. 7, 1992. www.c-r.org/our-work/accord/mozambique/agreement-partial-ceasefire. php (accessed Sept. 7, 2009).

Control Risk. *RiskMap 2008*. London: Control Risks, 2007. www.controlrisks. com/default.aspx?page=1096 (accessed Sept. 4, 2009).

Cooley, Alexander, and James Ron. "The NGO Scramble: Organizational Insecurity and the Political Economy of Transnational Action." *International Security* 27, no. 1 (2002): 5–39.

Crisp, Jeff, Marika Fahlen, Frances Christie, Phil O'Keefe, Jon Danilowicz, and Shirley De Wolf. "Rebuilding a War-Torn Society: A Review of the UNHCR Reintegration Programme for Mozambican Returnees." *Refugee Studies Quarterly* 16, no. 2 (1997).

Crocker, Chester A., Fen Osler Hampson, and Pamela R. Aall. *Turbulent Peace: The Challenges of Managing International Conflict*. Washington, D.C.: United States Institute of Peace Press, 2001.

———. *Leashing the Dogs of War: Conflict Management in a Divided World*. Washington, D.C.: United States Institute of Peace Press, 2007.

Dobbins, James. *The UN's Role in Nation-Building: From the Congo to Iraq*. Santa Monica, Calif.: RAND, 2005.

Doyle, Michael W., and Nicholas Sambanis. *Making War and Building Peace: United Nations Peace Operations*. Princeton, N.J.: Princeton University Press, 2006.

Dzinesa, Gwinyayi A. "Postconflict Disarmament, Demobilization, and Reintegration of Former Combatants in Southern Africa." *International Studies Perspectives* 8, no. 1 (2007): 73–89.

Eckstein, Harry. "Case Study and Theory in Political Science." In *Handbook of Political Science*. Edited by Fred I. Greenstein and Nelson W. Polsby. Reading, Mass.: Addison-Wesley, 1975.

Economist Intelligence Unit. "Country Report." 1996–2009. www.eiu.com (subscription only, accessed Sept. 1, 2009).

———. "Country Report: Mozambique Malawi." October 1996. www.eiu.com (subscription only, accessed Sept. 1, 2009).

————. "Country Report: Mozambique Malawi." October 1997. www.eiu.com (subscription only, accessed Sept. 1, 2009).

————. "Country Report: Democratic Republic of Congo." March 2004. www.eiu.com (subscription only, accessed Sept. 1, 2009).

————. "Country Profile 2008: Democratic Republic of Congo." Sept. 19, 2008. www.eiu.com (subscription only, accessed Sept. 1, 2009).

————. "Country Report: Serbia." 2000–2008. www.eiu.com (subscription only, accessed Sept. 1, 2009).

Ekehaug, Vidar, and Chernor Bah. "'Will You Listen?' Young Voices from Conflict Zones." Report, UN Office for the Special Representative for Children and Armed Conflict, 2006. www.reliefweb.int/rw/RWB.NSF/db900SID/KH-II-7A24NQ?OpenDocument (accessed Aug. 1, 2009).

Erlanger, Steven. "U.S. Ready to Resume Sanctions against Serbs over Kosovo Strife." *New York Times*, June 6, 1998.

Fearon, J. D., and D. D. Laitin. "Ethnicity, Insurgency, and Civil War." *American Political Science Review* 97, no. 1 (2003): 75–90.

Ferizi, Sokol, and Novi Sad. "Youth Despair of Decent Future in Kosovo." Balkan Investigative Reporting Network, Nov. 15, 2007. www.birn.eu.com/en/113/10/5821/ (accessed Sept. 8, 2009).

Fukuyama, Francis, Thomas Carothers, Edward D. Mansfield, Jack Snyder, and Sheri Berman. "The Debate on 'Sequencing.'" *Journal of Democracy* 18, no. 3 (2007): 5–22.

Fund for Peace. Failed States Index, 2007. www.fundforpeace.org/web/index.php?option=com_content&task=view&id=99&Itemid=140 (accessed Sept. 1, 2009).

Galtung, Johan, *Peace by Peaceful Means: Peace and Conflict, Development and Civilization*. London: SAGE, 1996.

Goldstone, Jack. "Youth and Conflict: A Toolkit for Intervention." USAID, Office of Conflict Management and Mitigation. Conflict Toolkit, 2004. www.usaid.gov/our_work/cross-cutting_programs/conflict/publications/docs/CMM_Youth_and_Conflict_Toolkit_April_2005.pdf (accessed Sept.1, 2009).

Government of Democratic Republic of the Congo. "Programme National de Désarmement, Démobilization et Réinsertion—PNDDR." 2006. http://unddr.org/docs/Programme%20National%20de%20DDR-7.5.pdf (accessed Sept. 1, 2009).

Graduate Institute of International Studies, Geneva. *Small Arms Survey 2004: Rights at Risk*. Oxford: Oxford University Press, 2004.

Greenhill, Kelly, and Solomon Major. "The Perils of Profiling: Civil War Spoilers and the Collapse of Intrastate Peace Accords." *International Security* 31, no. 3 (2006): 7–40.

Greste, Peter. "Congolese Children Forced to Fight." *BBC News*, Goma, Nov. 12, 2008. http://news.bbc.co.uk/2/hi/africa/7724088.stm (accessed Sept. 1, 2009).

Hartzell, Caroline, Matthew Hoddie, and Donald Rothchild. "Stabilizing the Peace after Civil War: An Investigation of Some Key Variables." *International Organization* 55, no. 1 (2001): 183–208.

Hobson, Matt. "Forgotten Casualties of War: Girls in Armed Conflict." Report, Save the Children, 2005. www.reliefweb.int/rw/lib.nsf/db900SID/EVIU-6BSFEG?OpenDocument (accessed Sept. 1, 2009).

Hoddie, Matthew, and Caroline Hartzell. "Signals of Reconciliation: Institution-Building and the Resolution of Civil Wars." *International Studies Review* 7, no. 1 (2005): 21–40.

Human Rights Watch. "Kosovo: Failure of NATO, U.N. to Protect Minorities." Human Rights Watch News, July 26, 2004. www.hrw.org/en/news/2004/07/26/kosovo-failure-nato-un-protect-minorities (accessed Aug. 1, 2009).

———. "DR Congo: Army Should Stop Use of Child Soldiers." Human Rights Watch News, April 19, 2007. www.hrw.org/en/news/2007/04/19/dr-congo-army-should-stop-use-child-soldiers (accessed Sept. 1, 2009).

———. "DR Congo: Massive Increase in Attacks on Civilians." July 2, 2009. www.hrw.org/en/news/2009/07/02/dr-congo-massive-increase-attacks-civilians (accessed Sept. 1, 2009).

Independent International Commission on Kosovo. *Kosovo Report: Conflict, International Response, Lessons Learned.* Oxford: Oxford University Press, 2000.

International Crisis Group. "EU Visas and the Western Balkans." *Europe Report* no. 168, 2005. www.crisisgroup.org/home/index.cfm?id=3809 (accessed Sept. 1, 2009).

———. "Beyond Victimhoood: Women's Peacebuilding in Sudan, Congo and Uganda." Africa Report no. 112, 2006. www.crisisgroup.org/home/index.cfm?id=4185&CFID=13912551&CFTOKEN=5093512 (accessed Sept. 1, 2009).

Kassa, Michel. "Humanitarian Assistance in the DRC." In *Challenges of Peace Implementation: The UN Mission in the Democratic Republic of Congo.* Edited by Mark Malan and João Gomes Porto. Pretoria: Institute for Security Studies, 2004.

Kemper, Yvonne. "Youth in War-to-Peace Transitions. Approaches by International Organizations." *Berghof Report* no. 10 (2005). www.berghof-center.org/uploads/download/br10e.pdf (accessed Sept. 5, 2009).

KosovaLive. "Kosovo Albanian Students Rally in Support of Independence." *BBC Worldwide Monitoring,* Oct. 10, 2007.

Kostovicova, Denisa. *Kosovo: The Politics of Identity and Space.* London: Routledge, 2005.

Lecoutere, Els, and Kristof Titeca. "Les Opec Boys en Ouganda, Trafiquants de Petrole et Acteurs Politiques." *Politique Africaine* 103 (2006): 143–59.

Leurdijk, Dick A., and Dick Zandee. *Kosovo: From Crisis to Crisis.* Aldershot, UK: Ashgate, 2000.

Lischer, Sarah Kenyon. "Collateral Damage: Humanitarian Assistance as a Cause of Conflict." *International Security* 28, no. 1 (2003): 79–109.

———. *Dangerous Sanctuaries: Refugee Camps, Civil War, and the Dilemmas of Humanitarian Aid.* Ithaca, N.Y.: Cornell University Press, 2005.

Lowicki, Jane, and Allison A. Pillsbury. "Making the Choice for a Better Life: Promoting the Protection and Capacity of Kosovo's Youth." Report, Women's Commission, 2001. www.womenscommission.org/pdf/yu_adol.pdf (accessed Sept. 1, 2009).

Lumsden, Malvern. "Breaking the Cycle of Violence." *Journal of Peace Research* 34, no. 4 (1997): 377–83.

Lusaka Cease-fire Agreement. 1999. www.usip.org/library/pa/drc/pa_drc.html (accessed Sept. 1, 2009).

Machel, Graça. "The Impact of Armed Conflict on Children." Report for UNICEF, 1996. www.unicef.org/graca/ (accessed Sept. 1, 2009).

Malan, Mark, and João Gomes Porto. *Challenges of Peace Implementation: The UN Mission in the Democratic Republic of the Congo.* Pretoria: Institute for Security Studies, 2004.

Maslen, Stuart. "The Reintegration of War-Affected Youth: The Experience of Mozambique." Report, International Labour Office, Geneva, 1997. www.ilo.org/public/english/employment/crisis/download/maslen.pdf (accessed Aug. 25, 2009).

Mathews, J. T. "Power Shift." *Foreign Affairs* 76, no. 1 (1997).

Máusse, Miguel A. "The Social Reintegration of the Child Involved in Armed Conflict in Mozambique." In Monograph no. 37, "Child Soldiers in Africa," 1999. www.iss.co.za/Pubs/Monographs/No37/TheSocialReintegration.html (accessed Sept. 7, 2009).

McEvoy-Levy, Siobhán. "Youth as Social and Political Agents: Issues in Post-Settlement Peace Building." Kroc Institute Occasional Paper no. 21, 2001. www.ciaonet.org/wps/mcs01/index.html (accessed Sept. 9, 2009).

———, ed. *Troublemakers or Peacemakers? Youth and Post-Accord Peace Building.* South Bend, Ind.: University of Notre Dame Press, 2006.

McIntyre, Angela. "Children and Youth in Sierra Leone's Peace-Building Process." *African Security Review* 12, no. 2 (2003).

Merriam-Webster's Collegiate Dictionary, 11th ed.

Mertus, Julie. "Improving International Peacebuilding Efforts: The Example of Human Rights Culture in Kosovo." *Global Governance* 10, no. 3 (2004): 333–51.

Mina News Agency. "Pristina Students Protest against Decentralization of Kosovo." BBC Monitoring Worldwide, May 3, 2006.

Minter, William. *Apartheid's Contras: An Inquiry into the Roots of War in Angola and Mozambique.* Johannesburg: Witwatersrand University Press, 1994.

Mo Ibrahim Foundation. 2008 Ibrahim Index of African Governance. www.moibrahimfoundation.org/the-index.asp (accessed Sept. 1, 2009).

Moran, Mary H., and M. Anne Pitcher. "The 'Basket Case' and the 'Poster Child': Explaining the End of Civil Conflicts in Liberia and Mozambique." *Third World Quarterly* 25, no. 3 (2004): 501–19.

Multi-Country Demobilization and Reintegration Program (MDRP), "Status of the MDRP in the Democratic Republic of the Congo." Multi-Country Demobilization and Reintegration Program Status Report, 2007. www.mdrp.org/PDFs/N&N_10_07.pdf (accessed Sept. 1, 2009).

Myers, Mary, and Judy El-Bushra. "Mid-Term Evaluation of Search for Common Ground (Centre Lokolé) 'Supporting Congo's Transition towards Sustainable Peace' Programme in Democratic Republic of the Congo (DRC)." DFID Final Report, March 2006. www.sfcg.org/sfcg/evaluations/drc2006.pdf (accessed Sept. 1, 2009).

Newitt, Malyn. *A History of Mozambique*. Bloomington, Ind.: Indiana University Press, 1995.

Onyejekwe, Chineze J. "Women, War, Peace-Building and Reconstruction." *International Social Science Journal* 57, no. 2 (2005): 277–83.

Parker, Lynette. "Organizing Ex-Combatants for Peace in Mozambique." *Restorative Justice Online,* 2007. www.restorativejustice.org/editions/2007/april2007/mozambique (accessed Sept. 1, 2009).

Paul, Katie. "The Bloodiest War: Civilians from the Eastern Congo Tell Their Stories." *Newsweek* Web Exclusive. www.newsweek.com/id/170763/page/1 (accessed June 29, 2009).

Peters, Krjin. "From Weapons to Wheels: Young Sierra Leonean Ex-combatants Become Motorbike Taxi-Riders." *Journal of Peace Conflict and Development* 10, no. 10 (2007).

Posthumus, Bram. *Struggles in Peacetime: Working with Ex-combatants in Mozambique: Their Work, Their Frustrations and Successes.* Amsterdam: NiZA, 2006.

Power, Samantha. "Bystanders to Genocide." *Atlantic Monthly* 288, no. 2 (Sept. 2001).

Pozhidaev, Dmitry, and Ravza Andzhelich. "Beating Swords to Ploughshares: Reintegration of Former Combatants in Kosovo." Report, Center for Political and Social Research, Pristina, 2005. http://unddr.org/docs/Beating%20Swords%20Into%20Plowshares.pdf (accessed Sept. 1, 2009).

Quinn, J. Michael, T. David Mason, and Mehmet Gurses. "Sustaining the Peace: Determinants of Civil War Recurrence." *International Interactions* 33, no. 2 (2007): 167–93.

Rehn, Elisabeth, and Ellen Johnson Sirleaf. "Women, War and Peace: The Independent Experts' Assessment on the Impact of Armed Conflict on Women and Women's Role in Peace-Building." Report, United Nations Development Fund for Women, 2002. www.unifem.org/resources/item_detail.php?ProductID=17 (accessed Sept. 1, 2009).

Repa, Jan. "Ethnic Cleansing: Revival of an Old Tradition." *BBC News*, March 29, 1999. http://news.bbc.co.uk/2/hi/special_report/1998/kosovo2/307261.stm (accessed Sept. 1, 2009).

Salopek, Paul. "The Guns of Africa: Violence-Wracked Nations Are Dumping Grounds for World's Arsenals." *Chicago Tribune* via *Seattle Times*, Feb. 27, 2002.

Schwartz, Stephen. *Kosovo: Background to a War*. London: Anthem, 2000.

Search for Common Ground. "DR Congo Update." www.sfcg.org/programmes/drcongo/archive/march2007.pdf (accessed Sept. 1, 2009).

———. "Search for Common Ground in the Democratic Republic of Congo: Programme Overview." 2009. www.sfcg.org/programmes/drcongo/programmes_drcongo.html (accessed Sept. 1, 2009).

Seelye, Katharine Q. "Crisis in the Balkans: Washington; Clinton Blames Milosevic, Not Fate, for Bloodshed." *New York Times*, May 14, 1999. www.nytimes.com/1999/05/14/world/crisis-in-the-balkans-washington-clinton-blames-milosevic-not-fate-for-bloodshed.html?pagewanted=all (accessed Sept. 1, 2009).

Seigel, Steve, Frederick Barton, and Karin Von Hippel. *Engaging Youth to Build Safer Communities: A Report of the CSIS Post-conflict Reconstruction Project, August 2006*. Washington, D.C.: CSIS Press, 2006.

Singer, P. W. *Children at War*. New York: Pantheon, 2005.

Sommers, Marc, and Peter Buckland. "Parallel Worlds: Rebuilding the Education System in Kosovo." Working document, UNESCO International Institute for Educational Planning, 2004. www.unesco.org/iiep/PDF/pubs/kosovo.pdf (accessed Sept. 1, 2009).

———. "Negotiating Kosovo's Educational Minefield." *Forced Migration Review*, no. 22 (2005): 38–39.

Stedman, Stephen J. "Spoiler Problems in Peace Processes." *International Security* 22, no. 2 (1997): 5–53.

Swarbrick, Peter. "DDRRR: Political Dynamics and Linkages." In *Challenges of Peace Implementation: The UN Mission in the Democratic Republic of Congo*. Edited by Mark Malan and João Gomes Porto. Pretoria: Institute for Security Studies, 2004.

Synge, Richard. *Mozambique: UN Peacekeeping in Action, 1992–1994*. Washington, D.C.: United States Institute of Peace Press, 1997.

Takala, Tuomas. "Making Educational Policy under the Influence of External Assistance and National Politics—a Comparative Analysis of the Education Sector Policy Documents of Ethiopia, Mozambique, Namibia and Zambia." *International Journal of Educational Development* 18, no. 4 (1998): 319–35.

UNAIDS. "Democratic Republic of the Congo." 2008. www.unaids.org/en/CountryResponses/Countries/democratic_republic_of_the_congo.asp (accessed Sept. 23, 2009).

UNDP. "Effective Youth Empowerment Strategy (Kos/02/005)." UNDP Project Summary, 2004. www.kosovo.undp.org/Projects/YEP/yep.htm (accessed April 2008).

———. "Human Development Report Kosovo 2004." www.ks.undp.org/repository/docs/KHDR2004.pdf (accessed Sept. 1, 2009).

———. "UNDP in Kosovo: Youth Post-conflict Participation Project." UNDP Project Summary. 2002. www.kosovo.undp.org/Projects/YPCPP/ypcpp.htm (accessed April 2008).

———. "Youth: A New Generation for a New Kosovo." Human Development Report, UNDP, 2006. Edited by Jeffrey Arthur Hoover (English). www.ks.undp.org/repository/docs/hdr_eng.pdf (accessed Sept. 1, 2009).

UNICEF. "The State of the World's Children 1996." www.unicef.org/sowc96/ (accessed Sept. 1, 2009).

———. "Youth in Kosovo." Report, June 2004. www.unicef.org/kosovo/kosovo_media_pub_youth.010.04.pdf (accessed Aug. 1, 2009).

———. "Mozambique—Background and Statistics." Aug. 2004. www.unicef.org/infobycountry/mozambique_statistics.html#25 (accessed Sept. 1, 2009).

———. "Democratic Republic of the Congo." Aug. 2006. www.unicef.org/infobycountry/drcongo_636.html (accessed Sept. 1, 2009).

———. "Understanding the Convention on the Rights of the Child." Feb. 2008. www.unicef.org/crc/index_understanding.html (accessed June 27, 2009).

United Nations. "Convention on the Rights of the Child," A/RES/44/25 of 20 November 1989. www.un.org/documents/ga/res/44/a44r025.htm (accessed Sept. 10, 2009).

———. Rome Statute of the International Criminal Court. Adopted July 17, 1998. http://untreaty.un.org/cod/icc/statute/romefra.htm (accessed Aug. 11, 2009).

———. "Optional Protocol to the Convention on the Rights of the Child on the Sale of Children, Child Prostitution and Child Pornography." A/RES/54/263 May 25, 2000. www2.ohchr.org/english/law/crc-sale.htm (accessed Sept. 1, 2009).

———. "S/2004/650: Third Special Report of the Secretary General on the United Nations Organization Mission in the Democratic Republic of the Congo." Aug. 16, 2004. http://daccessdds.un.org/doc/UNDOC/GEN/N04/457/42IMG/N0445742.pdf?OpenElement (accessed Sept. 1, 2009).

———. United Nations Security Council Resolution 1565. Oct. 1, 2004. http://daccess-ods.un.org/access.nsf/Get?Open&DS=S/RES/1565%20(2004)&Lang=E&Area=UNDOC (accessed Jan. 2008).

———. "Press Conference on the Democratic Republic of Congo." 2005. www.un.org/News/briefings/docs/2005/051006_DRC_PC.doc.htm (accessed April 2, 2008).

———. "MONUC: Background." 2005. www.un.org/Depts/dpko/missions/monuc/background.html (accessed April 5, 2008).

————. "World Youth Report." 2005. www.un.org/esa/socdev/unyin/wyr05.htm (accessed Sept. 1, 2009).

————. "S/2006/389: Report of the Secretary-General on Children and Armed Conflict in the Democratic Republic of Congo." June 13, 2006. http://daccess-ods.un.org/TMP/6174745.html (accessed Aug. 5, 2009).

————. "S/2007/391: Report of the Secretary-General on Children and Armed Conflict in the Democratic Republic of the Congo." June 28, 2007. www.un.org/Docs/sc/sgrep07.htm (accessed Sept. 1, 2009).

————. "The Millennium Development Goals Report, 2007." www.un.org/millenniumgoals/pdf/mdg2007.pdf (accessed Sept. 1, 2009).

————. "Democratic Republic of Congo – MONUC – Mandate." 2008. www.un.org/Depts/dpko/missions/monuc/mandate.html (accessed Sept. 1, 2009).

————. "MONUC: DDR." 2008. www.monuc.org/news.aspx?newsID=716 (accessed April 2, 2008).

————."Integrated Disarmament, Demobilization and Reintegration Standards: Module 5.20 Youth and DDR." 2009. www.unddr.org/iddrs/framework.php (accessed Sept. 1, 2009).

————. "MONUC: Facts and Figures." 2009. www.un.org/Depts/dpko/missions/monuc/facts.html (accessed Sept. 1, 2009).

UNMIK. "Kosovo State of the Environment Report." 2002. http://enrin.grida.no/htmls/kosovo/SoE/index.htm (accessed Sept. 1, 2009);

Urdal, Henrik. "A Clash of Generations? Youth Bulges and Political Violence." *International Studies Quarterly* 50, no. 3 (2006): 607–29.

————. "USAID/OTI DRC Field Report." 2005. www.usaid.gov/our_work/cross-cutting_programs/transition_initiatives/country/congo/rpt1005.html (accessed Sept. 1, 2009).

————. "USAID/OTI DROC Success Story," March 2006. www.usaid.gov/our_work/cross-cutting_programs/transition_initiatives/country/congo/topic0206a.html (accessed Sept. 1, 2009).

————. "Transition Initiatives: Democratic Republic of Congo." Sept. 2007. www.usaid.gov/our_work/cross-cutting_programs/transition_initiatives/country/congo/index.html (accessed Sept. 1, 2009).

USAID, "Children and War: The Mozambique Experience." Undated project report. http://pdf.usaid.gov/pdf_docs/PNABY287.pdf (accessed Sept. 1, 2009).

U.S. Census Bureau. "International Data Base." Sept. 2009. www.census.gov/ipc/www/idb/ (accessed Sept. 1, 2009).

U.S. Department of State. "Background Note: Mozambique." Aug. 2009. www.state.gov/r/pa/ei/bgn/7035.htm (accessed Sept. 1, 2009).

Van Evera, Stephen. *Guide to Methods for Students of Political Science.* Ithaca, N.Y.: Cornell University Press, 1997.

Verhey, Beth. "Going Home: Demobilising and Reintegrating Child Soldiers in the Democratic Republic of Congo." Report, Save the Children, 2003. www.savethechildren.org.uk/en/54_5151.htm (accessed Sept. 1, 2009).

Vision of Humanity. "Global Peace Index 2007." 2008. www.visionofhumanity.org/gpi/results/rankings/2007/ (accessed Sept. 1, 2009).

———. "Serbia: Global Peace Index 2007." 2008. www.visionofhumanity.org/gpi/results/serbia/2007/ (accessed Sept. 1, 2009).

Watchlist on Children and Armed Conflict. "Struggling to Survive: Children in Armed Conflict in the Democratic Republic of Congo." 2006. www.watchlist.org/reports/dr_congo.php (accessed July 2009).

Walker, Peter. "Mozambique: Reintegration Strategy." Unpublished report, UNHCR, 1994.

Watson, Keith. "Language, Education and Ethnicity: Whose Rights Will Prevail in an Age of Globalisation?" *International Journal of Educational Development* 27, no. 3 (2007): 252–65.

Wilson, K. B. "Cults of Violence and Counter-Violence in Mozambique." *Journal of Southern African Studies* 18, no. 3 (1992): 527–82.

Women's Commission for Refugee Women and Children. "Youth Speak Out: New Voices on the Protection and Participation of Young People Affected by Armed Conflict." Report, 2005. www.womenscommission.org/pdf/cap_ysofinal_rev.pdf (accessed Aug. 25, 2009).

World Bank. *Education in the Democratic Republic of Congo: Priorities and Options for Regeneration*. Washington, D.C.: World Bank, 2005.

———. "Project Appraisal Document on a Proposed Grant in the Amount of SDR 99.2 Million to the Democratic Republic of Congo for an Education Sector Project." 2007. www-wds.worldbank.org/external/default/WDSContentServer/WDSP/IB/2007/05/14/000020953_20070514115336/Rendered/PDF/39704.pdf [Comp. and proofreader: URL is correct as written.](accessed Oct. 20, 2009).

———. "Key Development Data and Statistics." 2009. http://web.worldbank.org/WBSITE/EXTERNAL/DATASTATISTICS/0,,contentMDK:20535285~menuPK:1390200~pagePK:64133150~piPK:64133175~theSitePK:239419,00.html (accessed Sept. 1, 2009).

Zakaria, Fareed. "The Politics of Rage." *Newsweek*, Oct. 15, 2001, 14–33.

Index

About the Author

Stephanie Schwartz is a senior program assistant at the United States Institute of Peace's Center for Mediation and Conflict Resolution. She graduated with high honors from Wesleyan University, with a BA in government and a certificate in international relations. Her scholarly interests include youth involvement in peacebuilding, conflict resolution, and social change in conflict environments.

United States Institute of Peace Press

Since its inception, the United States Institute of Peace Press has published over 150 books on the prevention, management, and peaceful resolution of international conflicts—among them such venerable titles as Raymond Cohen's *Negotiating Across Cultures; Herding Cats* and *Leashing the Dogs of War* by Chester A. Crocker, Fen Osler Hampson, and Pamela Aall; and I. William Zartman's *Peacemaking and International Conflict*. All our books arise from research and fieldwork sponsored by the Institute's many programs. In keeping with the best traditions of scholarly publishing, each volume undergoes both thorough internal review and blind peer review by external subject experts to ensure that the research, scholarship, and conclusions are balanced, relevant, and sound. As the Institute prepares to move to its new headquarters on the National Mall in Washington, D.C., the Press is committed to extending the reach of the Institute's work by continuing to publish significant and sustainable works for practicioners, scholars, diplomats, and students.

VALERIE NORVILLE
DIRECTOR

United States Institute of Peace

The United States Institute of Peace is an independent, nonpartisan, national institution established and funded by Congress. Its goals are to help prevent and resolve violent conflicts, promote post-conflict stability and development, and increase peacebuilding capacity, tools, and intellectual capital worldwide. The Institute does this by empowering others with knowledge, skills, and resources, as well as by directly engaging in peacebuilding efforts around the globe.

Board of Directors

The book is set in Caslon 540 LT Standard; the display type is Adobe Caslon Bold. Richard von Zimmer designed the book's cover, and Christian Feuerstein did the page makeup.